GETTING UP TO SPEED
THE FUTURE OF
SUPERCOMPUTING

Susan L. Graham, Marc Snir, and Cynthia A. Patterson, *Editors*

Committee on the Future of Supercomputing

Computer Science and Telecommunications Board
Division on Engineering and Physical Sciences

NATIONAL RESEARCH COUNCIL
OF THE NATIONAL ACADEMIES

THE NATIONAL ACADEMIES PRESS
Washington, D.C.
www.nap.edu

THE NATIONAL ACADEMIES PRESS   500 Fifth Street, N.W.   Washington, DC 20001

NOTICE: The project that is the subject of this report was approved by the Governing Board of the National Research Council, whose members are drawn from the councils of the National Academy of Sciences, the National Academy of Engineering, and the Institute of Medicine. The members of the committee responsible for the report were chosen for their special competences and with regard for appropriate balance.

Support for this project was provided by the Department of Energy under Sponsor Award No. DE-AT01-03NA00106. Any opinions, findings, conclusions, or recommendations expressed in this publication are those of the authors and do not necessarily reflect the views of the organizations that provided support for the project.

International Standard Book Number 0-309-09502-6 (Book)
International Standard Book Number 0-309-54679-6 (PDF)
Library of Congress Catalog Card Number 2004118086

Cover designed by Jennifer Bishop.

Cover images (clockwise from top right, front to back)
  1. Exploding star. Scientific Discovery through Advanced Computing (SciDAC) Center for Supernova Research, U.S. Department of Energy, Office of Science.
  2. Hurricane Frances, September 5, 2004, taken by GOES-12 satellite, 1 km visible imagery. U.S. National Oceanographic and Atmospheric Administration.
  3. Large-eddy simulation of a Rayleigh-Taylor instability run on the Lawrence Livermore National Laboratory MCR Linux cluster in July 2003. The relative abundance of the heavier elements in our universe is largely determined by fluid instabilities and turbulent mixing inside violently exploding stars.
  4. Three-dimensional model of the structure of a *ras* protein. Human Genome Program, U.S. Department of Energy, Office of Science.
  5. Test launch of Minuteman intercontinental ballistic missile. Vandenberg Air Force Base.
  6. A sample of liquid deuterium subjected to a supersonic impact, showing the formation of a shock front on the atomic scale. The simulation involved 1,320 atoms and ran for several days on 2,640 processors of Lawrence Livermore National Laboratory's ASCI White. It provided an extremely detailed picture of the formation and propagation of a shock front on the atomic scale. Accelerated Strategic Computing Initiative (ASCI), Department of Energy, Lawrence Livermore National Laboratory.
  7. Isodensity surfaces of a National Ignition Facility ignition capsule bounding the shell, shown at 200 picosec (left), 100 picosec (center), and near ignition time (right). An example of ASCI White three-dimensional computer simulations based on predictive physical models. ASCI, Lawrence Livermore National Laboratory.

Copies of this report are available from the National Academies Press, 500 Fifth Street, N.W., Lockbox 285, Washington, DC 20055; (800) 624-6242 or (202) 334-3313 in the Washington metropolitan area; Internet, http://www.nap.edu

Printed in the United States of America

THE NATIONAL ACADEMIES
Advisers to the Nation on Science, Engineering, and Medicine

The **National Academy of Sciences** is a private, nonprofit, self-perpetuating society of distinguished scholars engaged in scientific and engineering research, dedicated to the furtherance of science and technology and to their use for the general welfare. Upon the authority of the charter granted to it by the Congress in 1863, the Academy has a mandate that requires it to advise the federal government on scientific and technical matters. Dr. Bruce M. Alberts is president of the National Academy of Sciences.

The **National Academy of Engineering** was established in 1964, under the charter of the National Academy of Sciences, as a parallel organization of outstanding engineers. It is autonomous in its administration and in the selection of its members, sharing with the National Academy of Sciences the responsibility for advising the federal government. The National Academy of Engineering also sponsors engineering programs aimed at meeting national needs, encourages education and research, and recognizes the superior achievements of engineers. Dr. Wm. A. Wulf is president of the National Academy of Engineering.

The **Institute of Medicine** was established in 1970 by the National Academy of Sciences to secure the services of eminent members of appropriate professions in the examination of policy matters pertaining to the health of the public. The Institute acts under the responsibility given to the National Academy of Sciences by its congressional charter to be an adviser to the federal government and, upon its own initiative, to identify issues of medical care, research, and education. Dr. Harvey V. Fineberg is president of the Institute of Medicine.

The **National Research Council** was organized by the National Academy of Sciences in 1916 to associate the broad community of science and technology with the Academy's purposes of furthering knowledge and advising the federal government. Functioning in accordance with general policies determined by the Academy, the Council has become the principal operating agency of both the National Academy of Sciences and the National Academy of Engineering in providing services to the government, the public, and the scientific and engineering communities. The Council is administered jointly by both Academies and the Institute of Medicine. Dr. Bruce M. Alberts and Dr. Wm. A. Wulf are chair and vice chair, respectively, of the National Research Council.

www.national-academies.org

Preface

Igh-performance computing is important in solving complex problems in areas from climate and biology to national security. Several factors have led to the recent reexamination of the rationale for federal investment in research and development in support of high-performance computing, including (1) continuing changes in the various component technologies and their markets, (2) the evolution of the computing market, particularly the high-end supercomputing segment, (3) experience with several systems using the clustered processor architecture, and (4) the evolution of the problems, many of them mission-driven, for which supercomputers are used.

The Department of Energy's (DOE's) Office of Science expressed an interest in sponsoring a study by the Computer Science and Telecommunications Board (CSTB) of the National Research Council (NRC) that would assess the state of U.S. supercomputing capabilities and relevant research and development. Spurred by the development of the Japanese vector-based Earth Simulator supercomputer, the Senate's Energy and Water Development Appropriations Committee directed the Advanced Simulation and Computing (ASC) program of the National Nuclear Security Administration (NNSA) at DOE to commission, in collaboration with DOE's Office of Science, a study by the NRC. Congress also commissioned a study by the JASONs[1] to identify the distinct requirements of the stockpile stewardship program and its relation to the ASC acquisition strategy.

---

[1]Formed in 1959, the JASONs are a select group of scientific advisors who consult with the federal government, chiefly on classified research issues.

CSTB convened the Committee on the Future of Supercomputing to assess prospects for supercomputing technology research and development in support of U.S. needs, to examine key elements of context—the history of supercomputing, the erosion of research investment, the changing nature of the problems demanding supercomputing, and the needs of government agencies for supercomputing capabilities—and to assess opportunities for progress. The 18 distinguished members of the study committee (see Appendix A for their biographies) were drawn from academia, industry, and government research organizations in the United States. Several committee members have had previous government and/or industry service. Their collective expertise includes software, computer architecture, performance assessment, applications using supercomputing, economics, and policy matters.

The committee did its work through its own expert deliberations and by soliciting input from key officials in its sponsoring agency (DOE) and numerous experts in both the United States and Japan, including government officials, academic researchers, supercomputer manufacturers, software vendors, supercomputer center managers, and application users of supercomputing systems (see Appendix B). In addition to meeting six times, the committee hosted a workshop attended by more than 20 scientists from a broad range of disciplines to explore the supercomputing needs and opportunities of key scientific domains in the coming decade and to discuss the supercomputing technologies that will facilitate supercomputer use in these domains. Many of the workshop participants provided white papers (see Appendix C for a list) expressing their views on computational challenges in supercomputing, which informed both the workshop and this report.

The committee also visited five DOE supercomputer centers and the National Security Agency's (NSA's) Supercomputer Center (see Appendix B). A subset of the committee received classified briefings from the Department of Energy on stockpile stewardship and from the NSA on signals intelligence that helped illuminate how these mission requirements drive supercomputing needs now and in the future. Given that a significant fraction of government funding of supercomputing is for classified national security programs, the committee believed such briefings were needed to ensure that its report would be useful for the entire supercomputing community. Having received the briefings, the committee believes that the needs of the classified supercomputing applications reinforce, but do not change, the committee's findings and recommendations for the future of supercomputing. This unclassified report does not have a classified annex, nor is there a classified version.

To facilitate communication within the broader community, the committee hosted a town hall meeting at the annual 2003 Supercomputing

Conference in Phoenix, Arizona. In addition, a subset of the committee spent one week in Japan meeting with senior colleagues from the Japanese government, industry, and academia to discuss scientific, technical, and policy issues of mutual interest and to better understand both the similarities and the differences in how the two countries approach supercomputing. They visited several sites in Japan, including the Earth Simulator; the government ministry responsible for funding the Earth Simulator; a university supercomputer center; Japan's Aerospace Exploration Agency; and an auto manufacturer. On the committee's behalf, the National Academy of Engineering co-sponsored with the Engineering Academy of Japan a 1-day forum in Tokyo on the future of supercomputing. Twenty-five Japanese supercomputing experts participated in the forum. The sharing of ideas in those meetings provided important perspectives that contributed to the completeness and accuracy of this report. It is the hope of the committee that activities such as the Tokyo forum will lead to future collaboration between Japan and the United States in areas that will advance supercomputing in both countries.

In July 2003, the committee released an interim report[2] that provided a high-level description of the state of U.S. supercomputing, the needs of the future, and the factors that contribute to meeting those needs. That report generated a number of comments that helped to guide the committee in its work for this final report. Additional inputs helpful to committee members and staff came from professional conferences, the technical literature, and government reports.

The committee is grateful to the many people who contributed to this complex study and its comprehensive report. First and foremost, the committee thanks the sponsors, DOE's Office of Science (Fred Johnson and Dan Hitchcock) and DOE's NNSA (Dimitri Kusnezov, Edgar Lewis, and José Muñoz), not only for their financial support but also for their help in facilitating meetings with people with whom its members wished to speak.

The committee appreciates the thoughtful testimony received from many individuals at its plenary sessions (see Appendix B for a complete list of briefers). The NSA and DOE site visits provided critical input to the committee deliberations. These site visits would not have been possible without the assistance of people at each locale. The committee and staff thank the following people for their help: Gary D. Hughes (NSA), Lynn Kissel (Lawrence Livermore National Laboratory), James S. Peery (Los Alamos National Laboratory), Horst D. Simon (Lawrence Berkeley Na-

---

[2]National Research Council (NRC). 2003. *The Future of Supercomputing: An Interim Report.* Washington, D.C.: The National Academies Press.

tional Laboratory), Robert Thomas (Sandia National Laboratories), Rick Stevens (Argonne National Laboratory), and Thomas Zacharia (Oak Ridge National Laboratory).

The committee thanks the workshop participants for the insights they contributed through their white papers (see Appendix C for a list of papers), discussions, breakout sessions, and subsequent interactions. The committee is particularly grateful to Warren Washington (National Center for Atmospheric Research), Charles McMillan (Lawrence Livermore National Laboratory), Jeffrey Saltzman (Merck Research Laboratory), and Phillip Colella (Lawrence Berkeley National Laboratory) for their thoughtful plenary presentations.

Many people were instrumental in making the trip to Japan a success. The committee is extremely grateful to Kenichi Miura (Fujitsu fellow) and Tadashi Watanabe (NEC) for their assistance before and during the trip. The 1-day Japan–U.S. Forum on the Future of Supercomputing would not have been possible without the support of the Engineering Academy of Japan and the National Academy of Engineering. The committee learned a lot from insightful presentations and discussions from all the Japanese forum participants. The committee and staff also thank the individuals at each site who took time to meet with the committee. In particular, they thank Tetsuya Sato at the Earth Simulator Center and Harumasa Miura at the Ministry of Education, Culture, Sports, Science, and Technology. Maki Haraga provided excellent translation services and logistical help for the committee's entire trip.

The committee was fortunate to receive many thoughtful and perceptive comments from the reviewers as well as from the Monitor and the Coordinator of this report. These comments were instrumental in helping the committee to sharpen and improve its report.

Finally, the committee thanks the various members of the NRC staff who helped to move this report from vision to reality. Cynthia Patterson provided continuing wisdom, guidance, encouragement, and friendship, in concert with her hard work on the report. Margaret Huynh's skills in organizing the committee's meetings and supporting its efforts and Phil Hilliard's research support were key contributions to the work of the committee. Liz Fikre edited the final manuscript for publication. Kevin Hale and Machelle Reynolds successfully facilitated the security clearances and security review necessary to complete this study in a timely manner. Janice Mehler and Liz Panos were very helpful in facilitating and expediting the review process.

                              Susan L. Graham and Marc Snir, Co-chairs
                              Committee on the Future of Supercomputing

Acknowledgment of Reviewers

This report has been reviewed in draft form by individuals chosen for their diverse perspectives and technical expertise, in accordance with procedures approved by the National Research Council's (NRC's) Report Review Committee. The purpose of this independent review is to provide candid and critical comments that will assist the institution in making the published report as sound as possible and to ensure that the report meets institutional standards for objectivity, evidence, and responsiveness to the study charge. The review comments and draft manuscript remain confidential to protect the integrity of the deliberative process. We wish to thank the following individuals for their review of this report:

Mark E. Dean, IBM,
Steven Gottlieb, Indiana University,
Shane Mitchell Greenstein, Northwestern University,
Sidney Karin, University of California, San Diego,
Ken Kennedy, Rice University,
Richard Loft, National Center for Atmospheric Research,
J. Andrew McCammon, University of California, San Diego,
Kenichi Miura, National Institute of Informatics,
Michael Norman, University of Illinois, Urbana-Champaign,
Richard Proto, National Security Agency (retired),
Daniel A. Reed, University of North Carolina, Chapel Hill,
Ahmed Sameh, Purdue University,
Gary Smaby, Smaby Group, Inc.,

Burton J. Smith, Cray Inc.,
Allan Edward Snavely, San Diego Supercomputing Center,
William W. Stead, Vanderbilt University, and
Paul Tackley, University of California, Los Angeles.

Although the reviewers listed above have provided many constructive comments and suggestions, they were not asked to endorse the conclusions or recommendations, nor did they see the final draft of the report before its release. The review of this report was overseen by Elsa Garmire of Dartmouth University and Samuel H. Fuller of Analog Devices, Inc. Appointed by the NRC, they were responsible for making certain that an independent examination of this report was carried out in accordance with institutional procedures and that all review comments were carefully considered. Responsibility for the final content of this report rests entirely with the authoring committee and the institution.

Contents

Executive Summary

Supercomputing is very important to the United States for conducting basic scientific research and for ensuring the physical and economic well-being of the country. The United States has a proud history of leadership in supercomputing, which has contributed not only to its international standing in science and engineering and to national health and security but also to the commercial strength of many industries, including the computing industry. Supercomputing has become a major contributor to the economic competitiveness of our automotive, aerospace, medical, and pharmaceutical industries. The discovery of new substances and new techniques, as well as cost reduction through simulation rather than physical prototyping, will underpin progress in a number of economically important areas. The use of supercomputing in all of these areas is growing, and it is increasingly essential to continued progress.

However, in recent years our progress in supercomputing has slowed, as attention turned to other areas of science and engineering. The advances in mainstream computing brought about by improved processor performance have enabled some former supercomputing needs to be addressed by clusters of commodity processors. Yet important applications, some vital to our nation's security, require technology that is only available in the most advanced custom-built systems. We have been remiss in attending to the conduct of the long-term research and development we will one day need and to the sustenance of the industrial capabilities that will also be needed. The Japanese Earth Simulator has served as a wake-up call, reminding us that complacency can cause us to lose not only our competitive advantage but also, and more importantly, the national competence that we need to achieve our own goals.

To maintain our level of achievement in supercomputing and its applications, as well as to keep us from falling behind relative to other nations and to our own needs, a renewed national effort is needed. That effort must have the following components:

- Government leadership in maintaining a national planning activity that is sustained, ongoing, and coordinated and that drives investment decisions.
- Continuing progress in creating hardware, software, and algorithmic technologies that enable the application of supercomputing to important domain-specific problems. Such progress will require continuing government investment.
- International collaborations in all aspects of supercomputing except those that would demonstrably compromise national security.

Supercomputing has always been a specialized form of computing at the cutting edge of technology. As the computing field has grown and matured, computing has become broader and more diverse. From an economic perspective, there are large new markets that are distinct from supercomputing—for example, personal computing devices of various kinds, computers invisibly embedded in many kinds of artifacts, and applications that use large amounts of computing in relatively undemanding ways. As a consequence, potential providers of supercomputing systems and software and potential creators of future supercomputing technology are fewer in number than they once were. In the face of continuing need and the competing demands that weaken supply, the committee recommends that the following actions and policies be initiated.

> **Overall Recommendation: To meet the current and future needs of the United States, the government agencies that depend on supercomputing, together with the U.S. Congress, need to take primary responsibility for accelerating advances in supercomputing and ensuring that there are multiple strong domestic suppliers of both hardware and software.**

The government is the primary user of supercomputing. Government-funded research that relies on supercomputing is pushing the frontiers of knowledge and bringing important societal benefits. Because supercomputing is essential to maintain U.S. military superiority, to achieve the goals of stockpile stewardship, and to maintain national security, the government must ensure that the U.S. supercomputing infrastructure advances sufficiently to support our needs in the coming years.

These needs are distinct from those of the broad information technology industry. They involve platforms and technologies that are unlikely on their own to have a broad enough market in the short term to satisfy government needs.

To guide the government agencies and Congress in assuming that responsibility, the committee makes eight recommendations.

Recommendation 1. To get the maximum leverage from the national effort, the government agencies that are the major users of supercomputing should be jointly responsible for the strength and continued evolution of the supercomputing infrastructure in the United States, from basic research to suppliers and deployed platforms. The Congress should provide adequate and sustained funding.

A small number of government agencies are the primary users of supercomputing, either directly, through acquisitions, or indirectly, by awarding contracts and grants to other organizations that purchase supercomputers. At present, those agencies include the Department of Energy (DOE), including its National Nuclear Security Administration (NNSA) and its Office of Science; the Department of Defense (DoD), including its National Security Agency (NSA); the National Aeronautics and Space Administration (NASA); the National Oceanic and Atmospheric Administration (NOAA); and the National Science Foundation (NSF). (The increasing use of supercomputing in biomedical applications suggests that the National Institutes of Health (NIH) should be added to the list.) Although the agencies have different missions and different needs, they could benefit from the synergies of coordinated planning and acquisition strategies and coordinated support for R&D. For instance, many of the technologies, in particular the software technology, need to be broadly available across all platforms. Therefore, those agencies must be jointly responsible and jointly accountable. Moreover, for the agencies to meet their own mission responsibilities and also take full advantage of the investments made by other agencies, collaboration and coordination must become much more long range. The agencies that are the biggest users of supercomputing must develop and execute an integrated plan.

The committee emphasizes the need for developing an integrated plan rather than coordinating distinct supercomputing plans through a diffuse interagency structure. An integrated plan is not an integrated budget. Such a plan would not preclude agencies from individual activities, nor would it prevent them from setting their own priorities. Also, it must not be used to the exclusion of unanticipated needs and opportunities. Rather, the intent is to identify common needs at an early stage, and to leverage shared efforts for meeting those needs, while minimizing duplicative efforts. Different agencies should pick the activities that best match their missions; for example, long-term basic research best matches NSF's mission, while industrial supercomputing R&D is more akin to the mission of the Defense Advanced Research Projects Agency (DARPA).

Recommendation 2. The government agencies that are the primary users of supercomputing should ensure domestic leadership in those technologies that are essential to meet national needs.

Current U.S. investments in supercomputing and current plans are not sufficient to provide the supercomputing capabilities that our country will need. It needs supercomputers that satisfy critical requirements in areas such as cryptography and stockpile stewardship, as well as systems that will enable breakthroughs for the broad scientific and technological progress underlying a strong and robust U.S. economy. The committee is less concerned that the top-ranked computer in the TOP500 list (as of June 2004) was located in Japan. U.S. security is not necessarily endangered if a computer in a foreign country is capable of doing some computations faster than U.S.-based computers. The committee believes that had the United States at that time made an investment similar to the Japanese investment in the Earth Simulator, it could have created a powerful and equally capable system. The committee's concern is that the United States has not been making the investments that would guarantee its ability to create such a system in the future.

Leadership is measured by the ability to acquire and exploit effectively machines that can best reduce the time to solution of important computational problems. From this perspective, it is not the Earth Simulator system per se that is worrisome but rather the fact that the construction of this system might turn out to have been a singular event. It appears that custom high-bandwidth processors such as those used by the Earth Simulator are not viable products without significant government support. Two of the three Japanese companies that were manufacturing such processors do not do so anymore, and the third (NEC) may also bow to market realities in the not-too-distant future, since the Japanese government seems less willing now to subsidize the development of cutting-edge supercomputing technologies. Only by maintaining national leadership in these technologies can the U.S. government ensure that key supercomputing technologies, such as custom high-bandwidth processors, will be available to satisfy its needs. The U.S. industrial base must include suppliers on whom the government can rely to build custom systems to solve problems arising from the government's unique requirements. Since only a few units of such systems are ever needed, there is no broad market for the systems and hence no commercial off-the-shelf suppliers. Domestic supercomputing vendors can become a source of both the components and the engineering talent needed for building these custom systems.

Recommendation 3. To satisfy its need for unique supercomputing technologies such as high-bandwidth systems, the government needs to ensure the viability of multiple domestic suppliers.

Supercomputers built out of commodity components satisfy a large fraction of supercomputing applications. These applications benefit from the fast evolution and low cost of commodity technology. But commodity components are designed for the needs of large markets in data processing or personal computing and are inadequate for many supercomputing applications. The use of commodity clusters results in lower sustained performance and higher programming costs for some demanding applications. This is especially true of some security-related computations where shorter time to solution is of critical importance, justifying the use of custom-built, high-bandwidth supercomputers even at a higher cost per solution.

It is important to have multiple suppliers for any key technology in order to maintain competition, to prevent technical stagnation, to provide diverse supercomputing ecosystems that will address diverse needs, and to reduce risk. However, it is unrealistic to expect that such narrow markets will attract a large number of vendors. As is true for many military technologies, there may be only a few suppliers.

To ensure their continuing existence, domestic suppliers must follow a viable business model. For a public company, that means having a predictable and steady revenue stream recognizable by the financial market. A company cannot continue to provide leadership products without R&D. At least two models have been used successfully in the past: (1) an implicit guarantee for the steady purchase of supercomputing systems, giving the companies a steady income stream with which to fund ongoing R&D and (2) explicit funding of a company's R&D. Stability is a key issue. Suppliers of such systems or components are often small companies that can cease to be viable; additionally, uncertainty can mean the loss of skilled personnel to other sectors of the computing industry or the loss of investors. Historically, government priorities and technical directions have changed more frequently than would be justified by technology lifetimes, creating market instabilities. The chosen funding model must ensure stable funding.

Recommendation 4. The creation and long-term maintenance of the software that is key to supercomputing requires the support of those agencies that are responsible for supercomputing R&D. That software includes operating systems, libraries, compilers, software development and data analysis tools, application codes, and databases.

Supercomputer software is developed and maintained by the national laboratories, by universities, by vertically integrated hardware vendors, and by small independent companies. An increasing amount of the software used in supercomputing is developed in an open source model. Many of the supercomputing software vendors are small and can disappear from the marketplace. The open source model may suffer from having too few developers of supercomputing software with too many other demands on their time.

The successful evolution and maintenance of complex software systems are critically dependent on institutional memory—that is, on the continuous involvement of the few key developers that understand the software design. Stability and continuity are essential to preserve institutional memory. Whatever model of support is used, it should be implemented so that stable organizations with lifetimes of decades can maintain and evolve the software. At the same time, the government should not duplicate successful commercial software packages but should instead invest in new technology. When new commercial providers emerge, the government should purchase their products and redirect its own efforts toward technology that it cannot otherwise obtain.

Barriers to the replacement of application programming interfaces are very high, owing to the large sunk investments in application software. Any change that significantly enhances our nation's ability to program very large systems will entail the radical, coordinated change of many technologies, creating a new ecosystem. To facilitate this change, the government needs long-term, coordinated investments in a large number of interlocking technologies.

Recommendation 5. The government agencies responsible for supercomputing should underwrite a community effort to develop and maintain a roadmap that identifies key obstacles and synergies in all of supercomputing.

The challenges in supercomputing are very significant, and the amount of ongoing research is limited. To make progress, it is important to identify and address the key roadblocks. Furthermore, technologies in different domains are interdependent: Progress on a new architecture may also require specific advances in packaging, interconnects, operating system structures, programming languages and compilers, and the like. Thus, investments need to be coordinated. To drive decisions, one needs a roadmap of all the technologies that affect supercomputing. The roadmap needs to have quantitative and measurable milestones. Its creation and maintenance should be an open process that involves a broad community. It is important that a supercomputing roadmap be driven both top-down by application needs and bottom-up by technology barriers and that mission needs as well as science needs be incorporated. It should focus on the evolution of each specific technology and on the interplay between technologies. It should be updated annually and undergo major revision at suitable intervals.

The roadmap should be used by agencies and by Congress to guide their long-term research and development investments. Those roadblocks that will not be addressed by industry without government intervention must be identified, and the needed research and development must be initiated. Metrics must be developed to support the quantitative aspects of the roadmap. It is important also to invest in some high-risk, high-return research ideas that are not indicated by the roadmap, to avoid being blindsided.

> **Recommendation 6. Government agencies responsible for supercomputing should increase their levels of stable, robust, sustained multiagency investment in basic research. More research is needed in all the key technologies required for the design and use of supercomputers (architecture, software, algorithms, and applications).**

The peak performance of supercomputers has increased rapidly in the last decades, but their sustained performance has lagged, and the productivity of supercomputing users has lagged. Over the last decade the advance in peak supercomputing performance was largely due to the advance in microprocessor performance driven by increased miniaturization, with some contribution from increased parallelism. Perhaps because a large fraction of supercomputing improvements resulted from these advances, few novel technologies were introduced in supercomputer systems, and supercomputing research investments decreased. However, many important applications have not benefited from these advances in mainstream computing, and it will be harder for supercomputing to benefit from increased miniaturization in the future. Fundamental breakthroughs will be needed that will require an increase in research funding.

The research investments should be informed by the supercomputing roadmap but not constrained by it. It is important to focus on technologies that have been identified as roadblocks and that are beyond the scope of industry investments in computing. It is equally important to support long-term speculative research in potentially disruptive technical advances. The research investment should also be informed by the "ecosystem" view of supercomputing—namely, that progress is often needed on a broad front of interrelated technologies rather than as individual breakthroughs.

Research on supercomputing hardware and software should include a mix of small, medium, and large projects. Many small individual projects are necessary for the development of new ideas. A smaller number of large projects that develop technology demonstrations are needed to bring these ideas to maturity and to study the interaction between various technologies in a realistic environment. Such demonstration projects (which are different from product prototyping activities) should not be expected to be stable platforms for exploitation by users, because the need to maintain a stable platform conflicts with the ability to use the platform for experiments. It is important that the development of such demonstration systems have the substantial involvement not only of academic researchers but also of students, to support the education of the new generation of researchers and to increase the supercomputing workforce. It is also important that the fruits of such projects not be proprietary. The committee estimated the necessary investments in such projects at about $140 million per year. This estimate does not include investments in the development and use of application-specific software.

In its early days, supercomputing research generated many ideas that eventually became broadly used in the computing industry. Such influences will continue in the future. Many of the technical roadblocks faced today by supercomputing are roadblocks that will affect all computing over time. There can be little doubt that solutions developed to solve this problem for supercomputers will eventually influence the broader computing industry, so that investment in basic research in supercomputing is likely to be of widespread benefit to all of information technology.

> **Recommendation 7. Supercomputing research is an international activity; barriers to international collaboration should be minimized.**

Research has always benefited from the open exchange of ideas and the opportunity to build on the achievements of others. The national leadership advocated in these recommendations is enhanced, not compromised, by early-stage sharing of ideas and results. In light of the relatively small community of supercomputing researchers, international collaborations are particularly beneficial. The climate modeling community, for one, has long embraced that view.

Collaboration with international researchers must include giving them access to domestic supercomputing systems; they often spend time in the United States to work closely with resident scientists. Many of the best U.S. graduate students come from other countries, although they often remain as permanent residents or new citizens. Access restrictions based on citizenship hinder collaboration and are contrary to the openness that is essential to good research.

Restrictions on the import of supercomputers to the United States have not benefited the U.S. supercomputing industry and are unlikely to do so in the future. Some kinds of export controls—on commodity systems, especially—lack any clear rationale, given that such systems are built from widely available commercial components. It makes little sense to restrict sales of commodity systems built from components that are not export controlled. Because restrictions on the export of supercomputing technology may damage international collaboration, the benefit of using export controls to prevent potential adversaries or proliferators from accessing key supercomputing technology has to be carefully weighed against that damage.

Since supercomputer systems are multipurpose (nuclear simulations, climate modeling, and so on), their availability need not compromise the domestic leadership needed for national defense, so long as safeguards are in place to protect critical applications.

Recommendation 8. The U.S. government should ensure that researchers with the most demanding computational requirements have access to the most powerful supercomputing systems.

Access to the most powerful supercomputers is important for the advancement of science in many disciplines. A model in which top supercomputing capabilities are provided by different agencies with different missions is healthy. Each agency is the primary supporter of certain research or mission-driven communities; as such, each agency should have a long-term plan and budget for the acquisition of the supercomputing systems that are needed to support its users. The planning and funding process followed by each agency must ensure stability from the viewpoint of its users.

The users should be involved in the planning process and should be consulted in setting budget priorities for supercomputing. The mechanisms for allocating supercomputing resources must ensure that almost all of the computer time on capability systems is allocated to jobs for which that capability is essential. Budget priorities should be reflected in the high-end computing plan proposed in Recommendation 1. In Chapter 9, the committee estimates the cost of a healthy procurement process at about $800 million per year. Such a process would satisfy the capability supercomputing needs (but not the capacity needs) of the main agencies using supercomputing and would include the platforms primarily used for research. It would include both platforms used for mission-specific tasks and platforms used to support science.

The NSF supercomputing centers have traditionally provided open access to a broad range of academic users. However, some of these centers have increased the scope of their activities in order to support high-speed networking and grid computing and to expand their education mission. The increases in scope have not been accompanied by corresponding increases in funding, so less attention is paid to supercomputing, and support for computational scientists with capability needs has been diluted.

It is important to repair the current situation at NSF, in which the computational science users of supercomputing centers appear to have too little involvement in programmatic and budgetary planning. All the research communities in need of supercomputing capability have a shared responsibility to provide direction for the supercomputing infrastructure they use and to ensure that resources are available for sustaining the supercomputing ecosystems. Funding for the acquisition and operation of the research supercomputing infrastructure should be clearly separated from funding for computer and computational science and engineering research. It should compete on an equal basis with other infrastructure needs of the science and engineering disciplines. That is not now the case.

1

Introduction and Context

Supercomputers are used to solve complex problems, including the simulation and modeling of physical phenomena such as climate change, explosions, and the behavior of molecules; the analysis of data such as national security intelligence, genome sequencing, and astronomical observations; and the intricate design of engineered products. Their use is important for national security and defense, as well as for research and development in many areas of science and engineering. Supercomputers can advance knowledge and generate insight that would not otherwise be possible or that could not be captured in time to be actionable. Supercomputer simulations can augment or replace experimentation in cases where experiments are hazardous, expensive, or even impossible to perform or to instrument; they can even enable virtual experiments with imaginary worlds to test theories beyond the range of observable parameters. Further, supercomputers have the potential to suggest entirely novel experiments that can revolutionize our perspective of the world. They enable faster evaluation of design alternatives, thus improving the quality of engineered products. Most of the technical areas that are important to the well-being of humanity use supercomputing in fundamental and essential ways.

As the uses of computing have increased and broadened, supercomputing has become less dominant than it once was. Many interesting applications require only modest amounts of computing, by today's standards. Yet new problems have arisen whose computational demands for scaling and timeliness stress even our current supercomputers. Many of those problems are fundamental to the government's ability to address important national issues. One notable example is the Department of Energy's (DOE's) computational requirements for stockpile stewardship.

The emergence of mainstream solutions to problems that formerly required supercomputing has caused the computer industry, the research and development community, and some government agencies to reduce their attention to supercomputing. Recently, questions have been raised about the best ways for the government to ensure that its supercomputing needs will continue to be satisfied in terms of both capability and cost-effectiveness. At the joint request of the DOE's Office of Science and the Advanced Simulation and Computing[1] (ASC) Program of the National Nuclear Security Administrations (NNSA) at DOE, the National Research Council's (NRC's) Computer Science and Telecommunications Board convened the Committee on the Future of Supercomputing to conduct a 2-year study to assess the state of supercomputing in the United States. Specifically, the committee was charged to do the following:

- Examine the characteristics of relevant systems and architecture research in government, industry, and academia and the characteristics of the relevant market.
- Identify key elements of context such as the history of supercomputing, the erosion of research investment, the needs of government agencies for supercomputing capabilities, and historical or causal factors.
- Examine the changing nature of problems demanding supercomputing (e.g., stockpile stewardship, cryptanalysis, climate modeling, bioinformatics) and the implications for systems design.
- Outline the role of national security in the supercomputer market and the long-term federal interest in supercomputing.
- Deliver an interim report in July 2003 outlining key issues.
- Make recommendations in the final report for government policy to meet future needs.

STUDY CONTEXT

Much has changed since the 1980s, when a variety of agencies invested in developing and using supercomputers. In the 1990s the High Performance Computing and Communications Initiative (HPCCI) was conceived and subsequently evolved into a broader and more diffuse pro-

---

[1]ASC was formerly known as the Accelerated Strategic Computing Initiative (ASCI). This report uses ASC to refer collectively to these programs.

gram of computer science research support.[2] Over the last couple of decades, the government sponsored numerous studies dealing with supercomputing and its role in science and engineering research.[3]

Following the guidelines of the *Report of the Panel on Large Scale Computing in Science and Engineering* (the Lax report),[4] the National Science Foundation (NSF) established three supercomputer centers and one advanced prototype in 1985 and another center in 1986. Major projects on innovative supercomputing systems were funded—for instance, the Caltech Cosmic Cube, the New York University (NYU) Ultracomputer, and the Illinois Cedar project. The other recommendations of the report (to increase research in the disciplines needed for an effective and efficient use of supercomputers and to increase training of people in scientific computing) had only a modest effect. Following the renewal of four of the five NSF supercomputer centers in 1990, the National Science Board (NSB) commissioned the NSF Blue Ribbon Panel on High Performance Computing to investigate future changes in the overall scientific environment due to rapid advances in computers and scientific computing.[5] The panel's report, *From Desktop to Teraflop: Exploiting the U.S. Lead in High Performance Computing* (the Branscomb report), recommended a significant expansion in NSF investments, including accelerating progress in high-performance computing through computer science and computational science research. The impact of these recommendations on funding was small.

In 1991 Congress passed the High Performance Computing Act (P.L. 102-194),[6] which called for the President to establish a national program to set goals for federal high-performance computing research and development in hardware and software and to provide for interagency cooperation.

---

[2]The proliferation of PCs and the rise of the Internet commanded attention and resources, diverting attention and effort from research in high-end computing. There were, however, efforts into the 1990s to support high-performance computing. See, for example, NSF, 1993, *From Desktop to Teraflop: Exploiting the U.S. Lead in High Performance Computing*, NSF Blue Ribbon Panel on High Performance Computing, Arlington, Va.: NSF, August.

[3]The committee's interim report provides a more detailed summary of several key reports.

[4]National Science Board. 1982. *Report of the Panel on Large Scale Computing in Science and Engineering*. Washington, D.C., December 26 (the Lax Report).

[5]NSF. 1993. *From Desktop to Teraflop: Exploiting the U.S. Lead in High Performance Computing*. NSF Blue Ribbon Panel on High Performance Computing. Arlington, Va.: NSF, August.

[6]Bill summary and status are available online at <http://thomas.loc.gov/cgi-bin/bdquery/R?d102:FLD002:@1(102+194)>.

NSF formed a task force in 1995 to advise it on the review and management of the supercomputer centers program. The chief finding of the *Report of the Task Force on the Future of the NSF Supercomputer Centers Program* (the Hayes report)[7] was that the Advanced Scientific Computing Centers funded by NSF had enabled important research in computational science and engineering and had also changed the way that computational science and engineering contribute to advances in fundamental research across many areas. The recommendation of the task force was to continue to maintain a strong Advanced Scientific Computing Centers program. Congress asked the NRC's Computer Science and Telecommunications Board (CSTB) to examine the HPCCI.[8] CSTB's 1995 report *Evolving the High Performance Computing and Communications Initiative to Support the Nation's Infrastructure* (the Brooks/Sutherland report)[9] recommended the continuation of the HPCCI, funding of a strong experimental research program in software and algorithms for parallel computing machines, and HPCCI support for precompetitive research in computer architecture.

In 1997, following the guidelines of the Hayes report, NSF established two Partnerships for Advanced Computational Infrastructure (PACIs), one with the San Diego Supercomputer Center as a leading-edge site and the other with the National Center for Supercomputing Applications as a leading-edge site. Each partnership includes participants from other academic, industry, and government sites. The PACI program ended on September 30, 2004. The reports did not lead to increased funding, and no major new projects resulted from the recommendations of the Brooks/Sutherland report.

In 1999, the President's Information Technology Advisory Committee's (PITAC's) *Report to the President. Information Technology Research: Investing in Our Future* (the PITAC report) made recommendations

---

[7]NSF. 1995. *Report of the Task Force on the Future of the NSF Supercomputer Centers Program.* September 15.

[8]HPCCI was formally created when Congress passed the High-Performance Computing Act of 1991 (P.L. 102-194), which authorized a 5-year program in high-performance computing and communications. The goal of the HPCCI was to "accelerate the development of future generations of high-performance computers and networks and the use of these resources in the federal government and throughout the American economy" (Federal Coordinating Council for Science, Engineering, and Technology (FCCSET), 1992, *Grand Challenges: High-Performance Computing and Communications*, FY 1992 U.S. Research and Development Program, Office of Science and Technology Policy, Washington D.C.). The initiative broadened from four primary agencies addressing grand challenges such as forecasting severe weather events and aerospace design research to more than 10 agencies addressing national challenges such as electronic commerce and health care.

[9]NRC. 1995. *Evolving the High Performance Computing and Communications Initiative to Support the Nation's Infrastructure.* Washington, D.C.: National Academy Press.

similar to those of the Lax and Branscomb reports.[10] PITAC found that federal information technology R&D was too heavily focused on near-term problems and that investment was inadequate. The committee's main recommendation was to create a strategic initiative to support long-term research in fundamental issues in computing, information, and communications. In response to this recommendation, NSF developed the Information Technology Research (ITR) program. This program, which was only partly successful in meeting the needs identified by PITAC, is now being phased out.

In 2000, concern about the diminishing U.S. ability to meet national security needs led to a recommendation by the Defense Science Board that DoD continue to subsidize a Cray computer development program as well as invest in relevant long-term research.[11]

The Defense Advanced Research Projects Agency (DARPA) launched the High Productivity Computing Systems (HPCS) program in 2002 to provide a new generation of economically viable, high-productivity computing systems for the national security and industrial user community in 2007-2010. The goal is to address the gap between the capability needed to meet mission requirements and the current offerings of the commercial marketplace. HPCS has three phases: (1) an industrial concept phase (now completed), in which Cray, Silicon Graphics, Inc. (SGI), IBM, Hewlett-Packard, and Sun participated; (2) an R&D phase that was awarded to Sun, Cray, and IBM in July 2003 and lasting until 2006; and (3) full-scale development, to be completed by 2010, ideally by the two best proposals from the second phase.

In summary, while successive reports have emphasized the importance of increased investments in supercomputing and the importance of long-term, strategic research, investments in supercomputing seem not to have grown, and the focus has stayed on short-term research, one generation ahead of products. Research on the base technologies used for supercomputing (architecture, programming languages, compilers, operating systems, etc.) has been insufficient.

Computenik

In the spring of 2002 the Japanese installed the Earth Simulator (ES), a supercomputer to be used for geosciences applications. For over 2 years,

---

[10]PITAC. 1999. *Report to the President. Information Technology Research: Investing in Our Future.* February.

[11]Defense Science Board. 2000. *Report of the Defense Science Board Task Force on DoD Supercomputing Needs.* Washington, D.C.: Office of the Under Secretary of Defense for Acquisition and Technology. October 11.

the TOP500 list[12,13] has ranked it as the fastest performing supercomputer in the world. The ES was designed to use custom multiprocessor vector-based nodes and to provide good support for applications written in High Performance Fortran—technologies that were all but abandoned in the United States in favor of commodity scalar processors and message passing libraries. The emergence of that system has been fueling recent concerns about continued U.S. leadership in supercomputing. Experts have asserted that the Earth Simulator was made possible through long-term, sustained investment by the Japanese government. The U.S. Congress and several government agencies began to question what should be done to regain the supercomputing lead. While some experts have argued that maintaining an absolute lead in supercomputing (as measured by the TOP500 list) should not be an overriding U.S. policy objective, the Earth Simulator nonetheless offers important lessons about investment in, management of, and policy toward supercomputing.

The Defense Appropriations Bill for FY 2002 directed the Secretary of Defense to submit a development and acquisition plan for a comprehensive, long-range, integrated, high-end computing (IHEC) program. The resulting report, *High Performance Computing for the National Security Community*,[14] released in the spring of 2003 and known as the IHEC Report, recommends an applied research program to focus on developing the fundamental concepts in high-end computing and creating a pipeline of new ideas and graduate-level expertise for employment in industry and the national security community. The report also emphasizes the importance of high-end computing laboratories that will test system software on dedicated large-scale platforms; support the development of software tools and algorithms; develop and advance benchmarking, modeling, and simulations for system architectures; and conduct detailed technical re-

---

[12]The TOP500 project was started in 1993 to provide a reliable basis for tracking and detecting trends in high-performance computing. Twice a year, a list of the sites operating the 500 most powerful computer systems is assembled and released. The best performance on the Linpack benchmark is used for ranking the computer systems. The list contains a variety of information, including the system specifications and its major application areas (see <http://www.top500.org> for details).

[13]When Jack Dongarra, one of the people who maintains the TOP500 list (an authoritative source of the world's 500 most powerful supercomputers), announced that the Earth Simulator was the world's fastest supercomputer, the *New York Times* quoted him as saying, "In some sense we have a Computenik on our hands" (John Markoff, 2002, "Japanese Computer Is World's Fastest, as U.S. Falls Back," *The New York Times*, April 20, Page A1, C14).

[14]Available online at <http://www.hpcc.gov/hecrtf-outreach/bibliography/200302_hec.pdf>.

quirements analysis. The report suggests $390 million per year as the steady-state budget for this program. The program plan consolidates existing DARPA, DOE/NNSA, and National Security Agency (NSA) R&D programs and features a joint program office with Director of Defense Research and Engineering (DDR&E) oversight.

At the request of Congress, DOE commissioned (in addition to this study) a classified study by the JASONs to identify the distinct requirements of the Stockpile Stewardship Program and its relation to the ASC acquisition strategy. Roy Schwitters, the study leader, said that the report, released in 2003, concluded that "distinct technical requirements place valid computing demands on ASC that exceed present and planned computing capacity and capability."[15]

The 2003 Scales report, *A Science-Based Case for Large-Scale Simulation*,[16] presents a science-based case for balanced investment in numerous areas—such as algorithms, software, innovative architecture, and people—to ensure that the United States benefits from advances enabled by computational simulations.

The High-End Computing Revitalization Task Force (HECRTF) of the National Science Coordination Office for Information Technology Research and Development (NITRD) was chartered under the National Science and Technology Council to develop a plan and a 5-year roadmap to guide federal investments in high-end computing starting with FY 2005. The report, *Federal Plan for High-End Computing*,[17] released in May 2004, noted that the 1990s approach of building systems based on commercial off-the-shelf (COTS) components may not be suitable for many applications of national importance. It recommends research in alternative technologies to ensure U.S. leadership in supercomputing. The report also calls for an interagency collaborative approach.

The Senate Committee on Energy and Natural Resources held a hearing in June 2004 on the High-End Computing Revitalization Act of 2004 (S. 2176).[18] This bill calls for the Secretary of Energy to implement a research and development program in supercomputing and establish a high-end software development center. On July 8, 2004, the House passed and referred to the Senate Committee on Commerce, Science, and Transportation a similar bill, the Department of Energy High-End Computing

---

[15]Presentation to the committee on December 3, 2003.

[16]DOE, Office of Science. 2003. "A Science-Based Case for Large Scale Simulation." *Scales Workshop Report*, Vol. 1. July. Available online at <http://www.pnl.gov/scales/>.

[17]Available online at <http://www.hpcc.gov/pubs/2004_hecrtf/20040702_hecrtf.pdf>.

[18]See <http://thomas.loc.gov/cgi-bin/query/z?c108:S.2176:>.

Revitalization Act of 2004 (H.R. 4516), which omits the call for the software development center.[19] The Senate passed an amended version of H.R. 4516 on October 11, 2004; the House is expected to consider the legislation in late November 2004.[20] The House also passed and sent to the Senate the High-Performance Computing Revitalization Act of 2004 (H.R. 4218),[21] which amends the High-Performance Computing Act of 1991 and directs the President to establish a program to provide for long-term research on high-performance computing, including the technologies to advance the capacity and capabilities of high-performance computing. It also calls for the Director of the Office of Science and Technology Policy to develop and maintain a roadmap for high-performance computing.

ABOUT THE INTERIM REPORT

An interim report was presented in July 2003, approximately 6 months after the start of the study.[22] The report provides a preliminary outline of the state of U.S. supercomputing, the needs of the future, and the factors that will contribute to meeting those needs. The report notes that the United States had the lead, on the June 2003 TOP500 list, in the use and manufacture of supercomputers.[23] However, to meet the security and defense needs of our nation and to realize the opportunities to use supercomputing to advance knowledge, progress in supercomputing must continue. An appropriate balance is needed for investments that evolve current supercomputing architectures and software and investments that exploit alternative approaches that may lead to a paradigm shift. Balance is also needed between exploiting cost-effective advances in widely used hardware and software products and developing custom solutions that meet the most demanding needs. Continuity and stability in the government funding of supercomputing appear to be essential to the well-being of supercomputing in the United States.

ORGANIZATION OF THE REPORT

In this report the committee first examines the requirements of different classes of applications and the architecture, software, algorithm, and

---

[19]See <http://thomas.loc.gov/cgi-bin/bdquery/z?d108:HR04516:>.

[20]See <http://thomas.loc.gov/cgi-bin/query/R?r108:FLD001:S61181>.

[21]See <http://thomas.loc.gov/cgi-bin/query/D?c108:3:./temp/~c108qnbgq9::>.

[22]NRC. 2003. *The Future of Supercomputing: An Interim Report.* Washington, D.C.: The National Academies Press.

[23]Based on the June 2003 TOP500 list at <http://www.top500.org>.

cost challenges and trade-offs associated with these application classes. The report addresses not only present-day applications and technology, but also the context provided by history, by institutions and communities, and by international involvement in supercomputing. Chapter 2 defines supercomputing. Chapter 3 outlines a brief history of supercomputing. Chapter 4 describes many compelling applications that place extreme computational demands on supercomputing. Chapter 5 discusses the design of algorithms, computing platforms, and software environments that govern the performance of supercomputing applications. The institutions, computing platforms, system software, and the people who solve supercomputing applications can be thought of collectively as an ecosystem. Chapter 6 outlines an approach to supercomputing ecosystem creation and maintenance. Chapter 7 discusses the international dimension of supercomputing. Chapter 8 offers a framework for policy analysis. Chapter 9 describes the role of the government in ensuring that supercomputing appropriate to our needs is available both now and in the future. Chapter 10 contains the committee's conclusions and recommendations for action to advance high-end computing.

2

Explanation of Supercomputing

The term "supercomputer" refers to computing systems (hardware, systems software, and applications software) that provide close to the best currently achievable sustained performance on demanding computational problems. The term can refer either to the hardware/software system or to the hardware alone. Two definitions follow:

- From Landau and Fink[1] : "The class of fastest and most powerful computers available."
- From the Academic Press *Dictionary of Science and Technology*: "1. any of a category of extremely powerful, large-capacity mainframe computers that are capable of manipulating massive amounts of data in an extremely short time. 2. any computer that is one of the largest, fastest, and most powerful available at a given time."

"Supercomputing" is used to denote the various activities involved in the design, manufacturing, or use of supercomputers (e.g., "supercomputing industry" or "supercomputing applications"). Similar terms are "high-performance computing" and "high-end computing." The latter terms are used interchangeably in this report to denote the broader range of activities related to platforms that share the same technology as supercomputers but may have lower levels of performance.

---

[1]Rubin H. Landau and Paul J. Fink, Jr. 1993. *A Scientist's and Engineer's Guide to Workstations and Supercomputers.* New York, N.Y.: John Wiley & Sons.

The meaning of the terms supercomputing or supercomputer is relative to the overall state of computing at a given time. For example, in 1994, when describing computers subject to export control, the Department of Commerce's Bureau of Export Administration amended its definition of "supercomputer" to increase the threshold level from a composite theoretical performance (CTP) equal to or exceeding 195 million theoretical operations per second (MTOPS) to a CTP equal to or exceeding 1,500 MTOPS.[2] Current examples of supercomputers are contained in the TOP500 list of the 500 most powerful computer systems as measured by best performance on the Linpack benchmarks.[3]

Supercomputers provide significantly greater sustained performance than is available from the vast majority of installed contemporary mainstream computer systems. In applications such as the analysis of intelligence data, weather prediction, and climate modeling, supercomputers enable the generation of information that would not otherwise be available or that could not be generated in time to be actionable. Supercomputing can accelerate scientific research in important areas such as physics, material sciences, biology, and medicine. Supercomputer simulations can augment or replace experimentation in cases where experiments are hazardous, expensive, or even impossible to perform or to instrument. They can collapse time and enable us to observe the evolution of climate over centuries or the evolution of galaxies over billions of years; they can expand space and allow us to observe atomic phenomena or shrink space and allow us to observe the core of a supernova. They can save lives and money by producing better predictions on the landfall of a hurricane or the impact of an earthquake.

In most cases, the problem solved on a supercomputer is derived from a mathematical model of the physical world. Approximations are made when the world is represented using continuous models (partial differential equations) and when these continuous models are discretized. Validated approximate solutions will provide sufficient information to stimulate human scientific imagination or to aid human engineering judgment. As computational power increases, fewer compromises are made, and more accurate results can be obtained. Therefore, in many application domains, there is essentially no limit to the amount of compute power

---

[2]Federal Register, February 24, 1994, at <http://www.fas.org/spp/starwars/offdocs/940224.htm>.

[3]The TOP500 list is available at <http://www.top500.org>. The Linpack benchmark solves a dense system of linear equations; in the version used for TOP500, one picks a system size for which the computer exhibits the highest computation rate.

that can be usefully applied to a problem. As the committee shows in Chapter 4, many disciplines have a good understanding of how they would exploit supercomputers that are many orders of magnitude more powerful than the ones they currently use; they have a good understanding of how science and engineering will benefit from improvements in supercomputing performance in the years and decades to come.

One of the principal ways to increase the amount of computing achievable in a given period of time is to use parallelism—doing multiple coordinated computations at the same time. Some problems, such as searches for patterns in data, can distribute the computational workload easily. The problem can be broken down into subproblems that can be solved independently on a diverse collection of processors that are intermittently available and that are connected by a low-speed network such as the Internet.[4] Some problems necessarily distribute the work over a high-speed computational grid[5] in order to access unique resources such as very large data repositories or real-time observational facilities. However, many important problems, such as the modeling of fluid flows, cannot be so easily decomposed or widely distributed. While the solution of such problems can be accelerated through the use of parallelism, dependencies among the parallel subproblems necessitate frequent exchanges of data and partial results, thus requiring significantly better communication (both higher bandwidth and lower latency) between processors and data storage than can be provided by a computational grid. Both computational grids and supercomputers hosted in one machine room are components of a cyberinfrastructure, defined in a recent NSF report as "the infrastructure based upon distributed computer, information and communication technology."[6] This report focuses mostly on systems hosted in one machine room (such systems often require a large, dedicated room). To maintain focus, it does not address networking except to note its importance. Also, the report does not address special-purpose hardware accelerators. Special-purpose hardware has always played an important but

---

[4]A good example is SETI@home: The Search for Extraterrestrial Intelligence, <http://setiathome.ssl.berkeley.edu>.

[5]A computational grid is a hardware and software infrastructure that provides dependable, consistent, pervasive, and inexpensive access to high-end computational capabilities (I. Foster and C. Kesselman, 2003, *The Grid 2: Blueprint for a New Computing Infrastructure*, 2nd ed., San Francisco, Calif.: Morgan Kaufman).

[6]NSF. 2003. *Revolutionizing Science and Engineering Through Cyberinfrastructure*. NSF Blue-Ribbon Advisory Panel on Cyberinfrastructure.

limited role in supercomputing.[7] The committee has no evidence that this situation is changing. While it expects special-purpose hardware to continue to play an important role, the existence of such systems does not affect its discussion of general-purpose supercomputers.

Supercomputers in the past were distinguished by their unique (vector) architecture and formed a clearly identifiable product category. Today, clusters of commodity computers that achieve the highest performance levels in scientific computing are not very different from clusters of similar size that are used in various commercial applications. Thus, the distinction between supercomputers and mainstream computers has blurred. Any attempt to draw a clear dividing line between supercomputers and mainstream computers, e.g., by price or level of performance, will lead to arbitrary distinctions. Rather than attempting to draw such distinctions, the discussion will cover the topmost performing systems but will not exclude other high-performance computing systems that share to a significant extent common technology with the top-performing systems.

Virtually all supercomputers are constructed by connecting a number of compute nodes, each having one or more processors with a common memory, by a high-speed interconnection network (or switch). Supercomputer architectures differ in the design of their compute nodes, their switches, and their node-switch interface. The system software used on most contemporary supercomputers is some variant of UNIX; most commonly, programs are written in Fortran, C, and C++, augmented with language or library extensions for parallelism and application libraries.

Global parallelism is most frequently expressed using the MPI message passing library,[8] while OpenMP[9] is often used to express parallelism within a node. Libraries and languages that support global arrays[10] are

---

[7]The GRAPE (short for GRAvity PipE) family of special-purpose systems for astrophysics is one example. See the GRAPE Web site for more information: <http://grape.astron.s.u-tokyo.ac.jp/grape/>.

[8]MPI: A Message-Passing Interface Standard; see <http://www.mpi-forum.org/docs/mpi-11-html/mpi-report.html>.

[9]Leonardo Dagum and Ramesh Menon. 1998. "OpenMP: An Industry-Standard API for Shared-Memory Programming." *IEEE Journal of Computational Science and Engineering* (5)1.

[10]Tarek A. El-Ghazawi, William W. Carlson, and Jesse M. Draper, *UPC Language Specification (V 1.1.1)*, <http://www.gwu.edu/~upc/docs/upc_spec_1.1.1.pdf>; Robert W. Numrich and John Reid, 1998, "Co-array Fortran for Parallel Programming," *SIGPLAN Fortran Forum* 17(2), 1-31; J. Nieplocha, R.J. Harrison, and R.J. Littlefield, 1996, "Global Arrays: A Nonuniform Memory Access Programming Model for High-Performance Computers," *Journal of Supercomputing* 10, 197-220; Katherine Yelick, Luigi Semenzato, Geoff Pike, Carleton Miyamoto, Ben Liblit, Arvind Krishnamurthy, Paul Hilfinger, Susan Graham, David Gay, Philip Colella, and Alexander Aiken, 1998, "Titanium: A High-Performance Java Dialect," *Concurrency: Practice and Experience* 10, 825-836.

becoming more widely used as hardware support for direct access to remote memory becomes more prevalent.

Most of the traditional algorithm approaches must be modified so
that they scale effectively on platforms with a large number of processors. Supercomputers are used to handle larger problems or to introduce
more accurate (but more computationally intensive) physical models.
Both may require new algorithms. Some algorithms are very specialized
to a particular application domain, whereas others—for example, mesh
partitioners—are of general use.

Two commonly used measures of the overall productivity of high-
end computing platforms are capacity and capability. The largest supercomputers are used for capability or turnaround computing where the
maximum processing power is applied to a single problem. The goal is to
solve a larger problem, or to solve a single problem in a shorter period of
time. Capability computing enables the solution of problems that cannot
otherwise be solved in a reasonable period of time (for example, by moving from a two-dimensional to a three-dimensional simulation, using finer
grids, or using more realistic models). Capability computing also enables
the solution of problems with real-time constraints (e.g., intelligence processing and analysis). The main figure of merit is time to solution. Smaller
or cheaper systems are used for capacity computing, where smaller problems are solved. Capacity computing can be used to enable parametric
studies or to explore design alternatives; it is often needed to prepare for
more expensive runs on capability systems. Capacity systems will often
run several jobs simultaneously. The main figure of merit is sustained
performance per unit cost. There is often a trade-off between the two figures of merit, as further reduction in time to solution is achieved at the
expense of increased cost per solution; different platforms exhibit different trade-offs. Capability systems are designed to offer the best possible
capability, even at the expense of increased cost per sustained performance, while capacity systems are designed to offer a less aggressive reduction in time to solution but at a lower cost per sustained performance.[11]

A commonly used unit of measure for both capacity systems and capability systems is peak floating-point operations (additions or multiplications) per second, often measured in teraflops (Tflops), or 10^{12} floating-
point operations per second. For example, a 2003 report by the JASONs[12]

---

[11]Note that the capacity or capability of a system depends on the mix of application codes
it runs. The SETI@home grid system provides more sustained performance for its application than is possible on any single supercomputer platform; it would provide very low sustained performance on a weather simulation.

[12]JASON Program Office. 2003. *Requirements for ASCI.* July 29.

estimated that within 10 years a machine of 1,000 Tflops (1 petaflops) would be needed to execute the most demanding Advanced Simulation and Computing (ASC) application (compared to the then-existing ASC platforms of highest capability, the White at Lawrence Livermore National Laboratory and the Q at Los Alamos National Laboratory, of 12.3 Tflops and 20 Tflops, respectively). Although peak flops are a contributing factor to performance, they are only a partial measure of supercomputer productivity because performance as delivered to the user depends on much more than peak floating-point performance (e.g., on local memory bandwidth and latency or interconnect bandwidth and latency).

A system designed for high capability can typically be reconfigured into multiple virtual lower-capacity machines to run multiple less demanding jobs in parallel. There is much discussion about the use of custom processors for capacity computing (see Box 2.1). Commodity clusters are frequently used for capacity computing because they provide better cost/performance. However, for many capability applications, custom processors give faster turnaround—even on applications for which they are not the most cost-effective capacity machines.

A supercomputer is a scientific instrument that can be used by many disciplines and is not exclusive to one discipline. It can be contrasted, for example, with the Hubble Space Telescope, which has immense potential for enhancing human discovery in astronomy but little potential for designing automobiles. Astronomy also relies heavily on supercomputing to simulate the life cycle of stars and galaxies, after which results from simulations are used in concert with Hubble's snapshots of stars and galaxies at various evolutionary stages to form consistent theoretical views of the cosmos. It can be argued that supercomputing is no less important than the Hubble Telescope in achieving the goal of understanding the universe. However, it is likely that astronomers paid much less attention to ensuring that supercomputing resources would be available than they paid to carefully justifying the significant cost of the telescope. In astronomy, as in other disciplines, supercomputing is essential to progress but is not discipline-specific enough to marshal support to ensure that it is provided. Nevertheless, as the committee heard, the net contributions of supercomputing, when summed over a multitude of disciplines, are no less than monumental in their impact on overall human goals. Therefore, supercomputing in some sense transcends its individual uses and can be a driver of progress in the 21st century.

BOX 2.1 Custom Processors and Commodity Processors

Most supercomputers are built from commodity processors that are designed for a broad market and are manufactured in large numbers. A small number of supercomputers use custom processors that are designed to achieve high performance in scientific computing and are manufactured in small numbers. Commodity processors, because they benefit from economies of scale and sophisticated engineering, provide the shortest time to solution (capability) and the highest sustained performance per unit cost (capacity) for a broad range of applications that have significant spatial and temporal locality and therefore take good advantage of the caches provided by commodity processors. A small set of important scientific applications, however, has almost no locality. They achieve shorter time to solution and better sustained performance per unit cost on a custom processor that provides higher effective local memory bandwidth on access patterns having no locality. For a larger set of applications with low locality, custom processors deliver better time to solution but at a higher cost per unit of sustained performance.

Commodity processors are often criticized because of their low efficiency (the fraction of peak performance they sustain). However, peak performance, and hence efficiency, is the wrong measure. The system metrics that matter are sustained performance (on applications of interest), time to solution, and cost.

The rate at which operands can be transferred to/from the processor is the primary performance bottleneck for many scientific computing codes.[1,2] Custom processors differ primarily in the effective memory bandwidth that they provide on different types of access patterns. Whether a machine has a vector processor, a scalar processor, or a multithreaded processor is a secondary issue. The main issue is whether it has efficient support for irregular accesses (gather/scatter), high memory bandwidth, and the ability to hide memory latency so as to sustain this bandwidth. Vector processors, for example, typically have a short (if any) cache line and high memory bandwidth. The vectors themselves provide a latency hiding mechanism. Such features enable custom processors to more efficiently deliver the raw memory bandwidth provided by memory chips, which often dominate system cost. Hence, these processors can be more cost effective on applications that are limited by memory bandwidth.

Commodity processors are manufactured in high volume and hence benefit from economies of scale. The high volume also justifies sophisticated engineering—for example, the clock rate of the latest Intel Xeon processor is at least four times faster than the clock rate of the Cray X1. A commodity processor includes much of its memory system but little of its memory capacity on the processor chip, and this memory system is adapted for applications with high spatial and temporal locality. A typical commodity processor chip includes the level 1 and 2 caches on the chip and an external memory interface. This external interface limits sustained local memory bandwidth and requires local memory accesses to be performed in units of cache lines (typically 64 to 128 bytes in length[3]). Accessing memory in units of cache lines wastes a large fraction (as much as 94 percent) of local memory bandwidth when only a single word of the cache line is needed.

Many scientific applications have sufficient spatial and temporal locality that they provide better performance per unit cost on commodity processors than on custom processors. Some scientific applications can be solved more quickly using custom processors but at a higher cost. Some users will pay that cost; others will tolerate longer times to solution or restrict the problems they can solve to save money. A small set of scientific applications that are bandwidth-intensive can be solved both more quickly and more cheaply using custom processors. However, because this application class is small, the market for custom processors is quite small.[4]

In summary, commodity processors optimized for commercial applications meet the needs of most of the scientific computing market. For the majority of scientific applications that exhibit significant spatial and temporal locality, commodity processors are more cost effective than custom processors, making them better capability machines. For those bandwidth-intensive applications that do not cache well, custom processors are more cost effective and therefore offer better capacity on just those applications. They also offer better turnaround time for a wider range of applications, making them attractive capability machines. However, the segment of the scientific computing market—bandwidth-intensive and capability—that needs custom processors is too small to support the free market development of such processors.

The above discussion is focused on hardware and on the current state of affairs. As the gap between processor speed and memory speed continues to increase, custom processors may become competitive for an increasing range of applications. From the software perspective, systems with fewer, more powerful processors are easier to program. Increasing the scalability of software applications and tools to systems with tens of thousands or hundreds of thousands of processors is a difficult problem, and the characteristics of the problem do not behave in a linear fashion. The cost of using, developing, and maintaining applications on custom systems can be substantially less than the comparable cost on commodity systems and may cancel out the apparent cost advantages of hardware for commodity-based high-performance systems—for applications that will run only on custom systems. These issues are discussed in more detail in Chapter 5.

---

[1]L. Carrington, A. Snavely, X. Gao, and N. Wolter. 2003. *A Performance Prediction Framework for Scientific Applications.* ICCS Workshop on Performance Modeling and Analysis (PMA03). Melbourne, June.

[2]S. Goedecker and A. Hoisie. 2001. *Performance Optimization of Numerically Intensive Codes.* Philadelphia, Pa.: SIAM Press.

[3]The IBM Power 4 has a 512-byte level 3 cache line.

[4]This categorization of applications is not immutable. Since commodity systems are cheaper and more broadly available, application programmers have invested significant effort in adapting applications to these systems. Bandwidth-intensive applications are those that are not easily adapted to achieve acceptable performance on commodity systems. In many cases the difficulty seems to be intrinsic to the problem being solved.

3

Brief History of Supercomputing

This chapter touches on the role, importance, and special needs of supercomputing.[1] It outlines the history of supercomputing, the emergence of supercomputing as a market, the entry of the Japanese supercomputing manufacturers, and the impact of supercomputing on the broader computer market and on progress in science and engineering. It focuses on hardware platforms and only touches on other supercomputing technologies, notably algorithms and software. A more detailed discussion of current supercomputing technologies is provided in Chapter 5.

THE PREHISTORY OF U.S. SUPERCOMPUTING

The development of computer technology in the United States was inextricably linked to U.S. government funding for research on cryptanalysis, nuclear weapons, and other defense applications in its first several decades.[2] Arguably, the first working, modern, electronic, digital computer was the Colossus machine, put into operation at Bletchley Park,

---

[1]An expanded version of much of the analysis in this chapter will be found in "An Economic History of the Supercomputer Industry," by Kenneth Flamm, 2004.

[2]In Chapter 3, "Military Roots," of *Creating the Computer: Government, Industry, and High Technology* (Brookings Institution Press, 1988), Kenneth Flamm lays out the entire panorama of government-funded projects in the late 1940s and 1950s that essentially created the early U.S. computer industry. Another good but less comprehensive source ends in the very early 1950s, when high-volume production was 20 machines: N. Metropolis, J. Howlett, and Gian-Carlo Rota, *A History of Computing in the Twentieth Century* (Academic Press, 1980).

in the United Kingdom, in 1943. Although it was designed and employed to break a specific German cipher system, this machine was in fact a true electronic computer and could be used, in principle, on a range of problems. The existence of this machine was classified until the 1970s.

U.S. personnel working with Bletchley Park during World War II played a major role in creating the early U.S. computer industry in the decade following the war. In particular, U.S. engineers at the Naval Computing Machinery Laboratory (a National Cash Register plant in Dayton, Ohio, deputized into the war effort) were building copies or improved versions of Bletchley Park electronic cryptanalysis machines, as well as computers of their own design. American engineers involved in this effort included William Norris and Howard Engstrom—Norris later founded Engineering Research Associates (ERA), then Control Data; Engstrom was later deputy director of the National Security Agency (NSA)—and Ralph Palmer who was principal technical architect of IBM's move into electronic computers in the 1950s. Of the 55 people in the founding technical group at ERA, where Seymour Cray had his first design job in computers, 40 came from Navy communications intelligence in Washington, 5 from the Navy lab in Dayton, and 3 from the Naval Ordnance Laboratory.[3]

The ENIAC, built in 1945 at the University of Pennsylvania and often credited as the first functioning electronic computer, was a larger, plug-programmable computer designed to compute artillery ballistics tables.[4] Ironically, it came into existence, indirectly, as a result of the code-breaking efforts of the U.S. intelligence community. The U.S. Army's Ballistic Research Laboratory (BRL) had originally funded a ballistics computer project at National Cash Register and had turned down a competing proposal from J. Presper Eckert and John Mauchly at the University of Pennsylvania. BRL reconsidered this decision after the National Cash Register Dayton group was drafted into producing cryptanalysis machines for the Navy and finally decided to fund the ENIAC project.

---

[3]See Flamm, 1988, pp. 36-41, 43-45.

[4]As is the case for many other technologies, there has been a heated debate about who should be credited as the inventor of the first digital computer. In addition to the Colossus and the ENIAC, the following are worth mentioning: Konrad Zuse, working in Germany, built a relay-based automatic digital computer in Germany in 1939-1941. A similar system, the Automatic Sequence Controlled Calculator (ASCC), also called the Mark I, was conceived by Howard Aiken and designed and built by IBM in 1939-1944. John Vincent Atanasoff and Clifford Berry started building an electronic digital computer at Iowa State University in 1937-1942. Although the project was not completed, Atanasoff and Berry won a patent case against Eckert and Mauchly in 1973, invalidating the patent of the latter on ENIAC as the first automatic electronic computer.

Princeton mathematician and War Department consultant John von Neumann heard about the existence of the ENIAC project at the BRL and involved himself in the project.[5] It is reported that some of the early atomic bomb calculations (in which von Neumann was involved) made use of the ENIAC even before it was formally delivered to the Army. The link between both cryptanalytical and nuclear design applications and high-performance computing goes back to the very first computers.

ENIAC's designers, Eckert and Mauchly, built the first working stored program electronic computer in the United States in 1949 (the BINAC) and delivered it to Northrop Aircraft, a defense contractor. A number of advanced machines had been built in Britain by that time—Britain was actually leading in the construction of working electronic computers in the late 1940s. A massive U.S. government investment in computer technology in the 1950s was critical to the rapid rise of U.S. companies as the undisputed leaders in the field.

The second and third computers in the United States were the SEAC (built for the National Bureau of Standards, now renamed NIST) and the ERA 1101 (built for predecessors to the National Security Agency). Both went into operation in 1950, runners-up in the United States to the Eckert-Mauchly BINAC.

The first Eckert and Mauchly-designed computer targeting a commercial market, the UNIVAC, was delivered to the Census Bureau in 1951. The experimental MIT Whirlwind computer, built with Navy and later Air Force funding, also went into operation in 1951.

Von Neumann, who had brought British computing theoretician Alan Turing to Princeton in the 1930s and was much influenced by this contact, began work on the conceptual design of a general-purpose scientific computer for use in calculations of military interest in 1946, but a working machine was not completed until 1951. This machine was intended to be a tool for scientists and engineers doing numerical calculations of the sort needed in nuclear weapons design. Versions of the first machine installed at the Institute of Advanced Studies in Princeton, the IAS machine, were built and installed at Los Alamos (the MANIAC I) in 1952 and Oak Ridge (the ORACLE) in 1953; these were the first computers installed at the nuclear weapons laboratories.[6] The nuclear weapons labs-sponsored IAS design was highly influential. But the laboratories were so pressed for computing resources before these machines were delivered that they did

---

[5]Nancy Stern. 1981. *From ENIAC to UNIVAC: An Appraisal of the Eckert-Mauchly Computers.* Digital Press.

[6]The Argonne National Laboratory built AVIDAC (Argonne's Version of the Institute's Digital Automatic Computer), which was operational prior to IAS.

their calculations on the SEAC at the National Bureau of Standards and ran thermonuclear calculations on the floor of the UNIVAC factory in Philadelphia.

Volume computer production did not begin until 1953. In that year, the first ERA 1103 was delivered to the cryptanalysts in the intelligence community, as was the first IBM 701 Defense Calculator. Twenty ERA 1103s and 19 IBM 701s were built; all were delivered to DoD customers.

NSA was the primary sponsor of high-performance computing through most of the post-1103 1950s era. It sponsored the Philco 210 and the Philco 211 and cosponsored the IBM 7030 Stretch as part of its support for the Harvest system. DoD supported the development of the IBM 7090 for use in a ballistic missile early warning system.

Energy lab-sponsored computers did not play a leading role at the frontiers of high-performance computing until the late 1950s. The Atomic Energy Commission (AEC) set up a formal computer research program in 1956 and contracted with IBM for the Stretch system and with Sperry Rand (which acquired both the Eckert-Mauchly computer group and ERA in the 1950s) for the Livermore Advanced Research Computer (LARC). The cosponsorship of the Stretch system by NSA and AEC required IBM to meet the needs of two different customers (and applications) in one system. It was said that balancing those demands was an important factor in the success of IBM's system 360.

SUPERCOMPUTERS EMERGE AS A MARKET

With the emergence of specific models of computers built in commercial volumes (in that era, the double digits) in the 1950s, and the dawning realization that computers were applicable to a potentially huge range of scientific and business data processing tasks, smaller and cheaper computers began to be produced in significant numbers. In the early 1950s, machines produced in volume were typically separated by less than an order of magnitude in speed. By the late 1950s, the fastest, most expensive computers were three to four orders of magnitude more powerful than the smallest models sold in large numbers. By the early 1970s, that range had widened even further, with a spread now exceeding four orders of magnitude in performance between highest performance machines and small business or scientific computers selling in volume (see Figure 3.1).

In the late 1950s, the U.S. government, motivated primarily by national security needs to support intelligence and nuclear weapons applications, institutionalized its dominant role in funding the development of cutting-edge high-performance computing technology for these two sets of military applications. Arguably, the first supercomputers explicitly intended as such, designed to push an order of magnitude beyond the fast-

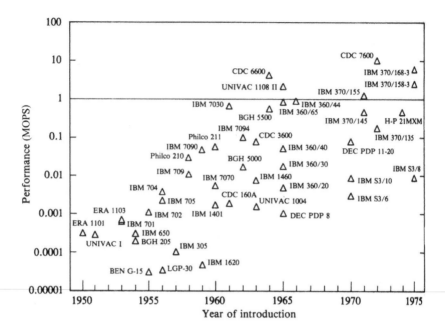

FIGURE 3.1 Early computer performance. Included in this figure are the best-performing machines according to value of installations, number of installations, and millions of operations per second (MOPS). SOURCE: Kenneth Flamm. 1988. *Creating the Computer: Government, Industry, and High Technology.* Washington, D.C.: Brookings Institution Press.

est available commercial machines, were the IBM 7030 Stretch and Sperry Rand UNIVAC LARC, delivered in the early 1960s.[7]

These two machines established a pattern often observed in subsequent decades: The government-funded supercomputers were produced in very limited numbers and delivered primarily to government users. But the technology pioneered in these systems would find its way into the industrial mainstream a generation or two later in commercial systems. For example, one typical evaluation holds that "while the IBM 7030 was not considered successful, it spawned many technologies incorporated in future machines that were highly successful. The transistor logic was the basis for the IBM 7090 line of scientific computers, then the 7040 and 1400 lines. Multiprogramming, memory protection, generalized interrupts, the

---

[7]The term "supercomputer" seems to have come into use in the 1960s, when the IBM 7030 Stretch and Control Data 6600 were delivered.

8-bit byte were all concepts later incorporated in the IBM 360 line of computers as well as almost all third-generation processors and beyond. Instruction pipelining, prefetch and decoding, and memory interleaving were used in later supercomputer designs such as the IBM 360 Models 91, 95, and 195, as well as in computers from other manufacturers. These techniques are now used in most advanced microprocessors, such as the Intel Pentium and the Motorola/IBM PowerPC."[8] Similarly, LARC technologies were used in Sperry Rand's UNIVAC III.[9]

Yet another feature of the supercomputer marketplace also became established over this period: a high mortality rate for the companies involved. IBM exited the supercomputer market in the mid-1970s. Sperry Rand exited the supercomputer market a few years after many of its supercomputer designers left to found the new powerhouse that came to dominate U.S. supercomputers in the 1960s—the Control Data Corporation (CDC).

CONTROL DATA AND CRAY

From the mid-1960s to the late 1970s, the global U.S. supercomputer industry was dominated by two U.S. companies: CDC and its offspring, Cray Research. Both companies traced their roots back to ERA, which had been absorbed by Sperry Rand in 1952. A substantial portion of this talent pool (including Seymour Cray) left to form a new company, CDC, in 1957. CDC was to become the dominant manufacturer of supercomputers from the mid-1960s through the mid-1970s. Government users, particularly the intelligence community, funded development of CDC's first commercial offering, the CDC 1604. In 1966 CDC shipped its first full-scale supercomputer, the CDC 6600, a huge success. In addition to offering an order of magnitude jump in absolute computational capability (see Figure 3.1), it did so very cost effectively. As suggested by Figure 3.2, computing power was delivered by the 6600 at a price comparable to or lower than that of the best cost/performance in mainstream commercial machines.[10]

---

[8]Historical information on the IBM 7030 is available online from the Wikipedia at <http://en.wikipedia.org/wiki/IBM_7030>.

[9]See <http://en.wikipedia.org/wiki/IBM_7030>; G. Gray, "The UNIVAC III Computer," *Unisys History Newsletter* 2(1) (revised 1999), <http://www.cc.gatech.edu/gvu/people/randy.carpenter/folklore/v2n1.html>.

[10]The benchmarks, the performance metrics, and the cost metrics used for that figure are considerably different from those used today, but the qualitative comparison is generally accepted.

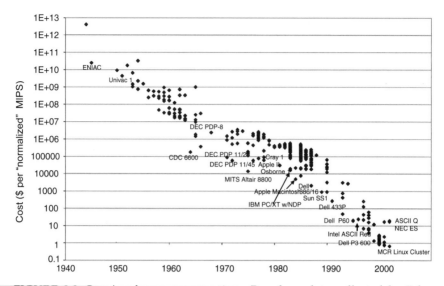

FIGURE 3.2 Cost/performance over time. Based on data collected by John McCallum at <http://www.jcmit.com/cpu-performance.htm>. NEC Earth Simulator cost corrected from $350 million to $500 million. Note that "normalized" MIPS (millions of instructions per second) is constructed by combining a variety of benchmarks run on these machines over this 50-year period, using scores on multiple benchmarks run on a single machine to do the normalization.

At this point, there was no such thing as a commodity processor. All computer processors were custom produced. The high computational performance of the CDC 6600 at a relatively low cost was a testament to the genius of its design team. Additionally, the software tools that were provided by CDC made it possible to efficiently deliver this performance to the end user.

Although the 6600 gave CDC economic success at the time, simply delivering theoretical computational power at a substantially lower price per computation was not sufficient for CDC to dominate the market. Then, as now, the availability of applications software, the availability of specialized peripherals and storage devices tailored for specific applications, and the availability of tools to assist in programming new software were just as important to many customers.

The needs of the government users were different. Because the specific applications and codes they ran for defense applications were often secret, frequently were tied to special-purpose custom hardware and peripherals built in small numbers, and changed quickly over time, the availability of low-cost, commercially available peripherals and software were often unimportant. The defense agencies typically invested in creating the software and computing infrastructure they needed (for example, NASTRAN[11] and DYNA[12]). When some of that software became available to commercial customers after it had been made available to the first government customers, these supercomputers became much more attractive to them.

In 1972, computer designer Seymour Cray left CDC and formed a new company, Cray Research. Although CDC continued to produce high-performance computers through the remainder of the 1970s (e.g., STAR100), Cray quickly became the dominant player in the highest performance U.S. supercomputer arena.[13] The Cray-1, first shipped to Los Alamos National Laboratory in 1976, set the standard for contemporary supercomputer design. The Cray-1 supported a vector architecture in which vectors of floating-point numbers could be loaded from memory into vector registers and processed in the arithmetic unit in a pipelined manner at much higher speeds than were possible for scalar operands.[14] Vector processing became the cornerstone of supercomputing. Like the CDC 6600, the Cray-1 delivered massive amounts of computing power at a price competitive with the most economical computing systems of the day. Figure 3.2 shows that the cost of sustained computing power on the Cray-1 was roughly comparable to that of the cost/performance champion of the day, the Apple II microcomputer.

During this period, IBM retreated from the supercomputer market, instead focusing on its fast-growing and highly profitable commercial computer systems businesses. Apart from a number of larger companies flirting with entry into the supercomputer business by building experimental machines (but never really succeeding) and several smaller com-

---

[11]NASTRAN (NASA Structural Analysis) was originally developed at Goddard Space Flight Center and released in 1971 (see <http://www.sti.nasa.gov/tto/spinoff2002/goddard.html>). There are now several commercial implementations.

[12]DYNA3D was originally developed in the 1970s at the Lawrence Livermore National Laboratory to simulate underground nuclear tests and determine the vulnerability of underground bunkers to strikes by nuclear missiles. Its successor, LS-DYNA, which simulates vehicle crashes, is commercially available.

[13]CDC ultimately exited the supercomputer business in the 1980s, first spinning off its supercomputer operations in a new subsidiary, ETA, and then shutting down ETA a few years later, in 1989.

[14]Vector processing first appeared in the CDC STAR100 and the Texas Instruments ASC, both announced in 1972. Much of the vector processing technology, including vectorizing compilers, originated from the Illiac IV project, developed at Illinois.

panies that successfully pioneered a lower-end, cost-oriented "mini-supercomputer" market niche, U.S. producers CDC and Cray dominated the global supercomputer industry in the 1970s and much of the 1980s.

Although it was not widely known or documented at the time, in addition to using the systems from CDC and Cray, the defense community built special-purpose, high-performance computers. Most of these computers were used for processing radar and acoustic signals and images. These computers were often "mil-spec'ed" (designed to function in hostile environments). In general, these systems performed arithmetic operations on 16- and 32-bit data. Fast Fourier transforms and digital filters were among the most commonly used algorithms. Many of the commercial array processor companies that emerged in the late 1970s were spin-offs of these efforts.

The commercial array processors, coupled with minicomputers from Digital Equipment Corporation and Data General, were often used as supercomputers. The resulting hybrid system combined a commodity host with a custom component. Unlike most other supercomputers of the period, these systems were air-cooled.

The 1970s also witnessed the shipment of the first simple, single-chip computer processor (or microprocessor) by the Intel Corporation, in November 1971. By the early 1980s, this technology had matured to the point where it was possible to build simple (albeit relatively low-performance) computers capable of "serious" computing tasks. The use of low-cost, mass-produced, high-volume commodity microprocessors was to transform all segments of the computer industry. The highest performance segment of the industry, the supercomputer, was the last to be transformed by this development.

ENTER JAPAN

By the mid-1980s, with assistance from a substantial government-subsidized R&D program launched in the 1970s and from a history of trade and industrial policy that effectively excluded foreign competitors from Japanese markets, Japanese semiconductor producers had pushed to the technological frontier in semiconductor manufacturing. Historically, the rationale for Japanese government support in semiconductors had been to serve as a stepping-stone for creating a globally competitive computer industry, since the semiconductor divisions of the large Japanese electronics companies had also produced computers sold in a protected Japanese market. Aided by their new capabilities in semiconductors and a successful campaign to acquire key bits of IBM's mainframe technology, by the mid-1980s Japanese computer companies were shipping cost-effective commercial computer systems that were competitive with, and often compatible with, IBM's mainframes.[15]

Thus it was that the United States viewed with some concern Japan's announcement of two government-funded computer R&D programs in the early 1980s explicitly intended to put Japanese computer producers at the cutting edge in computer technology. One was the Fifth Generation Computer System project, which was primarily focused on artificial intelligence and logic programming. The other was the High Speed Computing System for Scientific and Technological Uses project, also called the SuperSpeed project, which focused on supercomputing technology.[16] At roughly the same time, the three large Japanese electronics companies manufacturing mainframe computers began to sell supercomputers at home and abroad. The Japanese vendors provided good vectorizing compilers with their vector supercomputers. Although the Fifth Generation project ultimately would pose little threat to U.S. computer companies, it stimulated a substantial government effort in the United States to accelerate the pace of high-performance computing innovation. In the 1980s this effort, led by DARPA, funded the large Strategic Computing Initiative (SCI), which transformed the face of the U.S. supercomputer industry.

The prospect of serious competition from Japanese computer companies in mainstream markets also led to a series of trade policy responses by U.S. companies and their supporters in the U.S. government (see the discussion of trade policies in Chapter 8, Box 8.1). By the 1980s, Fujitsu, Hitachi, and NEC were all shipping highly capable supercomputers competitive with Cray's products, dominating the Japanese market and beginning to make inroads into European and American markets. The vast majority of Japanese supercomputers were sold outside the United States. There were some minimal sales to the United States in areas such as the petroleum industry but few sales to U.S. government organizations. Significant obstacles faced the sales of U.S.-made supercomputers in Japan as well. Responding to these market limitations in the 1980s, U.S. trade negotiators signed agreements with the Japanese government designed to open up government procurement in Japan to U.S. supercomputer producers. (In Japan, as in the United States, the government dominated the market for supercomputers.) In the mid-1990s, the U.S. government also supported U.S. supercomputer makers in bringing an antidumping case

---

[15]A good reference for the survey of supercomputer development in Japan is Y. Oyanagi, 1999, "Development of Supercomputers in Japan: Hardware and Software," *Parallel Computing* 25:1545-1567.

[16]D.K. Kahaner. 1992. "High Performance Computing in Japan: Supercomputing." Asian Technology Information Program. June.

against Japanese supercomputer makers in the U.S. market. That case ultimately forced Japanese companies out of the U.S. market until 2003, when a suspension agreement was signed.

INNOVATION IN SUPERCOMPUTING

While one part of the U.S. government reacted by building walls around the U.S. market, DARPA and its Strategic Computing Initiative (SCI), in concert with other government agencies and programs, took the opposite tack, attempting to stimulate a burst of innovation that would qualitatively alter the industry.[17] Computing technology was regarded as the cornerstone of qualitative superiority for U.S. weapons systems. It was argued that the United States could not regain a significant qualitative lead in computing technology merely by introducing faster or cheaper computer components, since Japanese producers had clearly achieved technological parity, if not some element of superiority, in manufacturing them. Furthermore, many technologists believed that continued advances in computer capability based on merely increasing the clock rates of traditional computer processor designs were doomed to slow down as inherent physical limits to the size of semiconductor electronic components were approached. In addition, Amdahl's law was expected to restrict increases in performance due to an increase in the number of processors used in parallel.[18]

The approach to stimulating innovation was to fund an intense effort to do what had not previously been done—to create a viable new architecture for massively parallel computers, some of them built around commodity processors, and to demonstrate that important applications could benefit from massive parallelism. Even if the individual processors were less efficient in delivering usable computing power, as long as the parallel architecture was sufficiently scalable, interconnecting a sufficient number

---

[17]Investments in high-performance computing were only one area funded by the SCI, which funded over $1 billion in R&D from 1983 to 1993. There are no available data that break out this investment by technology area. Other areas were electronic components, artificial intelligence and expert systems, and large-scale prototype development of advanced military systems intended to explore new technology concepts. The committee is not aware of any objective assessment of the success and utility of the program as a whole. An excellent history of the program may be found in Alex Roland and Phillip Shiman, 2002, *Strategic Computing: DARPA and the Quest for Machine Intelligence, 1983-1993*, Cambridge, Mass.: MIT Press.

[18]Amdahl's law states that if a fraction of $1/s$ of an execution is sequential, then parallelism can reduce execution time by at most a factor of s. Conventional wisdom in the early 1980s was that for many applications of interest Amdahl's law will restrict gains in performance from parallelism to factors of tens or low hundreds.

of processors might potentially provide a great deal of computing capability. Once the hardware architectural details of how to scale up these systems were determined, very large parallel machines could be put to work, and supercomputers that were orders of magnitude faster would give the government agencies charged with national security new qualitative technological advantages. It was assumed that appropriate software technology would follow.

This was the dream that motivated the architects of the U.S. government's supercomputer technology investments in the late 1980s. Dozens of new industrial flowers bloomed in DARPA's Strategic Computing hothouse from the mid-1980s through the early 1990s. Old players and new ones received substantial support for experiments with new, parallel architectures.[19]

It has become commonplace to point to the high mortality rate among U.S. supercomputer manufacturers in the 1990s and the large amount of resources invested by the U.S. government in now defunct massively parallel supercomputer makers. Many critics believe that the DARPA program was a failure that harmed the market.[20] Most of these start-up companies went bankrupt or were sold.

Over this period, however, some important lessons were learned. One was the importance of node performance; another was the importance of high-bandwidth, low-latency, scalable interconnects. The evolution of the Thinking Machines products from the CM-1 (with bit serial processors and a relatively low-performing, single-stage bit-serial network) to the CM-5 (with a powerful SPARC node enhanced with a vector unit and a powerful, scalable multistage network) is a typical example. Over time,

---

[19]Gordon Bell's list of experiments includes ATT/Columbia (Non Von), BBN Labs, Bell Labs/Columbia (DADO), CMU (Production Systems), CMU Warp (GE and Honeywell), Encore, ESL, GE (like connection machine), Georgia Tech, Hughes (dataflow), IBM (RP3), MIT/Harris, MIT/Motorola (Dataflow), MIT Lincoln Labs, Princeton (MMMP), Schlumberger (FAIM-1), SDC/Burroughs, SRI (Eazyflow), University of Texas, Thinking Machines (Connection Machine). See Gordon Bell, "PACT 98," a slide presentation available at <http://www.research.microsoft.com/barc/gbell/pact.ppt>.

[20]A list of failed industrial ventures in this area, many inspired by SCI, includes Alliant, American Supercomputer, Ametek, AMT, Astronautics, BBN Supercomputer, Biin, CDC/ETA Systems, Chen Systems, Columbia Homogeneous Parallel Processor, Cogent, Cray Computer, Culler, Cydrome, Denelcor, Elxsi, Encore, E&S Supercomputers, Flexible, Goodyear, Gould/SEL, Intel Supercomputer Division, IPM, iP-Systems, Kendall Square Research, Key, Multiflow, Myrias, Pixar, Prevec, Prisma, Saxpy, SCS, SDSA, Stardent (Stellar and Ardent), Supercomputer Systems Inc., Suprenum, Synapse, Thinking Machines, Trilogy, VItec, Vitesse, Wavetracer (E. Strohmaier, J.J. Dongarra, and H.W. Meuer, 1999, "Marketplace of High-Performance Computing," *Parallel Computing* 25(13):1517-1544.

DARPA shifted its emphasis from hardware alone to complementary investments in software that would make the newly developed parallel hardware easier to program and use in important applications. These investments included modest support for the port of industrial codes to the new scalable architectures.

In the commercial supercomputing arena, there continued to be vector architectures as well as the increasing presence of scalable systems based on commodity processors. There were many common attributes among the supercomputers of this period. Among them were these:

• Device technology shifted to complementary metal oxide semiconductor (CMOS), both for commodity-based systems and for custom systems. As a result, custom systems lost the advantage of faster technology.

• The increase in clock and memory speeds coincided with Moore's law.

• The reduction of the size of the processor resulted in small-scale multiprocessor systems (two to four processors) being used as nodes in scalable systems; larger shared-memory configurations appeared as high-end technical servers.

• Vendors began supplying vectorizing and (in some cases) parallelizing compilers, programming tools, and operating systems (mostly UNIX-based), which made it easier to program.

The common architectural features—vector processing, parallel shared memory, and, later, message passing—also encouraged third parties to develop software for this class of computers. In particular, standard numerical libraries such as the BLAS[21] evolved to supply common high-level operations, and important scientific and engineering applications such as NASTRAN appeared in vectorized and parallelized versions. The development of this software base benefited all supercomputer manufacturers by expanding the total market for machines. Similarly, the availability of common software and a shared programming model benefited the entire user community, both government and commercial.

By accident or by design, the course correction effected by SCI had some important and favorable economic implications for the U.S. supercomputer industry. Suppose that technology were available to per-

---

[21]C.L. Lawson, R.J. Hanson, D.R. Kincaid, and F.T. Krogh, 1979, "Basic Linear Algebra Subprograms for Fortran Usage," *ACM Transactions on Mathematical Software* 5:308-325; J.J. Dongarra, J. Du Croz, S. Hammarling, and R.J. Hanson, 1988, "An Extended Set of Fortran Basic Linear Algebra Subprograms," *ACM Transactions on Mathematical Software* 14(1):1–17; J.J. Dongarra, J. Du Croz, S. Hammarling, and I.S. Duff, "A Set of Level 3 Basic Linear Algebra Subprograms," *ACM Transactions on Mathematical Software* 16(1):1-17.

mit large numbers of inexpensive, high-volume commodity microprocessors to divide up the work of a given computing task. Then the continuing steep declines in the cost of commodity processors would eventually make such a system a more economic solution for supplying computing capability than a system designed around much smaller numbers of very expensive custom processors that were falling in cost much less rapidly. If a richer and more portable software base became available for these systems, the cost of their adoption would be reduced. If so, the difference in price trends between custom and commodity processors would eventually make a parallel supercomputer built using commodity components a vastly more economically attractive proposition than the traditional approach using custom processors.

In the late 1980s and early 1990s, DARPA shifted more of its supercomputer investments into systems based on commercially available processors, at Thinking Machines (what was to become the CM-5, using SPARC processors), at Intel (what was to become its Paragon supercomputer line, using Intel's iPSC processor), and at Cray (its T3D system, using DEC's Alpha processor).[22] The net impact of this shift benefited the development and sales of commodity-based systems. This outcome was particularly important given the increasing and highly competent Japanese competition in the market for traditional vector supercomputers. Rather than backing an effort to stay ahead of the competition in an established market in which competitors had seized the momentum, research- and experience-rich U.S. companies threw the entire competition onto a whole new battlefield, where they had a substantial advantage over their competitors.

Some of these hardware and software characteristics also found their way into a new generation of supercomputers, called "mini-supercomputers" (e.g., Convex, Alliant, Multiflow). Unlike the products from Cray and CDC, the mini-supercomputers were air-cooled, had virtual memory operating systems, and sold for under $1 million. The mini-supercomputer systems included UNIX operating systems and automatic vectorizing/parallelizing compilers. This new generation of software systems was based on prior academic research. With UNIX came a wealth of development tools and software components (editors, file systems, etc). The systems also made extensive use of open standards used for I/O bus-

---

[22]The Myrinet commodity interconnects used in a number of commodity supercomputer systems were also developed with DARPA support at about this time (Alex Roland and Philip Shiman, 2002. *Strategic Computing: DARPA and the Quest for Machine Intelligence, 1983-1993*, Cambridge, Mass.: MIT Press. pp. 308-317; DARPA, *Technology Transition*, 1997, pp. 42, 45.

ses, peripheral devices, and networking (e.g., TCP/IP). This standardization made it easier for users and independent software vendors (ISVs) to move from one platform to another. Additionally, the client/server model evolved through the use of Ethernet and TCP/IP. The NSF-funded supercomputer centers helped promote the adoption of UNIX for supercomputers; the Cray systems at those centers were required to run UNIX. Also, DARPA required the use of UNIX as a standard operating system for many of the supercomputing projects it funded. Ultimately every supercomputer platform supported UNIX. That in turn increased the use of the programming language C, which became widely used to write numerically intense applications. The newer generation of compilers enabled applications written in standard Fortran and C to be optimized and tuned to the contemporary supercomputers. This led to the widespread conversion of ISV-developed software and consequently the widespread adoption of supercomputing by the commercial (non-government-sponsored) marketplace.

Moore's law continued to hold, and to a large degree it changed the face of supercomputing. The systems built in the 1980s were all built from CMOS or from ECL gate arrays. As the density of CMOS increased, it became possible to put an entire processor on one die, creating a microprocessor. This led to the attack of "killer micros."[23] The killer micro permitted multiple microprocessors to be coupled together and run in parallel. For applications that could be parallelized (both algorithmically and by localizing data to a particular processor/memory system), a coupled system of killer micros could outperform a custom-designed supercomputer. Just as important, the single-processor scalar performance of a killer micro often exceeded the single-processor scalar performance of a supercomputer. This next generation of supercomputer resulted in a change of architectures. High-performance vector systems began to be replaced by parallel processing, often massive—hundreds and thousands of microprocessors.

Thus, although it is true that there was an extraordinarily high mortality rate among the companies that developed parallel computer architectures in the 1980s and early 1990s, much was learned from the technical failures as well as the successes. Important architectural and conceptual problems were confronted, parallel systems were made to work at a much larger scale than in the past, and the lessons learned were

---

[23]The term "killer micro" was popularized by Eugene Brooks in his presentation to the Teraflop Computing Panel, "Attack of the Killer Micros," at Supercomputing 1989 in Reno, Nev. (see also <http://jargon.watson-net.com/jargon.asp?w=killer%20micro>).

absorbed by other U.S. companies, which typically hired key technical staff from defunct parallel supercomputer pioneers. Subsequently, there were five major new U.S. entrants into the high-performance computing (HPC) market in the 1990s—IBM, SGI, Sun, DEC/Compaq (recently merged into Hewlett-Packard), and Convex/HP—which today have survived with the lion's share (as measured in numbers of systems) of the HPC marketplace.

Though dreams of effortless parallelism seem as distant as ever, the fact is that the supercomputer marketplace today is dominated by a new class of useful, commodity-processor-based parallel systems that—while not necessarily the most powerful high-performance systems available—are the most widely used. The commercial center of gravity of the supercomputer market is today dominated by U.S. companies marketing commodity-processor parallel systems that capitalize on technology investments made by the U.S. government in large-scale parallel hardware (and to a lesser extent, software) technology in the 1980s and 1990s.

RECENT DEVELOPMENTS IN SUPERCOMPUTING

To some extent, the reasons for the dominance of commodity-processor systems are economic, as illustrated by the hardware costs shown in Figure 3.2. Contemporary distributed-memory supercomputer systems based on commodity processors (like Linux clusters) appear to be substantially more cost effective—by roughly an order of magnitude—in delivering computing power to applications that do not have stringent communication requirements. However, there has been little progress, and perhaps even some regress, in making scalable systems easy to program. Software directions that were started in the early 1980s (such as CM-Fortran and High-Performance Fortran) were largely abandoned. The payoff to finding better ways to program such systems and thus expand the domains in which these systems can be applied would appear to be large.

The move to distributed memory has forced changes in the programming paradigm of supercomputing. The high cost of processor-to-processor synchronization and communication requires new algorithms that minimize those operations. The structuring of an application for vectorization is seldom the best structure for parallelization on these systems. Moreover, despite some research successes in this area, without some guidance from the programmer, compilers are not generally able to detect enough of the necessary parallelism or to reduce sufficiently the interprocessor overheads. The use of distributed memory systems has led to the introduction of new programming models, particularly the message passing paradigm, as realized in MPI, and the use of parallel loops in shared memory subsystems, as supported by OpenMP. It also has forced significant reprogramming of libraries and applications to port onto the new architectures. Debuggers and performance tools for scalable systems have developed slowly, however, and even today most users consider the programming tools on parallel supercomputers to be inadequate.

THE U.S. HIGH-PERFORMANCE COMPUTING INDUSTRY TODAY

Today, the current tension in the industry is between a large number of applications that make acceptable use of relatively inexpensive super-computers incorporating large numbers of low-cost commodity proces-sors and a small number of highly important applications (predominantly the domain of government customers) in which the required performance can currently be provided only by highly tuned systems making use of expensive custom components. This tension is at the root of many of the policy issues addressed by this report.

Despite the apparent economic weakness of the sole remaining U.S. vector-based supercomputer maker, Cray (which makes supercomputers based on custom processors), available data on the supercomputer mar-ketplace (based on the TOP500 list of June 2004) show it is dominated by U.S. companies today. International Data Corporation (IDC) numbers paint a similar picture: In 2000, U.S. vendors had 93 percent of the high-performance technical computing market (defined to include all technical servers) and 70 percent of the capability market (defined as systems pur-chased to solve the largest, most performance-demanding problems). In 2002 the numbers were 95 percent and 81 percent and in 2003 they were 98 percent and 88 percent, respectively, showing a continued strengthen-ing of U.S. vendors. Ninety-four percent of technical computing systems selling for more than $1 million in 2003 were U.S. made.[24] It may be a legitimate matter of concern to U.S. policymakers that the fastest com-puter in the world was designed in Japan and has been located there for the last 2 years. But it would be inaccurate to assert that the U.S. super-computer industry is in trouble. Indeed, the competitive position of U.S. supercomputer producers is as strong as it has been in decades, and all signs point to continued improvement.

To characterize the current dynamics of the U.S. industry, the com-mittee turned to a detailed analysis of the TOP500 data (using the June 2004 list), which are available for the period 1993-2003.[25] While the TOP500

---

[24]Source: Earl Joseph, Program Vice President, High-Performance Systems, IDC; e-mail exchanges, phone conversations, and in-person briefings from December 2003 to October 2004.

[25]For details and the data used in the analysis that follows, see <http://www.top500.org>.

lists are the best publicly available source of information on supercomputing trends, it is important to keep in mind the limitations of this source of information.

The R_{max} Linpack metric used by the TOP500 ranking does not correlate well with performance on many real-life workloads; this issue is further discussed in the section on metrics in Chapter 5. While no one number can characterize the performance of a system for diverse workloads, it is likely that the R_{max} metric exaggerates by at least a factor of 2 the real performance of commodity platforms relative to custom platforms. Similarly, custom high-performance systems are significantly more expensive than commodity systems relative to their performance as measured by R_{max}. Thus, if R_{max} is used as a proxy for market share, then the TOP500 list greatly exaggerates the dollar value of the market share of commodity systems. The TOP500 data merit analyzing because the changes and the evolution trends identified in the analysis are real. However, one should not attach too much significance to the absolute numbers.

Some large deployed systems are not reported in the TOP500 list. In some cases, organizations may not want to have their computer power known, either for security or competitiveness reasons. Thus, companies that sell mainly to classified organizations may see their sales underreported in the TOP500 lists. In other cases, organizations may not see value in a TOP500 listing or may consider that running a benchmark is too burdensome. This is especially true for companies that assemble clusters on their own and need to provide continuous availability. Although Web search or Web caching companies own the largest clusters, they do not usually appear in the TOP500 lists. Many large clusters used by service companies and some large clusters deployed in academia are also missing from the TOP500 list, even though they could be there. It is reasonable to assume that this biases the TOP500 listing toward underreporting of commercial systems and overreporting of research systems, supporting the argument that use of high-performance computing platforms in industry does not seem to be declining. While custom systems will be underreported because of their heavier use in classified applications, clusters will be underreported because of their use in large service deployments. It is not clear whether these two biases cancel each other out.

TOP500 provides information on the platform but not on its usage. The size of deployed platforms may not be indicative of the size of parallel applications run on these platforms. Industry often uses clusters as capacity systems; large clusters are purchased to consolidate resources in one place, reducing administration costs and providing better security and control. On the other hand, computing tends to be less centralized in academia, and a cluster often serves a small number of top users. Thus, a

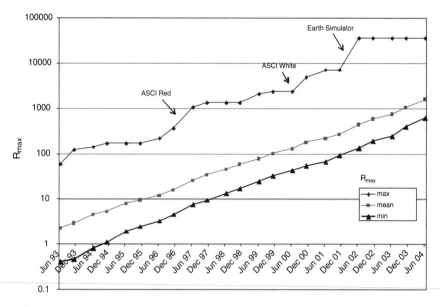

FIGURE 3.3 TOP500 Linpack performance.

good penetration of TOP500 platforms in industry does not necessarily indicate that applications in industry have scaled up in proportion to the scaling of TOP500 platforms over the years; the size of academic platforms is a better indicator of the scale of applications running on them.

Keeping those caveats in mind, many things can be learned from studying the TOP500 data.

There has been continuing rapid improvement in the capability of high-performance systems over the last decade (see Figure 3.3).[26] Mean Linpack performance has improved fairly steadily, by roughly an order of magnitude every 4 years (about 80 percent improvement annually). The performance of the very fastest machines (as measured by the R_{max}[27] of the machine) has shown much greater unevenness over this period but on average seems roughly comparable. Interestingly, the performance of the least capable machines on the list has been improving more rapidly than

---

[26]ASCI White and ASCI Red are two supercomputers installed at DOE sites as part of the ASC strategy. Information on all of the ASC supercomputers is available at <http://www.llnl.gov/asci/platforms/platforms.html>.

[27]The R_{max} is the maximal performance achieved on the Linpack benchmark—for any size system of linear equations.

mean performance, and the ratio between the least capable and the list mean is substantially smaller now than it was back in 1993. This reflects the fact that performance improvement in low-cost commodity microprocessors (used in lower-end TOP500 systems) in recent years has exceeded the already impressive rates of performance improvement in custom processors used in the higher-end systems; it also reflects the fact that in recent years, the average size of commonly available clusters has increased more rapidly than the size of the most powerful supercomputers.

There is no evidence of a long-term trend to widening performance gaps between the least and most capable systems on the TOP500 list (see Figure 3.4). One measure of this gap is the relative standard deviation of R_{max} of machines on this list, normalized by dividing by mean R_{max} in any given year. There was a significant jump in this gap in early 2002, when the Earth Simulator went operational, but it has since diminished to prior levels as other somewhat less fast machines made the list and as the least capable machines improved faster than the mean capability. Essentially the same story is told if one simply measures the ratio between greatest performance and the mean.

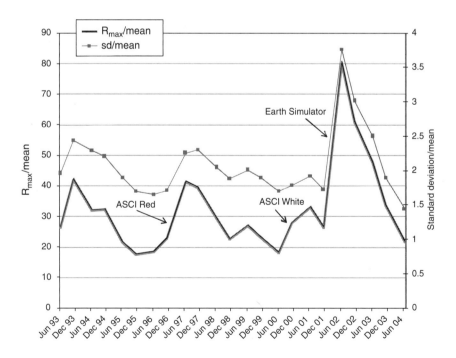

FIGURE 3.4 R_{max} dispersion in TOP500.

Increasingly, a larger share of high-end systems is being used by industry and a smaller share by academia. There has been a rapid increase in the share of TOP500 machines installed in industrial locations (see Figure 3.5). In the last several years, roughly 40 to 50 percent of the TOP500 systems (number of machines) have been installed in industry, as compared with about 30 percent in 1993. This contrasts with the situation in academia, which had a substantially smaller share of TOP500 systems in the late 1990s than in the early 1990s. There has been some increase in academic share in the last several years, accounted for mainly by Linux cluster-type systems, often self-built. It is tempting to speculate that the proliferation of relatively inexpensive, commodity-processor-based HPC systems is driving this development. There is one qualification to this picture of a thriving industrial market for high-end systems, however: The growing qualitative gap between the scale and types of systems used by industry and by cutting-edge government users, with industry using less and less of the most highly capable systems than it used to. There have been no industrial users in the top 20 systems for the last 3 years, contrast-

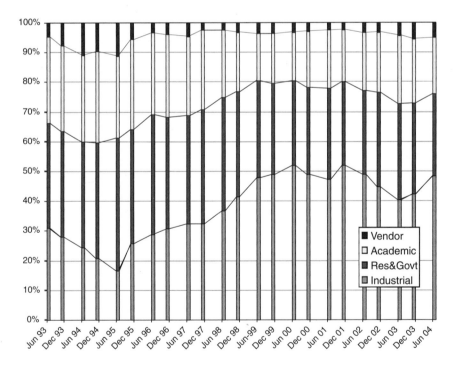

FIGURE 3.5 TOP500 by installation type.

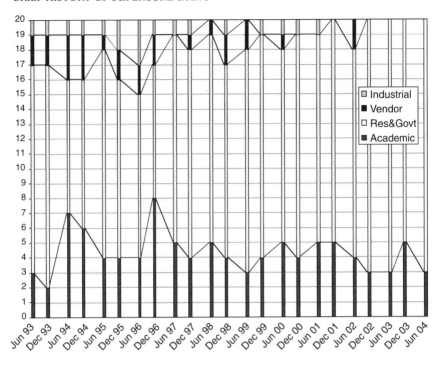

FIGURE 3.6 Top 20 machines by installation type.

ing with at least one industrial user in the top 20 at least once in each of the previous 9 years (see Figure 3.6).

U.S. supercomputer makers are performing strongly in global supercomputer markets. Their global market share has steadily increased, from less than 80 percent to more than 90 percent of TOP500 units sold (see Figure 3.7). Measuring market share by share of total computing capability sold (total R_{max}) is probably a better proxy for revenues and presents a more irregular picture, but it also suggests a significant increase in market share, by about 10 percentage points (see Figure 3.8). The conclusion also holds at the regional level. U.S. computer makers' share of European and other (excluding Japan) supercomputer markets also increased significantly, measured by either machines (Figure 3.9) or the capability proxy for revenues (Figure 3.10).

U.S. supercomputer capabilities are strong and competitive in the highest performing segment of the supercomputer marketplace (see Figure 3.11). Even if we consider only the 20 fastest computers in the world every year, the share manufactured by U.S. producers has been increasing steadily since the mid-1990s and is today about where it was in 1993—

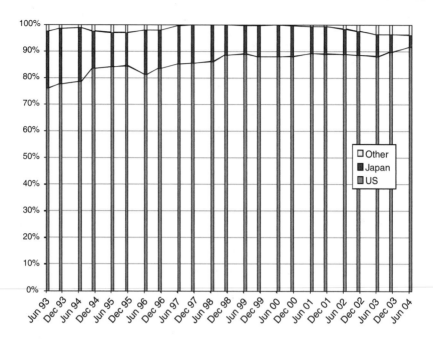

FIGURE 3.7 Share of TOP500 machines by country of maker.

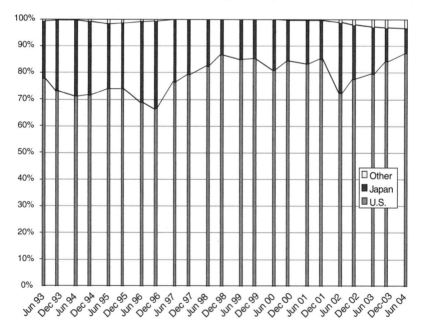

FIGURE 3.8 R_{max} share of TOP500 machines by maker.

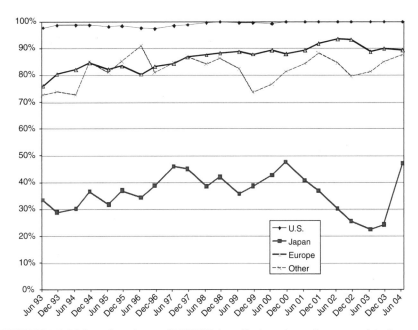

FIGURE 3.9 U.S. maker share of TOP500 installations in each geographical area.

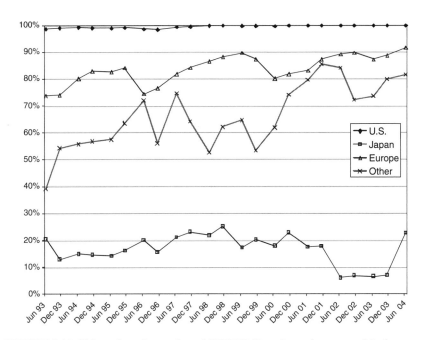

FIGURE 3.10 U.S. maker share of total TOP500 R_{max} in each geographical area.

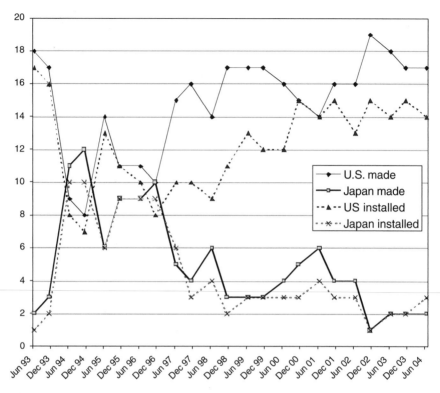

FIGURE 3.11 Top 20 machines by maker and country of installation.

with 17 of the top 20 machines worldwide made by U.S. producers. This trend reverses a plunge in the U.S. maker share of the fastest machines that took place in 1994 to 8 of the top 20 machines. Japanese producer performance is a mirror image of the U.S. picture, rising to 12 of the top 20 in 1994 and then falling steadily to 2 in 2003. The Japanese Earth Simulator was far and away the top machine from 2002 through mid-2004, but most of the computers arrayed behind it were American-made, unlike the situation in 1994.

A similar conclusion holds if we consider access by U.S. users to the fastest computers (Figure 3.11). Of the top 20, 14 or 15 were installed in the United States in the last 3 years, compared with lows of 7 or 8 observed earlier in the 1990s (a sharp drop from 1993, the initial year of the TOP500, when 16 or 17 of the TOP500 were on U.S. soil). Again, Japan is a mirror image of the United States, with 1 or 2 of the top 20 machines installed in Japan in 1993, peaking at 10 in 1994, then dropping fairly steadily, to 2 or 3 over the last 3 years.

There are indications that national trade and industrial policies may be having impacts on behavior in global markets. U.S. supercomputer makers now have effectively 100 percent of their home market, measured by machines (Figure 3.9) or capability (Figure 3.10). No machines on the TOP500 have been sold by Japan (the principal technological competitor of the United States) to this country since 2000, and only a handful on the list were sold in prior years going back to 1998. This contrasts with between 2 and 5 machines on the lists in years prior to 1998. (About half of the TOP500 systems currently installed in Japan are U.S. made.)

These data coincide with a period in which formal and informal barriers to purchases of Japanese supercomputers were created in the United States. Conversely, U.S. producer market share in Japan, measured in either units or capability, began to fall after the same 1998 watershed in trade frictions. While this analysis does not so prove, one might suspect a degree of retaliation, official or not, in Japan. Given that U.S. producers have been doing so well in global markets for these products, it is hard to argue that policies encouraging the erection of trade barriers in this sector would have any beneficial effect on either U.S. producers or U.S. supercomputer users. This is a subject to which the committee will return.

An Industrial Revolution

From the mid-1960s to the early 1980s, the supercomputer industry was dominated by two U.S. firms—first CDC, then Cray. The product these companies produced—highly capable, very expensive, custom-designed vector supercomputers, with individual models typically produced in quantities well under 100—was easily identified and categorized. This small, largely American world underwent two seismic shifts in the late 1980s.

Figure 3.12 sketches out the first of these changes. As described earlier, capable Japanese supercomputer vendors for the first time began to win significant sales in international markets. The Japanese vendors saw their share of vector computer installations double, from over 20 percent to over 40 percent over the 6 years from 1986 to 1992.[28]

The second development was the entry of new types of products—for example, non-vector supercomputers, typically massively parallel ma-

---

[28]These data are taken from H.W. Meuer, 1994, "The Mannheim Supercomputer Statistics 1986-1992," *TOP500 Report 1993*, J.J. Dongarra, H.W. Meuer, and E. Strohmaier, eds., University of Mannheim, pp. 1-15. See also Erich Strohmaier, Jack J. Dongarra, Hans W. Meuer, and Horst D. Simon, 1999, "The Marketplace of High Performance Computing," *Parallel Computing* 25(13-14):1517-1544.

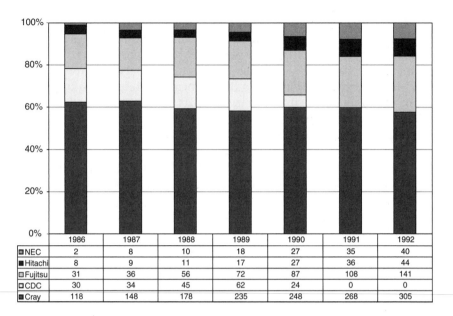

	1986	1987	1988	1989	1990	1991	1992
NEC	2	8	10	18	27	35	40
Hitachi	8	9	11	17	27	36	44
Fujitsu	31	36	56	72	87	108	141
CDC	30	34	45	62	24	0	0
Cray	118	148	178	235	248	268	305

FIGURE 3.12 Share of vector supercomputers installed.

chines built using large numbers of processors interconnected within a single system. One impetus for the development of these systems was DARPA's Strategic Computing Initiative in the 1980s, in part a reaction to the data depicted in Figure 3.12, discussed earlier, and other U.S. government initiatives that coordinated with and followed this initial effort. These new forms of supercomputing systems are not tracked in Figure 3.12.

The new types of supercomputing systems were initially built entirely from custom-designed and manufactured components used only in these proprietary supercomputer architectures. In the early 1990s, however, reacting to the high fixed costs of designing and manufacturing specialized processors that were only going to be used in machines to be built, in the most wildly optimistic estimate, in volumes in the hundreds, some of these machines began to make use of the most capable commercially available microprocessors and confined the proprietary elements of these supercomputer designs to the overall system architecture and interconnection components. To engineer a system that could be offered with more attractive cost/performance characteristics, there was a shift from a purely custom approach to building a high-performance machine, to a hybrid approach making use of COTS processor components.

Over the last 4 years, the high-end computing marketplace has undergone another fairly radical transformation, leaving makers of traditional supercomputers in an increasingly weakened position economically. The impetus for this transformation has been the growing availability of commodity high-performance interconnections, which, coupled to mass-produced, high-volume commodity microprocessors, are now being used to build true commodity supercomputers: systems built entirely from COTS hardware components. Although not commonly appreciated, over the last several years such commodity supercomputers have rapidly come to dominate the supercomputer marketplace.

To see this, the committee has categorized high-end systems into three groups. First, there are the so-called commodity systems, systems built using COTS microprocessors and COTS interconnections. The first such commodity system appeared on the TOP500 list in 1997.[29] Second, there are machines using custom interconnections linking COTS microprocessors, or machines making use of customized versions of COTS microprocessor chips. These systems are labeled as hybrid systems. Finally, there are machines using both custom processors and custom interconnects. These are labeled as full custom systems. All traditional vector supercomputers fall into this category, as do massively parallel systems using custom processors and interconnects.

Using this taxonomy, all supercomputers on the TOP500 list from June of 1993 through June of 2004 were categorized.[30] The results are summarized in Figure 3.13, which shows changes in mean R_{max} for each of these system types from 1993 to 2004. Commodity systems showed the greatest

---

[29]This was the experimental University of California at Berkeley network of workstations (NOW).

[30]The categorization used the following rules: All AP1000, Convex, Cray, Fujitsu, Hitachi, Hitachi SR8000, IBM 3090, Kendall Square, MasPar, Ncube, NEC, and Thinking Machines CM2 processor-based systems were categorized as custom. All AMD processor-based systems were categorized as commodity. All Alpha processor systems were commodity except those made by Cray, DEC/HP Alphaserver 8400 systems, and Alphaserver 8400, 4100, and 300 clusters, which were categorized as hybrid. All Intel processor-based systems were commodity, except those made by Intel (Sandia ASC Red, Delta, XP, other iPSC 860), Meiko, Cray, HP Superdome Itanium systems, and SGI Altix systems, which were categorized as hybrid. All Power processor systems were categorized as hybrid except IBM pSeries, for which use of commodity connections was noted in the TOP500 database, and the Param Padma cluster, which were categorized as commodity. All SPARC processor systems were hybrid except those that were "self-made" and categorized as commodity. All Hewlett-Packard processor systems were categorized as hybrid. All MIPS-based systems were hybrid, except for SGI Origin systems, for which the use of Ethernet interconnects was noted. The IBM Blue Gene system using the Power PC processor was hybrid; self-made and eServer blade systems using this processor were commodity.

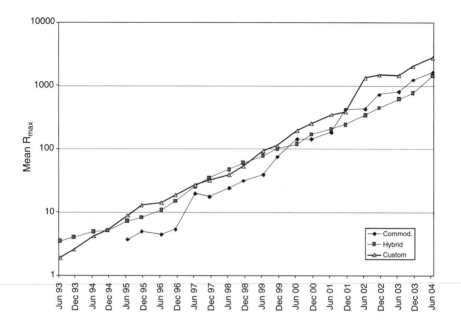

FIGURE 3.13 Mean R_{max} by system type.

annual growth rates in performance; hybrid systems showed the least growth in Linpack performance. Trend lines fitted to Figure 3.13 have slopes yielding annual growth rates in R_{max} of 111 percent for commodity systems, 94 percent for custom systems, and 73 percent for hybrid systems.[31] This is considerably faster than annual growth rates in single-processor floating-point performance shown on other benchmarks, suggesting that increases in the number of processors and improvements in the interconnect performance yielded supercomputer performance gains significantly greater than those due to component processor improvement alone for both commodity and custom systems. Hybrid system performance improvement, on the other hand, roughly tracked single-processor performance gains.

Nonetheless, the economics of using much less expensive COTS microprocessors was compelling. Hybrid supercomputer systems rapidly replaced custom systems in the early 1990s. Custom supercomputer sys-

---

[31]A regression line of the form $\ln R_{max} = a + b$ Time was fit, where Time is a variable incremented by one every half year, corresponding to a new TOP500 list. Annualized trend growth rates were calculated as $\exp(2b) - 1$.

tems, increasingly, were being used only in applications where software solutions making use of massively parallel hybrid systems were unsatisfactory or unavailable, or where the need for very high performance warranted a price premium.

Commodity high-performance computing systems first appeared on the TOP500 list in 1997, but it was not until 2001-2002 that they began to show up in large numbers. Since 2002, their numbers have swelled, and today commodity systems account for over 60 percent of the systems on the list (see Figure 3.14). Just as hybrid systems replaced many custom systems in the late 1990s, commodity systems today appear to be displacing hybrid systems in acquisitions. A similar picture is painted by data on R_{max}, which, as noted above, is probably a better proxy for systems revenues. Figure 3.15 shows how the distribution of total TOP500 system performance between these classes of systems has changed over time.

Furthermore, the growing marketplace dominance of commodity supercomputer systems is not just at the low end of the market. A similar

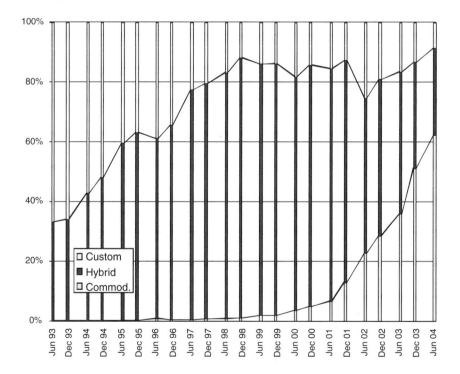

FIGURE 3.14 Share of TOP500 by system type.

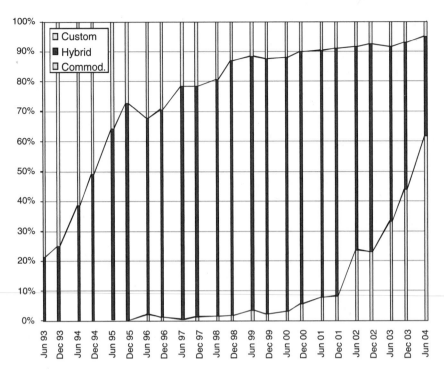

FIGURE 3.15 Share of TOP500 R_{max} by system type.

pattern has also been evident in the very highest performance systems. Figure 3.16 shows how the numbers of TOP20 systems in each of these categories has changed over time. A commodity system did not appear in the top 20 highest performing systems until mid-2001. But commodity supercomputers now account for 12 of the 20 systems with the highest Linpack scores. As was true with the entire TOP500 list, custom systems were replaced by hybrid systems in the 1990s in the top 20, and the hybrid systems in turn have been replaced by commodity systems over the last 3 years.

This rapid restructuring in the type of systems sold in the marketplace has had equally dramatic effects on the companies selling supercomputers. In 1993, the global HPC marketplace (with revenues again proxied by total R_{max}) was still dominated by Cray, with about a third of the market, and four other U.S. companies, with about another 40 percent of the market (three of those four companies have since exited the industry). The three Japanese vector supercomputer makers accounted for another 22 percent of TOP500 performance (see Figure 3.17).

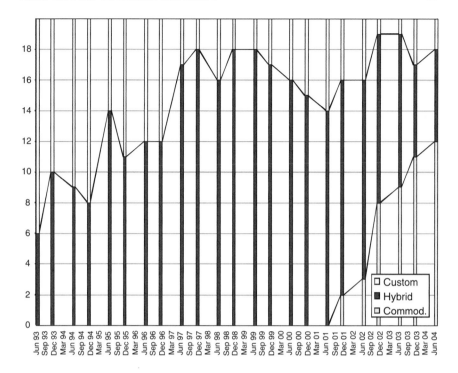

FIGURE 3.16 Share of top 20 machines by system type.

Of the five U.S. companies with significant market share on this chart, two (Intel and Thinking Machines, second only to Cray) were building hybrid systems and three (Cray, Hewlett-Packard, and Kendall Square Research) were selling custom systems.[32] The makers of traditional custom vector supercomputers (Cray and its Japanese vector competitors) have about half of the market share shown if only vector computers are considered (compare to Figure 3.12). Clearly, the HPC marketplace was undergoing a profound transformation in the early 1990s.

A decade later, after the advent of hybrid systems and then of commodity high-end systems, the players have changed completely (see Figure 3.18). A company that was not even present on the list in 1993 (IBM, marketing both hybrid and commodity systems) now accounts for over half of the market, Hewlett-Packard (mainly hybrid systems) now has

---

[32]Although some of the Thinking Machines systems counted here were using older proprietary processors, most of the Thinking Machines supercomputers on this chart were newer CM-5 machines using commodity SPARC processors.

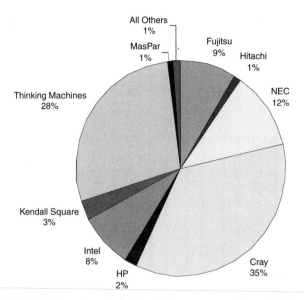

FIGURE 3.17 TOP500 market share (R_{max}) by company, June 1993.

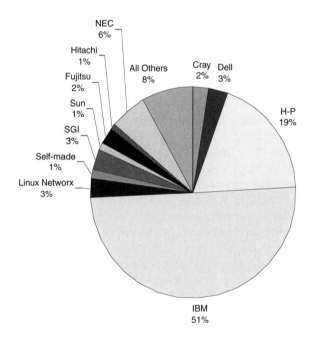

FIGURE 3.18 TOP500 market share (R_{max}) by company, June 2004.

roughly the same market share as all three Japanese producers did back in 1993, and other entirely new, pure-commodity U.S. vendors in this product space (Dell, Linux Networks) are now larger than two of the three traditional Japanese supercomputer vendors. The most successful Japanese producer, NEC, has about half of the TOP500 market share it had in 1993. Cray is a shadow of its former market presence, with only 2 percent of installed capability. Two other U.S. HPC vendors (Sun and SGI), which grew significantly with the flowering of hybrid systems in the late 1990s, have ebbed with the advent of commodity systems and now have shares of the market comparable to the pure commodity supercomputer vendors and self-made systems.

Over the last 15 years, extraordinary technological ferment has continuously restructured the economics of this industry and the companies surviving within its boundaries. Any policy designed to keep needed supercomputing capabilities available to U.S. government and industrial users must recognize that the technologies and companies providing these systems are living through a period of extremely rapid technological and industrial change.

IMPACTS

Throughout the computer age, supercomputing has played two important roles. First, it enables new and innovative approaches to scientific and engineering research, allowing scientists to solve previously unsolvable problems or to provide superior answers. Often, supercomputers have allowed scientists, engineers, and others to acquire knowledge from simulations. Simulations can replace experiments in situations where experiments are impossible, unethical, hazardous, prohibited, or too expensive; they can support theoretical experiments with systems that cannot be created in reality, in order to test the prediction of theories; and they can enhance experiments by allowing measurements that might not be possible in a real experiment. During the last decades, simulations on high-performance computers have become essential to the design of cars and airplanes, turbines and combustion engines, silicon chips or magnetic disks; they have been extensively used in support of petroleum exploration and exploitation. Accurate weather prediction would not be possible without supercomputing. According to a report by the Lawrence Berkeley National Laboratory (LBNL) for DOE, "Simulation has gained equal footing to experiments and theory in the triad of scientific process."[33] In-

---

[33]LBNL. 2002. *DOE Greenbook—Needs and Directions in High-Performance Computing for the Office of Science*. Prepared for the U.S. Department of Energy. April, p. 1.

deed, a significant fraction of the articles published in top scientific journals in areas such as physics, chemistry, earth sciences, astrophysics, and biology, depend for their results on supercomputer simulations.

The second major effect supercomputing technology has had on computing in general takes place through a spillover effect. Today's desktop computer has the capability of the supercomputers of a decade ago.

Direct Contributions

Supercomputers continue to lead to major scientific contributions. Supercomputing is also critical to our national security. Supercomputing applications are discussed in detail in Chapter 4. Here the committee highlights a few of the contributions of supercomputing over the years.

The importance of supercomputing has been recognized by many reports. The 1982 Lax report concluded that large-scale computing was vital to science, engineering, and technology.[34] It provided several examples. Progress in oil reservoir exploitation, quantum field theory, phase transitions in materials, and the development of turbulence were all becoming possible by combining supercomputing with renormalization group techniques (p. 5). Aerodynamic design using a supercomputer resulted in the design of an airfoil with 40 percent less drag than the design using previous experimental techniques (p. 5). Supercomputers were also critical for designing nuclear power plants (p. 6). The Lax report also praised supercomputers for helping to find new phenomena through numerical experiments, such as the discovery of nonergodic behavior in the formation of solitons and the presence of strange attractors and universal features common to a large class of nonlinear systems (p. 6). As supercomputers become more powerful, new applications emerge that leverage their increased performance. Recently, supercomputer simulations have been used to understand the evolution of galaxies, the life cycle of supernovas, and the processes that lead to the formation of planets.[35] Such simulations provide invaluable insight into the processes that shaped our universe and inform us of the likelihood that life-friendly planets exist. Simulations have been used to elucidate various biological mechanisms, such

---

[34]National Science Board. 1982. *Report of the Panel on Large Scale Computing in Science and Engineering.* Washington, D.C., December 26 (the Lax report).

[35]"Simulation May Reveal the Detailed Mechanics of Exploding Stars," ASC/Alliances Center for Astrophysical Thermonuclear Flashes, see <http://flash.uchicago.edu/website/home/>; "Planets May Form Faster Than Scientists Thought," Pittsburgh Supercomputer Center, see <http://www.psc.edu/publicinfo/news/2002/planets_2002-12-11.html>; J. Dubinski, R. Humble, U.-L. Pen, C. Loken, and P. Martin, 2003, "High Performance Commodity Networking in a 512-CPU Teraflops Beowulf Cluster for Computational Astrophysics," Paper submitted to the SC2003 conference.

as the selective transfer of ions or water molecules through channels in cellular membranes or the behavior of various enzymes.[36] Climate simulations have led to an understanding of the long-term effects of human activity on Earth's atmosphere and have permitted scientists to explore many what-if scenarios to guide policies on global warming. We have now a much better understanding of ocean circulation and of global weather patterns such as El Niño.[37] Lattice quantum chromodynamics (QCD) computations have enhanced our basic understanding of matter by exploring the standard model of particle physics.[38] Box 3.1 highlights the value of having a strong supercomputing program to solve unexpected critical national problems.

Codes initially developed for supercomputers have been critical for many applications, such as petroleum exploration and exploitation (three-dimensional analysis and visualization of huge amounts of seismic data and reservoir modeling), aircraft and automobile design (computational fluid mechanics codes, combustion codes), civil engineering design (finite element codes), and finance (creation of a new market in mortgage-backed securities).[39]

Much of the early research on supercomputers occurred in the laboratories of DOE, NASA, and other agencies. As the need for supercomputing in support of basic science became clear, the NSF supercomputing centers were initiated in 1985, partly as a response to the Lax report. Their mission has expanded over time. The centers have provided essential supercomputing resources in support of scientific research and have driven important research in software, particularly operating systems, compilers, network control, mathematical libraries, and programming languages and environments.[40]

Supercomputers play a critical role for the national security community according to a report for the Secretary of Defense.[41] That report iden-

---

[36]Benoit Roux and Klaus Schulten. 2004. "Computational Studies of Membrane Channels." *Structure* 12 (August): 1.

[37]National Energy Research Scientific Computing Center. 2002. "NERSC Helps Climate Scientists Complete First-Ever 1,000-Year Run of Nation's Leading Climate-Change Modeling Application." See <http://www.lbl.gov/Science-Articles/Archive/NERSC-1000-Year-climate-model.html>.

[38]D. Chen, P. Chen, N.H. Christ, G. Fleming, C. Jung, A. Kahler, S. Kasow, Y. Luo, C. Malureanu, and C.Z. Sui. 1998. "3 Lattice Quantum Chromodynamics Computations." This paper, submitted to the SC1998 conference, won the Gordon Bell Prize in the category Price-Performance.

[39]NRC. 1995. *Evolving the High Performance Computing and Communications Initiative to Support the Nation's Information Infrastructure.* Washington, D.C.: National Academy Press, p. 35.

[40]Ibid., p. 108.

[41]Office of the Secretary of Defense. 2002. *Report on High Performance Computing for the National Security Community.*

BOX 3.1 Sandia Supercomputers Aid in
Analysis of Columbia Disaster

Sandia National Laboratories and Lockheed Martin offered Sandia's technical support to NASA immediately after the February 1, 2003, breakup of the space shuttle *Columbia*. Sandia personnel teamed with analysts from four NASA Centers to provide timely analysis and experimental results to NASA Johnson Space Center accident investigators for the purpose of either confirming or closing out the possible accident scenarios being considered by NASA. Although Sandia's analysis capabilities had been developed in support of DOE's stockpile stewardship program, they contained physical models appropriate to the accident environment. These models were used where they were unique within the partnership and where Sandia's massively parallel computers and ASC code infrastructure were needed to accommodate very large and computationally intense simulations. Sandia external aerodynamics and heat transfer calculations were made for both undamaged and damaged orbiter configurations using rarefied direct simulation Monte Carlo (DSMC) codes for configurations flying at altitudes above 270,000 ft and continuum Navier-Stokes codes for altitudes below 250,000 ft. The same computational tools were used to predict jet impingement heating and pressure loads on the internal structure, as well as the heat transfer and flow through postulated damage sites into and through the wing. Navier-Stokes and DSMC predictions of heating rates were input to Sandia's thermal analysis codes to predict the time required for thermal demise of the internal structure and for wire bundle burn-through. Experiments were conducted to obtain quasi-static and dynamic material response data on the foam, tiles, strain isolation pad, and reinforced carbon-carbon wing leading edge. These data were then used in Sandia finite element calculations of foam impacting the thermal protection tiles and wing leading edge in support of accident scenario definition and foam impact testing at Southwest Research Institute.

The supercomputers at Sandia played a key role in helping NASA determine the cause of the space shuttle *Columbia* disaster. Sandia researchers' analyses and experimental studies supported the position that foam debris shed from the fuel tank and impacting the orbiter wing during launch was the most probable cause of the wing damage that led to the breakup of the *Columbia*.

NOTE: The committee thanks Robert Thomas and the Sandia National Laboratories staff for their assistance in drafting this box.

tified at least 10 defense applications that rely on high-performance computing (p. 22): comprehensive aerospace vehicle design, signals intelligence, operational weather/ocean forecasting, stealthy ship design, nuclear weapons stockpile stewardship, signal and image processing, the Army's future combat system, electromagnetic weapons, geospatial intelligence, and threat weapon systems characterization.

Spillover Effects

Advanced computer research programs have had major payoffs in terms of technologies that enriched the computer and communication industries. As an example, the DARPA VLSI program in the 1970s had major payoffs in developing timesharing, computer networking, workstations, computer graphics, windows and mouse user interface technology, very large integrated circuit design, reduced instruction set computers, redundant arrays of inexpensive disks, parallel computing, and digital libraries.[42] Today's personal computers, e-mail, networking, data storage all reflect these advances. Many of the benefits were unanticipated.

Closer to home, one can list many technologies that were initially developed for supercomputers and that, over time, migrated to mainstream architectures. For example, vector processing and multithreading, which were initially developed for supercomputers (Illiac IV/STAR100/TI ASC and CDC 6600, respectively), are now used on PC chips. Instruction pipelining and prefetch and memory interleaving appeared in early IBM supercomputers and have become universal in today's microprocessors. In the software area, program analysis techniques such as dependence analysis and instruction scheduling, which were initially developed for supercomputer compilers, are now used in most mainstream compilers. High-performance I/O needs on supercomputers, particularly parallel machines, were one of the motivations for Redundant Array of Inexpensive Disks (RAID)[43] storage, now widely used for servers. Scientific visualization was developed in large part to help scientists interpret the results of their supercomputer calculations; today, even spreadsheets can display three-dimensional data plots. Scientific software libraries such as LAPACK that were originally designed for high-performance platforms are now widely used in commercial packages running on a large range of

---

[42]NRC. 1995. *Evolving the High Performance Computing and Communications Initiative to Support the Nation's Information Infrastructure.* Washington, D.C.: National Academy Press, pp. 17-18.

[43]RAID is a disk subsystem consisting of many disks that increases performance and/or provides fault tolerance.

platforms. In the application areas, many application packages that are routinely used in industry (e.g., NASTRAN) were initially developed for supercomputers. These technologies were developed in a complex interaction involving researchers at universities, the national laboratories, and companies. The reasons for such a spillover effect are obvious and still valid nowadays: Supercomputers are at the cutting edge of performance. In order to push performance they need to adapt new hardware and software solutions ahead of mainstream computers. And the high performance levels of supercomputers enable new applications that can be developed on capability platforms and then used on an increasingly broader set of cheaper platforms as hardware performance continues to improve.

4

The Demand for Supercomputing

The committee now turns to a discussion of some of the key application areas that are using supercomputing and are expected to continue to do so. As each of these areas is reviewed, it is important to recognize that many of the areas are themselves supported by government research funds and contribute to broader societal objectives, ranging from national defense to the ability to make more informed decisions on climate policy. Also, as is discussed further in Chapter 5, the precise technology requirements for these different application areas differ. Additionally, several of them are subject to at least some degree of secrecy. As will be discussed in Chapter 8, a key issue in the effective management of and policy toward supercomputing involves understanding and choosing the degree of commitment, the degree of diversification, and the degree of secrecy associated with the technology.

Supercomputers are tools that allow scientists and engineers to solve computational problems whose size and complexity make them otherwise intractable. Such problems arise in almost all fields of science and engineering. Although Moore's law and new architectural innovations enable the computational power of supercomputers to grow, there is no foreseeable end to the need for ever larger and more powerful systems.

In most cases, the problem being solved on a supercomputer is derived from a model of the physical world. An example is predicting changes that Earth's climate might experience centuries into the future. Approximations are made when scientists use partial differential equations to model a physical phenomenon. To make the solution feasible, compromises must be made in the resolution of the grids used to discretize the equations. The coefficients of the matrices are represented as numbers expressed in scientific notation.[1] Therefore, the computation does not precisely emulate the real phenomenon but, rather, simulates it with enough fidelity to stimulate human scientific imagination or to aid human engineering judgment. As computational power increases, the fidelity of the models can be increased, compromises in the methods can be eliminated, and the accuracy of the computed answers improves. An exact solution is never expected, but as the fidelity increases, the error decreases and results become increasingly useful.

This is not to say that exact solutions are never achieved. Many problems with precise answers are also addressed by supercomputing. Examples are found in discrete optimization, cryptography, and mathematical fields such as number theory. Recently a whole new discipline, experimental mathematics, has emerged that relies on algorithms such as integer relation detection. These are precise calculations that require hundreds or even thousands of digits.[2,3] At the hardware level, these operations are most efficiently done using integer arithmetic. Floating-point arithmetic is sometimes used, but mostly to perform whole number operations.

By studying the results of computational models, scientists are able to glean an understanding of phenomena that are not otherwise approachable. Often these phenomena are too large and complex or too far away in time and space to be studied by any other means. Scientists model turbulence inside supernovae and material properties at the center of Earth. They look forward in time and try to predict changes in Earth's climate. They also model problems that are too small and too fast to observe, such as the transient, atomic-scale dynamics of chemical reactions. Material scientists can determine the behavior of compounds not known to exist in nature.

Supercomputers not only allow people to address the biggest and most complex problems, they also allow people to solve problems faster, even those that could fit on servers or clusters of PCs. This rapid time to solution is critical in some aspects of emergency preparedness and national defense, where the solutions produced are only valuable if they can be acted on in a timely manner. For example, predicting the landfall of a

---

[1]IEEE Standard 754, available at <http://cch.loria.fr/documentation/IEEE754/#SGI_man>.

[2]Jonathan M. Borwein and David H. Bailey. 2004. *Mathematics by Experiment: Plausible Reasoning in the 21st Century*. Natick, Mass.: A.K. Peters.

[3]Jonathan M. Borwein, David H. Bailey, and Roland Girgensohn. 2004. *Experimental Mathematics: Computational Paths to Discovery*. Natick, Mass.: A.K. Peters.

hurricane allows evacuation of the coastline that will be impacted (saving lives), while not disturbing the surrounding area (saving money). Rapid time to solution in a commercial arena translates into minimizing the time to market for new products and services. The ability to solve many problems in a reasonable time frame allows engineers to explore design spaces before committing to the time and expense of building prototypes.

An important phenomenon that cannot be underestimated is how the potential for making a scientific discovery can encourage human creativity. Few advances in science and technology are unplanned or unexpected, at least in hindsight. Discoveries almost always come in the wake of work that inspires or enables them. When one discovery opens up the possibility of another, the leading intellects of our time will focus tremendous time and energy on developing the algorithms needed to make a discovery that appears tantalizingly close. Supercomputing expands the space within which such new algorithms can be found by maximizing the resources that can be brought to bear on the problem.

Supercomputing allows pioneering scientists and engineers to invent solutions to problems that were initially beyond human ability to solve. Often, these are problems of great national importance. Dimitri Kusnezov, Director of the NNSA, put it this way when he testified before the U.S. Senate in June 2004:[4] "Simulating the time evolution of the behavior of an exploding nuclear device is not only a mammoth scientific enterprise from a computational perspective, it probably represents the confluence of more physics, chemistry and material science, both equilibrium and non-equilibrium, at multiple length and time scales than almost any other scientific challenge."

Over time and with increasing experience, the algorithms mature and become more efficient. Furthermore, smaller computing systems such as servers and personal computers become more powerful. These two trends make problems that were once addressable only by nation states now addressable by large research and engineering enterprises and, given enough time, eventually by individual scientists and engineers. Consider an example from mechanical dynamics. Starting in the 1950s, scientists at the nuclear weapons laboratories pioneered the use of explicit finite element programs to simulate the propagation of shocks through the devices they were developing. These codes became available to industrial users in the 1980s. Through the 1980s and into the 1990s, automotive companies ran

---

[4]Testimony of Dimitri Kusnezov, Director, Office of Advanced Simulation and Computing, NNSA, U.S. Department of Energy, before the U.S. Senate Committee on Energy and Natural Resources, Subcommittee on Energy, June 22, 2004.

their occupant safety problems on the same type of supercomputers used by the national laboratories. As the power of servers and PCs continued to increase, many of those engineering problems were able to move to departmental-scale systems in the late 1990s, and even to individual PCs today. Without the development of algorithms and software on super-computers in the 1980s and 1990s, such codes would not be available for broad use on servers and PCs today.

The example above should not be construed to suggest that there is no longer a need for supercomputing in mechanical engineering. On the contrary, while today's codes are very useful tools for supporting design and analysis, they are by no means predictive. One software vendor believes that his users in the automotive industry could productively employ computing power at least seven orders of magnitude greater than what they have today. There are many such examples, some of which are given later in the chapter.

The above discussion has focused on supercomputers as tools for research performed in other disciplines. By their very nature, super-computers push the boundaries of computer engineering in terms of scale. To effectively solve the most challenging problems requires that supercomputers be architected differently than standard PCs and servers. As the underlying technology (semiconductors, optics, etc.) from which they are constructed evolves, the design space for supercomputers changes rapidly, making supercomputers themselves objects of scientific curiosity. This last point will be taken up in Chapter 5.

COMPELLING APPLICATIONS FOR SUPERCOMPUTING

The Committee on the Future of Supercomputing has extensively investigated the nature of supercomputing applications and their present and future needs. Its sources of information have included its own membership as well as the many experts from whom it heard in committee meetings. The committee has talked with the directors of many super-computing centers and with scientists and engineers who run application programs at those centers. Subcommittees visited DOE weapons laboratories, DOE science laboratories, the National Security Agency, and the Japanese Earth Simulator. In addition, the committee held a 2-day applications workshop in Santa Fe, New Mexico, in September 2003, during which approximately 20 experts discussed their applications and their computing requirements. What follows is a consensus summary of the information from all of those sources.

Many applications areas were discussed either at the Santa Fe workshop or in presentations to the committee. In addition to furthering basic scientific understanding, most of these applications have clear practical benefits. A capsule summary of the areas is given first, followed by a detailed description. This is a far from complete list of supercomputing applications, but it does represent their broad range and complexity. Several other recent reports give excellent summaries of the high-end computational needs of applications. Among those reports are the HECRTF workshop report,[5] the Scales report,[6] the IHEC Report,[7] and the HECRTF final report.[8]

- *Stockpile stewardship.* Several of the most powerful computers in the world are being used as part of DOE's Advanced Simulation and Computing (ASC) to ensure the safety and reliability of the nation's stockpile of nuclear weapons. France's CEA (Atomic Energy Commission) has a similar project.
- *Intelligence/defense.* Very large computing demands are made by the DoD, intelligence community agencies, and related entities in order to enhance the security of the United States and its allies, including anticipating the actions of terrorists and of rogue states.
- *Climate prediction.* Many U.S. high-end computational resources and a large part of the Japanese Earth Simulator are devoted to predicting climate variations and anthropogenic climate change, so as to anticipate and be able to mitigate harmful impacts on humanity.
- *Plasma physics.* An important goal of plasma physics will be to produce cost-effective, clean, safe electric power from nuclear fusion. Very large simulations of the reactions in advance of building the generating devices are critical to making fusion energy feasible.
- *Transportation.* Whether it be an automobile, an airplane, or a spacecraft, large amounts of supercomputer resources can be applied to understanding and improving the vehicle's airflow dynamics, fuel consumption, structure design, crashworthiness, occupant comfort, and noise reduction, all with potential economic and/or safety benefits.
- *Bioinformatics and computational biology.* Biology has huge emerging computational needs, from data-intensive studies in genomics to

---

[5]NITRD High End Computing Revitalization Task Force (HECRTF). 2003. *Report of the Workshop on the Roadmap for the Revitalization of High-End Computing*. Daniel A. Reed, ed. June 16-20, Washington, D.C.

[6]DOE, Office of Science. 2003. "A Science-Based Case for Large-Scale Simulation," *Scales Workshop Report*, Vol. 1, July.

[7]Department of Defense, National Security Agency. 2002. Report on High Performance Computing for the National Security Community. July 1.

[8]NITRD HECRTF. 2004. *Federal Plan for High End Computing*. May.

computationally intensive cellular network simulations and large-scale systems modeling. Applications promise to provide revolutionary treatments of disease.

• *Societal health and safety.* Supercomputing enables the simulation of processes and systems that affect the health and safety of our society (for instance, pollution, disaster planning, and detection of terrorist actions against local and national infrastructures), thereby facilitating government and private planning.

• *Earthquakes.* Supercomputing simulation of earthquakes shows promise for allowing us to predict earthquakes and to mitigate the risks associated with them.

• *Geophysical exploration and geoscience.* Supercomputing in solid-earth geophysics involves a large amount of data handling and simulation for a range of problems in petroleum exploration, with potentially huge economic benefits. Scientific studies of plate tectonics and Earth as a geodynamo require immense supercomputing power.

• *Astrophysics.* Supercomputer simulations are fundamental to astrophysics and play the traditional scientific role of controlled experiments in a domain where controlled experiments are extremely rare or impossible. They allow vastly accelerated time scales, so that astronomical evolution can be modeled and theories tested.

• *Materials science and computational nanotechnology.* The simulation of matter and energy from first principles is very computationally intensive. It can lead to the discovery of materials and reactions having large economic benefits—for instance, superconductors that minimize transmission loss in power lines and reduce heating in computers.

• *Human/organizational systems studies.* The study of macroeconomics and social dynamics is also amenable to supercomputing. For instance, the behavior of large human populations is simulated in terms of the overall effect of decisions by hundreds of millions of individuals.

Common Themes and Synergies Across Applications Areas

The committee was struck by the many similarities across application areas in the importance of supercomputing to each scientific domain, the present use of computational equipment, and projected future supercomputing needs. Most of the applications areas use supercomputer simulations in one of three ways: (1) to extend the realization of complex natural phenomena so that they can be understood scientifically; (2) to test, via simulation, systems that are costly to design or to instrument, saving both time and money; or (3) to replace experiments that are hazardous, illegal, or forbidden by policies and treaties. The use of supercomputing provides information and predictions that are beneficial to the economy, to health, and to society at large. The applications areas all use supercomputing to accomplish tasks that are uneconomical—or even impossible—without it.

Whether the task is cracking a cryptographic code, incorporating new physics into a simulation, or detecting elusive targets, the real value of supercomputing is increased insight and understanding. Time to solution includes getting a new application up and running (the programming time), waiting for it to run (the execution time), and, finally, interpreting the results (the interpretation time). Applications areas have productivity problems because the time to program new supercomputers is increasing. While application codes and supercomputing systems have both become more complex, the compilers and tools that help to map application logic onto the hardware have not improved enough to keep pace with that complexity. The recent DARPA High Productivity Computing Systems (HPCS) initiative, having recognized this problem, has a strong focus on improving the programmability of supercomputers and on developing productivity metrics that will provide a measure of this improvement.[9]

It is well known that computational techniques span application areas. For example, astrophysics, aircraft design, climate modeling, and geophysics all need different models of fluid flow. Computational modeling used in applications that seek fundamental understanding enhances applications that solve real-world needs. Thus, basic understanding of plasma physics and materials facilitates stockpile stewardship, while basic results in weather prediction can facilitate climate modeling. These examples are illustrative, not a complete story.

In July 2003, Raymond Orbach, Director of the DOE Office of Science, testified before the U.S. House of Representatives Committee on Science. He said

> The tools for scientific discovery have changed. Previously, science had been limited to experiment and theory as the two pillars for investigation of the laws of nature. With the advent of what many refer to as "Ultra-Scale" computation, a third pillar, simulation, has been added to the foundation of scientific discovery. Modern computational methods are developing at such a rapid rate that computational simulation is possible on a scale that is comparable in importance with experiment and theory. The remarkable power of these facilities is opening new vistas for science and technology. Previously, we used computers to solve sets of equations representing physical laws too complicated to solve analytically.

---

[9]For more information on the HPCS program, see <http://www.darpa.mil/ipto/programs/hpcs/index.htm>.

Now we can simulate systems to discover physical laws for which there
are no known predictive equations.[10]

Dr. Orbach also remarked that computational modeling and simulation were among the most significant developments in the practice of scientific inquiry in the latter half of the 20th century. Supercomputing has
contributed to essentially all scientific research programs and has proved
indispensable to DOE's missions. Computer-based simulation can bridge
the gap between experimental data and simple mathematical models, thus
providing a means for predicting the behavior of complex systems.

Selected Application Areas

Stockpile Stewardship

In June 2004, Dimitri Kusnezov, Director of the Office of Advanced
Simulation and Computing at DOE's National Nuclear Security Administration, testified before the U.S. Senate Committee on Energy and Natural
Resources. He said "Since the dawn of the nuclear age, computation has
been an integral part of the weapons program and our national security.
With the cessation of testing and the advent of the science-based Stockpile
Stewardship Program, ASC simulations have matured to become a critical tool in stockpile assessments and in programs to extend the life of the
nation's nuclear deterrent."[11]

Even with simple, low-resolution physics models, weapons simulations have given insight and information that could not be obtained in
other ways.[12] Thus, the DOE nuclear weapons laboratories have always
been at the forefront of supercomputing development and use. The huge
challenge of nuclear weapons simulation is to develop the tools (hardware, software, algorithms) and skills necessary for the complex, highly
coupled, multiphysics calculations needed for accurate simulations. Under the DOE/NNSA Stockpile Stewardship Program, several of the larg-

---

[10]Testimony of Raymond L. Orbach, Director, Office of Science, U.S. Department of Energy, before the U.S. House of Representatives Committee on Science, July 16, 2003.

[11]Testimony of Dimitri Kusnezov, Director, Office of Advanced Simulation and Computing, NNSA, U.S. Department of Energy, before the U.S. Senate Committee on Energy and
Natural Resources, Subcommittee on Energy, June 22, 2004.

[12]This subsection is based on white papers by Charles F. McMillan et al., LLNL, "Computational Challenges in Nuclear Weapons Simulation," and by Robert Weaver, LANL, "Computational Challenges to Supercomputing from the Los Alamos Crestone Project: A Personal Perspective." Both papers were prepared for the committee's applications workshop
at Santa Fe, N.M., in September 2003.

est supercomputers in the world are being developed and used as part of the NNSA ASC program to ensure the safety and reliability of the nation's stockpile of nuclear weapons.

One of the fundamental problems that the national laboratories are attempting to solve with extremely complex (and obviously classified) codes is the simulation of the full physical operation of the nuclear weapons in the U.S. stockpile. This problem is important in order to continue to certify to the nation that the nuclear deterrent stockpile is safe and reliable in the absence of testing. Prior to the development of the current generation of National Laboratory codes, weapons designers had to rely on a more empirical solution to the complex, nonlinear coupled physics that occurs in a nuclear weapon. This procedure had to be augmented by an experimental test of the design.

In the absence of nuclear testing, the simulation codes must rely less on empirical results and must therefore be more refined. The simulations have evolved from two-dimensional models and solutions to three-dimensional ones. That evolution has required a more than 1,000-fold increase in computational resources. To achieve that capability, the simulations are developed and run on the most advanced platforms—systems that are prototype machines with few users. These platforms often lack the ideal infrastructure and stability, leading to new and unanticipated challenges, with the largest runs taking many months to a year to complete. Dr. Kusnezov noted that stockpile simulations "currently require heroic, nearly yearlong calculations on thousands of dedicated processors. It is essential that we provide the designers with the computational tools that allow such simulations to be completed in a reasonable time frame for systematic analysis. This is one of the requirements that drive us well into the petascale regime for future platforms."[13]

During the last 5 years, ASC has acquired a number of increasingly powerful supercomputing systems and plans to continue such acquisition. The vendors of these systems include Intel, IBM, Silicon Graphics, Cray, and Hewlett-Packard. The number of processors in these systems ranges from about 2,000 to a proposed 131,000, with peak performances ranging from 3 trillion floating-point operations per second (Tflops) to a proposed 360 Tflops. Portability of applications among the systems has become relatively smooth because of commitment in general to standard languages and programming models and avoidance of processor-specific optimizations. These practices have allowed the ASC community to begin taking advantage of new processor technology as it becomes available.

---

[13]Testimony of Dimitri Kusnezov, Director, Office of Advanced Simulation and Computing, U.S. Department of Energy, before the U.S. Senate Committee on Energy and Natural Resources, Subcommittee on Energy, June 22, 2004.

The ASC programming environment stresses software development tools because of the scale of the hardware architecture, software complexity, and the need for compatibility across ASC platforms. A multiphysics application code may take 4 to 6 years to become useful and may then have a lifespan of several decades. Thus, it is important that code development focus on present and future supercomputing systems. Almost all ASC applications, for example, use a combination of three programming models: the serial model, symmetric multiprocessing using OpenMP, and message passing using MPI. Programming is typically done in ANSI C, C++, and Fortran 90. Algorithm development attempts to balance the (often competing) requirements of high-fidelity physics, short execution time, parallel scalability, and algorithmic scalability[14]; not surprisingly, it is in some ways influenced by target architectures. It is interesting to note that, even with all this effort, codes running on the ASC White system typically attain from 1 percent to 12 percent of theoretical peak performance. It is not uncommon for complex scientific codes run on other platforms to exhibit similarly modest percentages. By contrast, the somewhat misleading Linpack benchmarks run at 59 percent of peak on that system.

Signals Intelligence

The computational challenges posed by the Signals Intelligence mission of the NSA are enormous.[15] The essence of this mission is to intercept and analyze foreign adversaries' communications signals, many of which are protected by encodings and other complex countermeasures. NSA must collect, process, and disseminate intelligence reports on foreign intelligence targets in response to intelligence requirements set at the highest levels of the government. The Signals Intelligence mission targets capabilities, intentions, and activities of foreign powers, organizations, or persons. It also plays an important counterintelligence role in protecting against espionage, sabotage, or assassinations conducted for or on behalf of foreign powers, organizations, persons, or international terrorist groups or activities.

The context and motivation that the Signals Intelligence mission pro-

---

[14]Parallel scalability means near-linear decrease in execution time as an increasing number of processors are used; algorithm scalability means moderate (near-linear) increase in computer time as problem size increases.

[15]This subsection is based on excerpts from the white paper "Computational Challenges in Signals Intelligence," prepared by Gary Hughes, NSA, and William Carlson and Francis Sullivan, Institute for Defense Analyses, Center for Computational Science, for the committee's Santa Fe, N.M., applications workshop, September 2003.

vides are essential to understanding its demands on supercomputing. Two characteristics are key: problem choice and timeliness of solutions. The highest priority problems to be solved are chosen not by NSA itself but rather by the very entities that pose the greatest danger: foreign adversaries. They do this when they choose communication methods. This single characteristic puts phenomenal demands on both the development of solutions and their deployment on available computing platforms. Solutions must also be timely—the intelligence derived from the communication "attack at dawn" is, to say the least, far less valuable at noon. Timeliness applies to both the development of solutions and their deployment. While these specific mission-driven requirements are unique to the Signals Intelligence mission, their effect is seen across a fairly broad spectrum of mission agencies, both inside and outside the defense community. This is in contrast to computing that targets broad advances in technology and science. In this context, computations are selected more on the basis of their match to available resources and codes.

There are two main uses of supercomputing driven by the Signals Intelligence mission: intelligence processing (IP) and intelligence analysis (IA). Intelligence processing seeks to transform intercepted communications signals into a form in which their meaning can be understood. This may entail overcoming sophisticated cryptographic systems, advanced signal processing, message reconstruction in the presence of partial or corrupted data, or other complex signaling or communications subsystems. Intelligence analysis begins with the output of IP and seeks to transform the blizzard of communication messages into a complete mosaic of knowledge so that adversaries' intentions can be discerned and actionable intelligence provided to national leadership and others with a need to know.

The key computational characteristics of Signals Intelligence problems differ greatly from those of the other scientific problems discussed in this section. There is extensive use of bit operations and operations in non-standard algebraic systems; floating point is used on only a tiny percentage of problems. A significant portion of the problem space is easily amenable to all forms of parallel processing (e.g., "embarrassingly parallel") techniques. Yet another significant portion of the problem space uses computations needing random access to extremely large data sets in memory and sustained, but unpredictable, interprocessor communication. In fact, the designers of cryptographic systems do their best to ensure there is no way to segment the code-breaking problem. Additionally, the knowledge discovery problem requires the understanding of extremely large graph networks with a dynamic collection of vertices and edges. The scale of this knowledge discovery problem is significantly larger than the largest commercial data mining operations.

Computational systems for Signals Intelligence include workstations, workstation farms, Beowulf clusters, massively parallel supercomputers, vector supercomputers, "handmade" FPGA-enhanced systems, and others. Operating systems used are mainly UNIX and Linux and programming is done mainly in C and Universal Parallel C (UPC).[16] Interprocessor communication is essential for the most demanding computations, yet MPI and related message passing models are not used because the added overhead of message passing systems is much too high a price to pay. Instead, SHMEM, a message-passing library developed for the Cray T3E and related systems, is employed.

Defense

A Mitre Corporation survey documented in June 2001[17] listed 10 DoD applications for supercomputing, which are still valid today:

- Weather and ocean forecasting.
- Planning for dispersion of airborne/waterborne contaminants.
- Engineering design of aircraft, ships, and other structures.
- Weapon (warhead/penetrators) effect studies and improved armor design.
- Cryptanalysis.
- Survivability/stealthiness.
- Operational intelligence, surveillance, and reconnaissance (ISR).
- Signal and image processing research to develop new exploitation.
- National missile defense.
- Test and evaluation.

Many of these defense applications require computational fluid dynamics (CFD), computational structural mechanics (CSM), and computational electromagnetics (CEM) calculations similar to those needed by

---

[16]Tarek A. El-Ghazawi, William W. Carlson, and Jesse M. Draper, "UPC Language Specification (V 1.1.1)," <http://www.gwu.edu/~upc/docs/upc_spec_1.1.1.pdf>; Robert W. Numrich and John Reid, 1998, "Co-array Fortran for Parallel Programming," *SIGPLAN Fortran Forum* 17(2):1-31; J. Nieplocha, R.J. Harrison, and R.J. Littlefield, 1996, "Global Arrays: A Nonuniform Memory Access Programming Model for High-Performance Computers," *Journal of Supercomputing* 10:197-220; Katherine Yelick, Luigi Semenzato, Geoff Pike, Carleton Miyamoto, Ben Liblit, Arvind Krishnamurthy, Paul Hilfinger, Susan Graham, David Gay, Philip Colella, and Alexander Aiken, 1998, "Titanium: A High-Performance Java Dialect," *Concurrency: Practice and Experience* 10:825-836.

[17]Richard Games. 2001. *Survey and Analysis of the National Security High Performance Computing Architectural Requirements.* MITRE Corp. June 4.

other supercomputing applications areas discussed in this report. One defense application that relies critically on supercomputing is comprehensive aerospace vehicle design, such as the design of the F-35 Joint Strike Fighter, and this reliance will only accelerate. Future aerospace development programs will involve hypersonic capabilities requiring more comprehensive physics models for accurate simulation in these harsh flight regimes. Two distinct types of computational science are required. CFD is used in the engineering design of complex flow configurations, including external airflow, and for predicting the interactions of chemistry with fluid flow for combustion and propulsion. CEM is used to compute electromagnetic signatures of tactical ground, air, sea, and space vehicles. Currently, we have the capability to model the external airflow, propulsion performance, vehicle signature, and materials properties in vehicle design with reasonable predictive accuracy on current systems, provided that these aspects are computed independently. But what is desired is the ability to combine these independent modeling efforts into an interactive modeling capability that would account for the interplay among model components. For example, engineers could quickly see the effect of proposed changes in the propulsion design on the vehicle's radar and infrared signature. Exceptional supercomputing performance and exceptional programmability are jointly required to enable a fine-grained, full-airframe combined CFD and CEM simulation of a vehicle like the Joint Strike Fighter.[18]

Climate Modeling

Comprehensive three-dimensional modeling of the climate has always required supercomputers.[19] To understand the role of supercomputing in climate modeling, it is important to first describe the composition of a climate model. Present-day climate models are made up of several major components of the climate system. In a sense they are now really Earth system models designed to deal with the issue of global change. The standard components are an atmosphere model, an ocean model, a combined land-vegetation-river transport (hydrological) model (which is sometimes a part of the atmospheric model), and a sea ice model. Some of

---

[18]High-End Crusader. 2004. "HEC Analysis: The High-End Computing Productivity Crisis." *HPC Wire* 13(15).

[19]This subsection is based on white papers by Warren M. Washington, NCAR, "Computer Architectures and Climate Modeling," and by Richard D. Loft, NCAR, "Supercomputing Challenges for Geoscience Applications," both prepared for the committee's applications workshop in Santa Fe, N.M., in September 2003.

the climate models have embedded chemical cycles such as carbon, sulfate, methane, and nitrogen cycles, which are treated as additional aspects of the major components. Indeed, climate modeling is similar to astrophysics and plasma physics in that it is a multiscale and multiphysical discipline. Although all relevant processes ultimately interact at the 10,000-km scale of the planet, the most important and least parameterizable influence on climate change is the response of cloud systems; clouds are best treated by embedding explicit submodels with grid sizes down to 1 km into a coarser climate grid. Similarly, the most important aspect of the oceanic part of climate change deals with changes in the Gulf Stream and the associated thermohaline overturning in the North Atlantic, where horizontal grid spacing in the hydrodynamics is required to be only a few kilometers in order to resolve the fundamental length scales. Southern Ocean processes, which involve both the sea-ice cover as it affects marine biological productivity and the stability of the antarctic ice cap as it affects global sea level, also occur mainly at this small space scale. Land component models should represent the biological properties of multiple types of vegetation and soil at a resolution of 1 km, and models of the global carbon cycle must represent the complex chemical and biological reactions and processes in the free atmosphere, the land surface, and the full-depth ocean. Even then, some processes must be prescribed separately on the basis of laboratory and process studies into such phenomena as cloud microphysics, small-scale ocean mixing, chemical reactions, and biological interactions.

Even with the highest performing supercomputers available today, climate simulations of 100 to 1,000 years require thousands of computational hours. Climate modeling requires multi-thousand-year simulations to produce equilibrium climate and its signals of natural variability, multi-hundred-year simulations to evaluate climate change beyond equilibrium (including possible abrupt climatic change), many tens of runs to determine the envelope of possible climate changes for a given emission scenario, and a multitude of scenarios for future emissions of greenhouse gases and human responses to climate change. However, these extended simulations require explicit integration of the nonlinear equations using time steps of only seconds to minutes in order to treat important phenomena such as internal waves and convection.

During each time step of a climate model, there is a sizeable amount of floating-point calculation, as well as a large amount of internal communication within the machine. Much of the spatial communication derives inherently from the continuum formulations of atmospheric and oceanic dynamics, but additional communication may arise from numerical formulations such as atmospheric spectral treatment or oceanic implicit free-surface treatments. Because of the turbulent nature of the underlying fluids, large volumes of model output must be analyzed to understand the underlying dynamics; this requires large external storage devices and efficient means of communicating with them.

As already indicated, an important aspect of the climate model is the grid resolution, both vertically and horizontally. In particular, the presence of moisture leads to a new class of small-scale fluid motions—namely, moist convection—which requires very high horizontal and vertical resolution (on the order of a kilometer) to resolve numerically. To resolve moist convection, the governing equations must include nonhydrostatic effects. This set of governing equations is considerably more difficult to solve than the hydrostatic primitive equations traditionally used in lower resolution atmospheric models. While direct numerical simulation at a global 1-km grid scale remains impractical for the foreseeable future, even so-called super parameterizations that attempt to realistically capture the sub-grid-scale properties of the underlying moist dynamics are dramatically more computationally expensive than current physics packages in operational models.

Resolution increases in hurricane modeling made possible by super-computing upgrades since 1998 have improved the ability to forecast hurricane tracks, cutting the track error in half and providing advance information to reduce loss of life and property in threatened areas.[20] Resolution increases will improve predictions of climate models, including the statistics of severe events in the face of climatic change.

All of the above considerations point to a massive need for increased computational resources, since current climate models typically have grid sizes of hundreds of kilometers, have few components and oversimplified parameterizations, have rarely reached equilibrium, and have rarely simulated future climate changes beyond a century. Moreover, they are seldom run in ensembles or for multiple-emission scenarios. Today, the climate modeler must make compromises in resolution in order to perform a realistic set of simulations. As advances in technology increase the speed of the supercomputers, history shows that the model complexity grows correspondingly, bringing both improved treatment of physical processes (such as clouds, precipitation, convection, and boundary layer fluxes) and the need for finer grid resolution.

Recently, climate models running on the most advanced U.S. super-computers have approached grid sizes of 100 km. In particular, simulations with the Community Climate System Model (CCSM),[21] running

---

[20]CNN. 2004. "Supercomputers Race to Predict Storms." September 16.
[21]See <http://www.ccsm.ucar.edu/> for more information.

mainly at the National Center for Atmospheric Research (NCAR) in support of the important Fourth Assessment of the Intergovernmental Panel on Climate Change (IPCC),[22] have used a 100-km ocean grid and an atmospheric grid of about 140 km. Very compute-intensive ocean-only simulations have been carried out at 10 km for simulated periods of only a few decades at several DOE and DoD sites and for longer periods on the Earth Simulator, and the results show a striking increase in the realism of strong currents like the Gulf Stream. Also, the initialization of the ocean component of climate models using four-dimensional data assimilation has used enormous amounts of supercomputer time at NCAR and the San Diego Supercomputer Center while still being carried out at relatively coarse resolution.

Notwithstanding the implied need for high internal bandwidth and effective communication with external storage, the requirement for sustained computational speed can be taken as a measure of computing needs for climate modeling. A 100- to a 1,000-fold increase in compute power over the next 5 to 10 years would be used very effectively to improve climate modeling. For example, the embedding of submodels of cloud systems within climate model grids removes much of the uncertainty in the potential climatic response to increasing greenhouse gases but increases the computing time by a factor of 80. Ocean components of climate models should be run a few thousand years at the desired 10-km resolution to test their ability to simulate long-term equilibrium conditions from first principles. Additional aspects of atmospheric chemistry and oceanic chemistry and biology are needed to move toward a proper treatment of the global carbon cycle and its vulnerability to greenhouse gases and industrial pollutants.

Continuing progress in climate prediction can come from further increases in computing power beyond a factor of 1,000. One detailed study of computational increases needed for various facets of climate modeling has shown the need for an ultimate overall increase in computer power of at least a billion-fold.[23] (Such a large increase could also be used for complex systems in plasma physics and astrophysics.) The breakdown of ultimate needs for increased computing power in climate modeling is as follows:

---

[22]More information is available at <http://www.ipcc.ch/about/about.htm>.

[23]Robert Malone, John Drake, Philip Jones, and Douglas Rotman. In press. "High-End Computing in Climate Modeling." *A Science-Based Case for Large-Scale Simulation.* D. Keyes, ed. Philadephia, Pa.: SIAM Press.

• Increase the spatial resolution of the grids of the coupled model components. The resolution targets are about 10 km in both the atmosphere and ocean, but for different reasons. It has been demonstrated that 10-km resolution is needed to resolve oceanic mesoscale eddies. A similar resolution is needed in the atmospheric component to obtain predictions of surface temperature and precipitation in sufficient detail to analyze the regional and local implications of climate change. This increases the total amount of computation by a factor of 1,000.

• Increase the completeness of the coupled model by adding to each component model important interactive physical, chemical, and biological processes that heretofore have been omitted owing to their computational complexity. Inclusion of atmospheric chemistry, both tropospheric and stratospheric, and biogeochemistry in the ocean are essential for understanding the ecological implications of climate change. This increases computation by a factor of 100.

• Increase the fidelity of the model by replacing parameterizations of subgrid physical processes by more realistic and accurate treatments as our understanding of the underlying physical processes improves, often as the result of observational field programs. This increases computation by a factor of 100.

• Increase the length of both control runs and climate-change-scenario runs. Longer control runs will reveal any tendency for the coupled model to drift and will also improve estimates of model variability. Longer climate-change-scenario runs will permit examination of critical issues such as the potential collapse of the global thermohaline circulation that may occur on time scales of centuries in global warming scenarios. Computation increases by a factor of 10.

• Increase the number of simulations in each ensemble of control runs or climate-change-scenario runs. Increase the number of climate-change scenarios investigated. These issues are both examples of perfectly parallel extensions of present-day simulations: Each instance of another scenario or ensemble member is completely independent of every other instance. Ensemble members are distinguished by small perturbations in their initial conditions, which are quickly amplified by the nonlinearity of the equations. The use of ensembles provides an important measure of the range of variability of the climate system. Computation increases by a factor of 10.[24]

---

[24]Ibid.

Plasma Physics

A major goal of plasma physics research is to produce cost-effective, clean, safe electric power from nuclear fusion.[25] Very large simulations of the reactions in advance of building the generating devices can save billions of equipment dollars. Plasmas comprise over 99 percent of the visible universe and are rich in complex, collective phenomena. Fusion energy, the power source of the Sun and other stars, occurs when forms of the lightest atom, hydrogen, combine to make helium in a very hot (~100 million degrees centigrade) ionized gas, or "plasma." The development of a secure and reliable energy system that is environmentally and economically sustainable is a truly formidable scientific and technological challenge facing the world in the 21st century. This demands basic scientific understanding that can enable the innovations to make fusion energy practical. Fusion energy science is a computational grand challenge because, in addition to dealing with space and time scales that can span more than 10 orders of magnitude, the fusion-relevant problem involves extreme anisotropy; the interaction between large-scale fluidlike (macroscopic) physics and fine-scale kinetic (microscopic) physics; and the need to account for geometric detail. Moreover, the requirement of causality (inability to parallelize over time) makes this problem among the most challenging in computational physics.

Supercomputing resources can clearly accelerate scientific research critical to progress in plasma science in general and to fusion research in particular. Such capabilities are needed to enable scientific understanding and to cost-effectively augment experimentation by allowing efficient design and interpretation of expensive new experimental devices (in the multi-billion-dollar range). In entering the exciting new physics parameter regimes required to study burning fusion plasmas, the associated challenges include higher spatial resolution, dimensionless parameters characteristic of higher temperature plasmas, longer simulation times, and higher model dimensionality. It will also be necessary to begin integrating these models together to treat nonlinear interactions of different phenomena. Various estimates indicate that increases in combined computational power by factors of 1,000 to 100,000 are needed. Associated challenges include advancing computer technology, developing algorithms, and improving theoretical formulation—all of which will contribute to better overall time-to-solution capabilities.

---

[25]This subsection is based on excerpts from the white paper "Plasma Science," prepared by W.M. Tang, Princeton University, for the committee's Santa Fe, N.M., applications workshop, September 2003.

Transportation

High-performance computing contributes to many aspects of transportation product engineering. It provides many benefits, such as reduced time to market, reduced requirements for physical prototypes, the ability to explore a larger design space, and a deeper understanding of vehicle behavior. The main problems addressed by high-performance computing include occupant safety (crash), noise, vibration, and harshness (NVH), durability, airflow, and heat transfer. These problems vary in time to solution from a few hours to days to weeks. The general goal is to achieve overnight turnaround times for all types of problems, which trades off the complexity of the models being run with the ability of engineers to utilize the results. The models need to have sufficient detail to provide a high degree of confidence in the accuracy of the results. Today's machines are not fast enough to compensate for the scaling limitations of many of these problems.[26]

Transportation manufacturers drastically reduce their development expenses and time to market by replacing physical models and car crashes with virtual tests run on supercomputers. According to Bob Kruse, GM's executive director for vehicle integration,[27] supercomputing will enable his company to shorten its product development cycle from the 48 months of a few years ago to 15 months. The company is performing fewer rounds of vehicle prototyping, which has reduced engineering costs by 40 percent. Kruse went on to say that GM has eliminated 85 percent of its real-world crash tests since moving to modeling crashes on its supercomputer. In theory, the company could do away with its $500,000 crash tests, but the National Highway Traffic Safety Administration still requires final real-world crash testing.

There is a long history of using high-performance computing in the automotive industry (see Box 4.1). Automotive computer-aided engineering (CAE) may well be the largest private-sector marketplace for such systems. In the 1980s and early 1990s, automotive companies worldwide deployed the same Cray vector supercomputers favored by government laboratories and other mission agencies. This changed in the late 1990s, when government-funded scientists and engineers began migrating to distributed memory systems. The main CAE applications used in the automotive industry contain millions of lines of code and have proven very

---

[26]Based on excerpts from the white paper "High Performance Computing in the Auto Industry," by Vincent Scarafino, Ford Motors, prepared for the committee's Santa Fe, N.M., applications workshop, September 2003.

[27]John Gartner. 2004. "Supercomputers Speed Car Design." *Wired News.* April 26.

**BOX 4.1 Automotive Companies and Their Use of
High-Performance Computers**

One of the main commercial users of supercomputing is the automotive industry. The largest car manufacturers in the United States, Europe, and the Far East all use supercomputing in one form or another for the design and validation cycle. This market segment is called mechanical computer-aided engineering (MCAE).

The use of computing in the automotive industry has come about in response to (1) the need to shorten the design cycle and (2) advances in technology that enable such reduction. One advance is the availability of large-scale high-performance computers. The automotive industry was one of the first commercial segments to use high-performance computers. The other advance is the availability of third-party application software that is optimized to the architecture of high-performance computers. Both advances operate in other industries as well; the existence of third-party application software for MCAE, electrical CAD, chemistry, and geophysics has increased the market for high-performance computers in many industries.

Since the use of supercomputing is integrated within the overall vehicle design, the time to solution must be consistent with the overall design flow. This requirement imposes various time constraints. To be productive, designers need two simulation runs a day (one in the morning and one overnight) or three (one in the morning, one in the afternoon, and one overnight). To meet that need, typical computer runs must complete in 4 to 8 hours or, at most, overnight. In many situations, the fidelity of the input is matched to this requirement. As additional compute power is added, the fidelity of the models is increased and additional design features simulated.

Demand for computing doubles every year. One measure of demand is the size of the model. Current models process 1 million elements. Larger models are not run now for two reasons: (1) processor capability is not powerful enough to process more than 1 million elements with manageable time-to-solution characteristics—that is, the single job takes too long to complete subject to operational requirements—and (2) the companies do not have adequate tools such as visualization to help them understand the outputs from larger simulations.

difficult to port to the distributed memory computational model. As a result, automotive companies have tended not to purchase capability systems in the last decade. Instead they have increased capacity and reduced their costs by replacing vector mainframes with shared memory multiprocessor (SMP) servers and, more recently, clusters of PCs.

Almost all software is supplied by third-party, independent software vendors (ISVs). There are several de facto standard codes that are used, among them the following:

- *MSC/NASTRAN (structural analysis).* NASTRAN generally runs on one processor and is I/O bound. Large jobs are run with limited parallelization on small SMP systems (four to eight processors).
- *PAMCRASH/LS-DYNA/RADIOSS (crash analysis).* These codes use modest degrees of parallelism, ranging from 12 to 100 processors in production automotive calculations today. At that scale, crash codes work well on clusters. While at least one of these codes has run on 1,024 processors,[1] load imbalances limit the effective scaling of these codes for today's automotive calculations.

In the past 10 years there has been considerable evolution in the use of supercomputing in the automotive industry. Ten years ago, CAE was used to simulate a design. The output of the simulation was then compared with the results from physical tests. Simulation modeled only one component of a vehicle—for example, its brake system—and only one "discipline" within that subsystem (for example, temperature, weight, or noise). There has been a transition to the current ability to do design verification—that is, a component is designed by human engineers but the properties of the design can be checked before the component is built and tested. In some cases multidisciplinary verification is possible. The longer-term goal is to automate the design of a vehicle, namely, to move from single subsystems to an integrated model, from single disciplines to multidisciplinary analysis, and from verifying a human design to generating the design computationally. Design definition will require optimization and first-order analysis based on constraints. Attaining this objective will reduce design cycle times and increase the reliability and safety of the overall design.

NOTE: The committee is grateful to Vince Scarafino, Ford Motor Company, for his assistance in developing this box. In addition, the committee thanks the several auto manufacturers who kindly provided anonymous input.

[1]Roger W. Logan and Cynthia K. Nitta. 2002. "Verification & Validation (V&V) Methodology and Quantitative Reliability at Confidence (QRC): Basis for an Investment Strategy." DOE paper UCRL-ID-150874.

This is not to say that there is no longer a demand for supercomputers in the automobile industry. In March of 2000, Toyota purchased 30 VPP5000 vector processors from Fujitsu. At the time, this was arguably the most powerful privately owned system in the world. As independent software vendor (ISV) CAE codes have matured to the point where they can effectively exploit hundreds of processors, automotive companies have responded by purchasing larger systems. GM recently announced the purchase of a large IBM system rated at 9 Tflops peak, which would place it within the top 20 systems in the June 2004 TOP500 list.[28] Frank Roney, a managing director at IBM, said GM's supercomputer would most likely be the most powerful computer owned by a private company. In May 2004, the Japan Agency for Marine-Earth Science and Technology announced that it would make the Earth Simulator available to the Japanese Automobile Industry Association starting in summer 2004.[29] According to a June 2004 report from Top500.org, automotive companies, including Ford, GM, Renault, VW, BMW, Opel, and Daimler Chrysler (three companies are anonymous), own 13 of the 500 fastest supercomputers in the world. The same report indicates that automakers dedicate nearly 50 percent of their supercomputing hours to crash test simulations.

Automotive engineers are continually expanding their computational requirements to exploit both available computing power and advances in software. Finite-element models of automobiles for crash simulation use mesh spacing of about 5 mm, resulting in problems that have as many as 1 million elements. The automotive engineering community would like to reduce the mesh size to 1 mm, resulting in 100 million elements. Today's crash test models typically include multiple dummies, folded front and side airbags, and fuel in the tanks. Deployment of airbags and sloshing of fuel are modeled with CFD. Engineers in the future will expect CAE tools to automatically explore variations in design parameters in order to optimize their designs. John Hallquist of Livermore Software Technology Corporation believes that fully exploiting these advances in automotive CAE will require a seven-order-of-magnitude increase beyond the computing power brought to bear today.[30] This would allow, among other things, much greater attention to occupant safety requirements, including aspects of offset frontal crash, side impact, out-of-position occupants, and more humanlike crash dummies.

While the use of supercomputers has historically been the most aggressive in the automotive industry, supercomputing facilitates engineer-

---

[28]Ibid.

[29]Summary translation of an article from *Nihn Keizai* newspaper, May 24, 2004, provided by the NSF Tokyo regional office.

[30]Based on excerpts from the white paper "Supercomputing and Mechanical Engineering," by C. Ashcraft, R. Grimes, J. Hallquist, and B. Maker, Livermore Software Technology Corporation, prepared for the committee's Santa Fe, N.M., applications workshop, September 2003.

ing in many other aspects of transportation. According to Ray Orbach, the DOE Office of Science's research accomplishments in transportation simulation have received accolades from corporations such as GE and GM.[31] When the Office of Science met with the vice presidents for research of these and other member companies of the Industrial Research Institute, it learned, for example, that GE is using simulation very effectively to detect flaws in jet engines. If the engine flaws identified by simulation were to go undetected, the life cycle of those GE engines would be reduced by a factor of 2, causing GE a loss of over $100,000,000. For example, the evaluation of a design alternative to optimize a compressor for a jet engine design at GE would require 3.1×10^{18} floating-point operations, or over a month at a sustained speed of 1 Tflops, which is near today's state of the art in supercomputing. To do this for the entire jet engine would require sustained computing power of 50 Tflops for the same period. This is to be compared with many millions of dollars, several years, and many designs and redesigns for physical prototyping.[32]

In summary, transportation companies currently save hundreds of millions of dollars using supercomputing in their new vehicle design and development processes. Supercomputers are used for vehicle crash simulation, safety models, aerodynamics, thermal and combustion analyses, and new materials research. However, the growing need for higher safety standards, greater fuel efficiency, and lighter but stronger materials demands dramatic increases in supercomputing capability that will not be met by existing architectures and technologies. Some of these problems are relatively well understood and would yield to more powerful computing systems. Other problems, such as combustion modeling inside pistons, are still open research challenges. Nevertheless, a supercomputing capability that delivered even 100 Tflops to these applications would save billions of dollars in product design and development costs in the commercial transportation sector.[33]

Bioinformatics and Computational Biology

The past two decades have witnessed the emergence of computation and information technology as arguably the most important disciplines

---

[31]Testimony of Raymond L. Orbach, Director, Office of Science, U.S. Department of Energy, before the U.S. House of Representatives Committee on Science, July 16, 2003.
[32]Ibid.
[33]Ibid.

for future developments in biology and biomedicine.[34] The explanation of biological processes in terms of their underlying chemical reactions is one of the great triumphs of modern science and underlies much of contemporary medicine, agriculture, and environmental science. An exciting consequence of this biochemical knowledge is that computational modeling methods developed to study fundamental chemical processes can now, at least in principle, be applied to biology. Many profound biological questions, such as how enzymes exhibit both exquisite selectivity and immense catalytic efficiency, are amenable to study by simulation. Such simulations could ultimately have two goals: (1) to act as a strong validation that all relevant features of a biochemical mechanism have been identified and understood and (2) to provide a powerful tool for probing or reengineering a biochemical process.

Computation also is essential to molecular biology, which seeks to understand how cells and systems of cells function in order to improve human health, longevity, and the treatment of diseases. The sheer complexity of molecular systems, in terms of both the number of molecules and the types of molecules, demands computation to simulate and codify the logical structure of these systems. There has been a paradigm shift in the nature of computing in biology with the decoding of the human genome and with the technologies this achievement enabled. Equations-of-physics-based computation is now complemented by massive-data-driven computations, combined with heuristic biological knowledge. In addition to deployment of statistical methods for data processing, myriad data mining and pattern recognition algorithms are being developed and employed. Finding multiple alignments of the sequences of hundreds of bacterial genomes is a computational problem that can be attempted only with a new suite of efficient alignment algorithms on a petaflops supercomputer. Large-scale gene identification, annotation, and clustering expressed sequence tags are other large-scale computational problems in genomics.

In essence, computation in biology will provide the framework for understanding the flow of information in living systems. Some of the grand challenges posed by this paradigm are outlined below, along with the associated computational complexity:

---

[34]This subsection is based in part on excerpts from the white papers "Quantum Mechanical Simulations of Biochemical Processes," by Michael Colvin, LLNL, and "Supercomputing in Computational Molecular Biology," by Gene Myers, UC Berkeley, both prepared for the committee's Santa Fe, N.M., applications workshop, September 2003.

• Deciphering the genome continues to be a challenging computational problem. One of the largest Hewlett-Packard cluster systems ever developed was used to assemble the human genome. In the annotation of the genome (assigning functional roles), the computation can be extraordinarily complex. Multiple genome comparisons, which are practically impossible with current computers, are essential and will constitute a significant challenge in computational biomedicine for the future.

• There are typically a few hundred cell types in a mammal, and each type of cell has its own repertoire of active genes and gene products. Our understanding of human diseases relies heavily on figuring out the intracellular components and the machinery formed by the components. The advent of DNA microarrays has provided us with a unique ability to rapidly map the gene expression profiles in cells experimentally. While analysis of a single array is not a supercomputing problem, the collective analysis of a large number of arrays across time or across treatment conditions explodes into a significant computational task.

• Genes translate into proteins, the workhorses of the cell. Mechanistic understanding of the biochemistry of the cell involves intimate knowledge of the structure of these proteins and details of their function. The number of genes from various species is in the millions, and experimental methods have no hope of resolving the structures of the encoded proteins. Computational modeling and prediction of protein structures remain the only hope. This problem, called the protein-folding problem, is regarded as the holy grail of biochemistry. Even when knowledge-based constraints are employed, this problem remains computationally intractable with modern computers.

• Computer simulations remain as the only approach to understanding the dynamics of macromolecules and their assemblies. Early simulations were restricted to small macromolecules. In the past three decades, our ability to compute has helped us to understand large macromolecular assemblies like membranes for up to tens of nanoseconds. These simulations that scale as N^2 are still far from capable of calculating motions of hundreds of thousands of atoms for biologically measurable time scales.

• Understanding the characteristics of protein interaction networks and protein-complex networks formed by all the proteins of an organism is another large computational problem. These networks are small-world networks, where the average distance between two vertices in the network is small relative to the number of vertices. Small-world networks also arise in electric power networks and semantic networks for intelligence analysis and in models of the Web; understanding the nature of these networks, many with billions of vertices and trillions of edges, is critical to making them invulnerable to attacks. Simulations of small-world networks fall into three categories: topological, constraint-driven, and dynamic. Each of these categories involves complex combinatorial, graph theoretic, and differential equation solver algorithms and challenges any supercomputer. Current algorithmic and computational capabilities will not be able to address computational needs for even the smallest microorganism, Haemophilus influenza. There is an imminent need for the development of novel methods and computing technology.

  • The achievement of goals such as a cure for cancer and the prevention of heart diseases and neurovascular disorders continue to drive biomedicine. The problems involved were traditionally regarded as noncomputational or minimally computational problems. However, with today's knowledge of the genome and intracellular circuitry, we are in a position to carry out precise and targeted discovery of drugs that, while curing the pathology, will only minimally perturb normal function. This is rapidly emerging as a serious computational task and will become the preeminent challenge of biomedicine.

  • Much of our knowledge of living systems comes from comparative analysis of living species. Phylogenetics, the reconstruction of historical relationships between species or individuals, is now intensely computational, involving string and graph algorithms. In addition to being an intellectual challenge, this problem has a significant practical bearing on bioterrorism. Computation is the fastest and currently the only approach to rapidly profiling and isolating dangerous microorganisms.

In conclusion, we are at the threshold of a capability to perform predictive simulations of biochemical processes that will transform our ability to understand the chemical basis of biological functions. In addition to its value to basic biological research, this will greatly improve our ability to design new therapeutic drugs, treat diseases, and understand the mechanisms of genetic disorders.

Societal Health and Safety

Computational simulation is a critical tool of scientific investigation and engineering design in many areas related to societal health and safety, including aerodynamics; geophysics; structures; manufacturing processes with phase change; and energy conversion processes. Insofar as these mechanical systems can be described by conservation laws expressed as partial differential equations, they may be amenable to analysis using supercomputers. Trillions of dollars of economic output annually and the health and safety of billions of people rest on our ability to simulate such systems.

Incremental improvements in the accuracy and reliability of simulations are important because of huge multipliers. A very small (perhaps even 1 percent) improvement in the efficiency of heat exchangers or gas turbines could have a significant impact on the global environment and economy when aggregated over the lifetime of many such devices.[35]

The problem of monitoring the quality of air, water, and other utility networks has gained prominence in the wake of terrorist events like Tokyo's subway incident and London's poison gas bomb plot. One example of a computational problem of this type is optimizing the placement of sensors in municipal water networks to detect contaminants injected maliciously. Traditionally, this type of problem was studied using numerical simulation tools to see how a water supply network is impacted by the introduction of contaminant at a given point. Recently, combinatorial optimization formulations have been proposed to compute optimal sensor locations. Optimal sensor placement is desirable to ensure adequate coverage of the network's flow for detection and remediation of contaminants. The objective of one model is to minimize the expected fraction of the population that is at risk for an attack. An attack is modeled as the release of a large volume of harmful contaminant at a single point in the network with a single injection. For any particular attack, assume that all points downstream of the release point can be contaminated. In general, one does not know a priori where this attack will occur, so the objective is to place sensors to provide a compromise solution across all possible attack locations. Depending on the size of the water network, the amount of computation needed can be extremely large and can certainly require supercomputing performance for timely results, especially in an emergency.[36]

Earthquakes

An important application in geophysical exploration is earthquake modeling and earthquake risk mitigation. When an earthquake occurs, some areas the size of city blocks are shaken, while other areas are stable and not shaken. This effect is caused by the focusing or deflection of seismic waves by underground rock structures. If the underground rock struc-

---

[35]Based on excerpts from the white paper "Supercomputing for PDE-based Simulations in Mechanics," by David Keyes, Columbia University, prepared for the committee's Santa Fe, N.M., applications workshop, September 2003.

[36]Based on excerpts from the white paper "Supercomputing and Discrete Algorithms: A Symbiotic Relationship," by William Hart, Bruce Hendrickson, and Cindy Phillips, Sandia National Laboratories, prepared for the committee's Santa Fe, N.M., applications workshop, September 2003.

ture of an area in an earthquake-prone region could be simulated or imaged, damage mitigation strategies could include identifying dangerous areas and avoiding building on them and simulating many typical earthquakes, noting which areas are shaken and identifying dangerous areas.

Using forward simulation, one can match seismic simulation results with observed seismographic data. Then an image of the underground rock in a region can be deduced by repeatedly simulating the error from forward simulation by adjoint methods.[37]

Current earthquake simulation codes running at the California Institute of Technology and the Pittsburgh Supercomputer Center use frequencies up to 1 Hz, which equates to a resolution of several miles of rock. Seismographs can collect data up to 20 Hz or more, which yields a resolution of hundreds of feet of rock. This is a useful resolution for risk mitigation, since buildings are hundreds of feet in size. However, the computing power needed to process such data is on the order of 1 exaflops, or 1,000 Pflops (25,000 times the power of the Earth Simulator). For useful earthquake risk mitigation, the algorithms exist, the codes are written and debugged, and the input data exist. The consequence of not proceeding is continued loss of life and extensive property damage in earthquake-prone regions of the world.[38]

Geophysical Exploration and Geoscience

The simulation of petroleum reservoirs is a large consumer of supercomputing resources in this application area.[39] All of the major oil companies simulate petroleum reservoirs to predict future oil and gas production from the subsurface of Earth, where porous sandstone or limestone formations may hold oil and gas. Predictions are made using differential equations that represent flow in porous media in three dimensions. In addition to the simple case of flow of oil, water, and gas in the reservoirs, it is often necessary to include the phase behavior of multicomponent hydrocarbon fluids for enhanced-recovery processes and/or thermal effects for steam injection or in situ combustion recovery techniques.

---

[37]Erik P. DeBenedictus. 2004. "Completing the Journey of Moore's Law," Presentation at the University of Illinois, May 5.

[38]Ibid.

[39]This subsection is based on excerpts from the white paper "High Performance Computing and Petroleum Reservoir Simulation," by John Killough, Landmark Graphics Corporation, prepared for the committee's Santa Fe, N.M., applications workshop, September 2003.

The overall goal of the simulations is to maximize hydrocarbon liquid and gas recovery and net present value.

The motivation for using supercomputing in reservoir simulation has always existed. From the earliest simulation models, computing resources have been severely taxed simply because the level of complexity desired by the engineer almost always exceeded the speed and memory of the hardware. The high-speed vector processors of the late 1970s and early 1980s led to orders of magnitude improvement in the speed of computation and led to production models of several hundred thousand cells. The relief brought by these models was short lived. The desire for increased physics of compositional modeling and the introduction of geostatistically/structurally based geological models led to increases in computational complexity even beyond the large-scale models of the vector processors. Tens of millions of cells with complete reservoir parameters now became available for use by the engineer. Although upscaling or lumping provided a tool to dramatically reduce model sizes, the inherent assumptions of the upscaling techniques left the engineer with a strong desire to incorporate all of the available data in studies.

Scientific studies of Earth's interior are heavily dependent on supercomputer power. Two examples are illustrative. One is the geodynamo—i.e., an understanding of how Earth's magnetic field is generated by complicated magnetohydrodynamic convection and turbulence in its outer core, a long-standing grand challenge in fluid dynamics. Supercomputer simulations have enabled major breakthroughs in the last decade, including the first self-consistent dynamo solution and the first simulated magnetic reversal, both of which occurred in 1995. However, these simulated dynamos are still many orders of magnitude away from the "correct" parameter range. The second example comes from the need to understand the dynamics of Earth's plate tectonics and mantle convection, which drives continental drift, mountain building, etc. To do this simulation properly requires incorporating the correct multirheological behavior of rocks (elastic, brittle, viscous, plastic, history-dependent, and so forth), which results in a wide range of length scales and time scales, into a three-dimensional, spherical model of the entire Earth, another grand challenge that will require substantially more computing power to address.[40]

---

[40]For more information, see <http://sdcd.gsfc.nasa.gov/ESS/olson.finalreport/final_report.html>. A more general article is P.J. Tackley, J.R. Baumgardner, G.A. Glatzmaier, P. Olson, and T. Clune, 1999, "Three-Dimensional Spherical Simulations of Convection in Earth's Mantle and Core Using Massively-Parallel Computers," Advanced Simulations Technologies Conference, San Diego, pp. 95-100.

Astrophysics

Observation has always been fundamental to astronomy, but controlled experiments are extremely rare.[41] Thus, astronomical computer simulations have assumed the traditional scientific role of controlled experiments by making it possible to test scenarios when the underlying physical laws are known. Observations still provide a check, but they show the results of processes that cannot be controlled in a laboratory. Furthermore, the evolutionary time scales for most astronomical systems are so long that these systems seem frozen in time. Constructing evolutionary models purely from observation is therefore difficult. By observing many different systems of the same type (e.g., stars or galaxies), we can see many different stages of development and attempt to put them into a logical order, but we cannot watch a single system evolve. A supercomputer simulation is usually required to provide the evolutionary model that ties the different observed stages together using known physical laws and properties of matter.

Stellar evolution theory provides an excellent example of why astrophysicists have been forced to rely on computer simulation. Although one can perform laboratory experiments to determine the properties of the gaseous constituents in a star like the Sun, one cannot build an experimental star in the laboratory and watch it evolve. That must be done by computer simulation. Although one can make some simple arguments and estimates without using a computer, the physics involved in stellar evolution theory is complex and nonlinear, so one does not get very far in developing the theory without a computer.

Supercomputing power can be used to literally add a spatial dimension, turning a two-dimensional simulation of a supernova explosion into three-dimensional simulation, or it can be used to add treatments of new and important phenomena into a simulation. For example, magnetic fields could be added to global simulations of solar convection to address the operation of the dynamo that drives the sunspot cycle. For some problems, such as the development of large-scale structure in the expanding universe, simply getting more of the system under study into the computational problem domain by dramatically increasing the size of the computational grid should have a significant impact on scientific discovery. Alternatively, one might choose to simulate the same size system, using supercomputing power to treat structures on a much wider range of

---

[41]This subsection is based on excerpts from the white paper "Future Supercomputing Needs and Opportunities in Astrophysics," by Paul Woodward, University of Minnesota, prepared for the committee's Santa Fe, N.M., applications workshop, September 2003.

length and time scales. An excellent example is the cosmological problem, since it contains scales of interest ranging from that of a single star to that of a large cluster of galaxies.

Physicists trying to determine whether our universe will continue to expand or eventually collapse have gathered data from dozens of distant supernovae. By analyzing the data and simulating another 10,000 supernovae on supercomputers at NERSC, they have concluded that the universe is expanding—and at an accelerating rate.[42]

Materials Science and Computational Nanotechnology

The emerging fields of computational materials science examine the fundamental behavior of matter at atomic to nanometer length scales and picosecond to millisecond time scales in order to discover novel properties of bulk matter for numerous important practical uses.

Predictive equations take the form of first principles electronic structure molecular dynamics (FPMD) and quantum Monte Carlo (QMC) techniques for the simulation of nano-materials. The QMC methods are highly parallel across multiple processors but require high bandwidth to local memory, whereas the FPMD methods are demanding of both local and global bandwidth. The computational requirements of a materials science problem grow typically as the cube of the number of atoms in any simulation even when the newest and best computational algorithms are used—making the area an almost unlimited consumer of future increases in computer power. The most beneficial simulations in terms of practical applications require large numbers of atoms and long time scales—far more than presently possible in both of those aspects. For example, FPMD simulations are currently limited to a few hundred atoms for a few picoseconds. The promise of revolutionary materials and processes from materials science will routinely require several petaflops of computer power in the not too distant future.

As the Committee on the Future of Supercomputing heard in numerous presentations during its site visits, computational materials science is now poised to explore a number of areas of practical importance. Algorithms are well tested that will exploit 100 to 1,000 times the computing power available today. Materials scientists in a number of universities as well as in DOE laboratories are already targeting the largest future con-

---

[42]Testimony of Raymond L. Orbach, Director, Office of Science, U.S. Department of Energy, before the U.S. House of Representatives Committee on Science, July 16, 2003.

figurations of Cray X1 and IBM Blue Gene/L in order to advance their applications.

The promise of new materials and processes covers a wide variety of economically important areas. Among the most important are these:

- *Better electronic equipment.* Materials with superconducting properties are most useful when they can function at temperatures well above absolute zero. The negligible power loss of superconductors makes them ideal for constructing a range of devices from MRI machines to microprocessors, when cooling can be provided by relatively inexpensive liquid nitrogen (as opposed to more expensive liquid helium systems). A computational search is well under way for superconductors with higher critical temperatures than substances already found in the laboratory.
- *Improved power transmission.* It is possible that computational methods will discover synthetic materials with much better conducting properties at room temperatures than those presently available. The possibility of nearly loss-free power transmission has major economic implications. Even supercomputing itself would benefit greatly.
- *High-density data storage.* Some supercomputing applications will require magnetic storage densities of terabits per square inch in the relatively near future. The information will need to be stored in nanometer-scale particles or grains. A detailed understanding of the magnetism in nanometer particles will have to come from computational studies that will be validated with selected experiments. This is a new way to approach the science involving magnetic storage and constitutes a major opportunity for petaflops-scale computing.[43]
- *Photoelectric devices.* In selective-light-absorbing materials for solar energy, for photothermal energy conversion, or for optical sensors, the active semiconductor particles will contain millions of atoms to ensure sharp enough lines. With clever techniques exploiting special features to reduce the computational burden, the optical properties of such particles can be accurately evaluated, and even charging effects from electron excitations can be accounted for. Such calculations can now be performed only by using very large allocations of time on the most powerful computers available in the United States. To be useful for designing new structures and devices, such simulations need to be run almost routinely for configurations that do not have the special features currently being exploited.[44]

---

[43]Thomas Schulthess. 2004. "Ab-initio Monte Carlo for Nanomagnetism." ORNL White Paper.

[44]"Accelerating the Revolution in Computational Materials Science," 2002, <http://www.ultrasim.info/doe_docs/acc_mat_sci.pdf>.

• *Electric motors.* Scientists have recently achieved breakthrough quantum mechanical simulations of magnetic moments at high temperatures. Such simulations were limited to a few thousand atoms of pure iron. Understanding more complex substances is the key to designing materials for stronger magnets in order to build more efficient and powerful electrical generators and motors. For simulations to accurately model the dynamics of magnetic domains in more complex materials, much larger simulation sizes will be required. Award-winning algorithms of high quality exist, so the issue now is having a computing platform capable of sustaining the level of computation necessary to carry out the science.[45]

• *Catalysts.* The U.S. chemical, biochemical, and pharmaceutical industries are the world's largest producer of chemicals, ranging from wonder drugs to paints to cosmetics to plastics to new, more efficient energy sources. A key ingredient in nearly all such industrial processes is a type of chemical called a catalyst. The true computational design of practical catalysts for industrial and commercial applications will require the ability to predict, at the molecular level, the detailed behavior of the large, complex molecules and materials involved in catalytic processes. This level of detail is not available from experiments, and it is not feasible on currently available computer hardware. For example, to simulate the platinum catalyst in a car's catalytic converter requires the model to include hundreds to tens of thousands of platinum atoms. A realistic simulation of the actual process in a car engine would take decades on today's computer hardware. The design of new catalysts simply cannot wait this long if the U.S. chemical and pharmaceutical industries are to remain competitive. New computational capabilities will revolutionize the chemical industry, turning the art of catalysis creation into the science of catalyst design.[46]

• *Bioengineering.* Within the biology arena, the use of supercomputers will enable microscopic modeling of DNA repair mechanisms and drug/DNA interactions, effectively bringing quantum simulations into the realm of biology. In particular, nearly exact QMC results will represent valuable theoretical benchmarks that may help overcome some of the current limitations of experimental biology.[47]

---

[45]Ibid.

[46]"Computational Design of Catalysts: Building the Science Case for Ultrascale Simulations," 2002, <http://www.ultrasim.info/doe_docs/catalysis_redux2.pdf>.

[47]F. Gygi, G. Galli, J.C. Grossman, and V. Bulatov. 2002. "Impact of Earth-Simulator-Class Computers on Computational Nanoscience and Materials Science." DOE Ultrascale Simulation White Paper.

In summary, computational materials science is emerging as an important factor in providing the designer materials and processes that will underlie the economic progress of the nation in the coming decades. Simulating the complexity of large numbers of atoms and molecules over increasingly long time periods will challenge supercomputers of petaflops power and beyond.

Human/Organizational Systems Studies

The study of macroeconomics and social dynamics is amenable to simulation and study using supercomputing. In such applications, the behavior of large human populations is simulated in terms of the overall effect of decisions by hundreds of millions of individuals. The simulations can model physical or social structures with hundreds of thousands, or maybe even millions, of actors interacting with one another in a complex fashion. Supercomputing makes it possible to test different interactor (or interpersonal) relations to see what macroscopic behaviors can ensue. Simulations can determine the nature of the fundamental forces or interactions between actors. Some logistical examples include airline crew scheduling, inventory management, and package delivery scheduling (the FedEx problem).[48]

Sociotechnical systems of 10^6 to 10^9 agents (people, packets, commodities, and so on) with irregular interactions on time scales of seconds to years can be simulated using supercomputers at institutions like Los Alamos National Laboratory. However, the customers for such simulations are often organizations such as metropolitan planning offices, which do not generally have access to sophisticated supercomputing systems and therefore are limited to manipulating the amount of data that can be handled by COTS technology such as Linux clusters. Over the coming years, researchers will expand existing simulations of transportation, electricity distribution and markets, epidemiology, and mobile telecommunications on scales ranging from that of a city the size of Portland, Oregon (1.6 million people) to national scale. Sociotechnical simulations in the future will require coupling many large, heterogeneous, irregular simulation systems, which will require advanced supercomputing power to accomplish.[49]

---

[48]Testimony of Raymond L. Orbach, Director, Office of Science, U.S. Department of Energy, before the U.S. House of Representatives Committee on Science, July 16, 2003.

[49]Based on excerpts from the white paper "The Future of Supercomputing for Sociotechnical Simulation," by Stephen Eubank, LANL, prepared for the committee's Santa Fe, N.M., applications workshop, September 2003.

PROJECTED COMPUTING NEEDS FOR APPLICATIONS

The scientific and engineering applications that use supercomputing are diverse both in the nature of the problems and in the nature of the solutions. Most of these applications have unsatisfied computational needs. They were described in expert briefings to the committee as computing-limited at present and very much in need of 100 to 1,000 times more computing power over the next 5 to 10 years. Increased computing power would be used in a variety of ways:

- To cover larger domains, more space scales, and longer time scales;
- To solve time-critical problems (e.g., national security ones) in shorter times;
- To include more complete physics and/or biogeochemistry;
- To use more sophisticated mathematical algorithms with desirable linear scaling; and
- To add more components to models of complex systems.

Various experts made estimates of the long-range computing power needed for their disciplines in units of petaflops. Most of the applications areas discussed would require a minimum sustained performance of 10 Pflops to begin to solve the most ambitious problems and realize practical benefits. To move toward a full solution of these problems would require capabilities of 100 Pflops and beyond.

The overall computing style in important application areas appears to be evolving toward one in which community models are developed and used by large groups. The individual developers may bring diverse backgrounds and expertise to modeling a complex natural system such as the climate system or to a daunting engineering effort like the development of a fusion power generator. In addition, the applications are moving toward first-principles methods, in which basic physical and biochemical relations are used as much as possible instead of ad hoc parameterizations involving approximations and poorly known constants. Both trends will greatly increase the amount of computing power required in various applications.

A common computational characteristic is the demand for both capacity and capability. Typically, each disciplinary area does many smaller simulations and parameter studies using machine capacity prior to large simulations that require machine capability, followed by analysis studies that use capacity. Many application areas could each use at least one large computing center almost continuously to attack multiple problems in this way.

Another computational characteristic is that each application area has a rather high degree of problem complexity. There may be multiple time and space scales, different component sub-models (e.g., magnetic, hydro-dynamic, or biochemical), different types of equations (e.g., nonlinear par-tial differential equations and ordinary differential equations), and differ-ent algorithms (spectral, finite-difference, finite-element, algebraic) covering a range of problems being studied in each area.

It is clear from the summary above that a 1,000-fold increase in com-puting power is needed almost immediately and a 1,000,000-fold increase will ultimately be needed by the current major applications. Some of this increase can be expected on the basis of Moore's law and greater numbers of processors per machine. Any increase in raw computing power in terms of raw flops will have to be accompanied by larger memories to accom-modate larger problems, and internal bandwidth will have to increase dramatically. As problems become more data-oriented, more effective parallel I/O to external devices will be needed, which will themselves have to be larger than today's disks and mass storage systems.

Table 4.1 summarizes six supercomputing system bottlenecks that of-ten limit performance on important applications and gives examples of the applications. It should be noted that the limitations/bottlenecks in application areas are heavily dependent on the problem-solving strate-gies and the algorithms used.

The ability of applications to be mapped onto hardware effectively is critically dependent on the software of the overall system, including both the operating system and the compilers. Application programmers and users will need software that exploits the features of any given machine without heroic efforts on the programmer's part. Software ideally should

TABLE 4.1 Six Limitations of Supercomputing Systems

Limitation/Bottleneck	Typical Areas of Application
Floating-point performance	Astrophysics, defense radar cross-sections, climate modeling, plasma physics
Memory size	Intelligence, materials science, genomics, automobile noise, vibration, and harshness
Memory bandwidth	Intelligence, climate modeling, materials science, astrophysics, biological systems modeling
Memory latency	Intelligence, nuclear simulation, climate modeling, astrophysics, biological systems modeling
Interconnect bandwidth	Intelligence, climate modeling, materials science, astrophysics, biological systems modeling
Interconnect latency	Intelligence, nuclear simulation, climate modeling, astrophysics, biological systems modeling

promote effective parallel processor usage and efficient memory use while hiding many of the details. Ideally, software should allow portability of well-designed application programs between different machine architectures, handle dynamic load balancing, and also have fault tolerance.

There is also a need for better ability to deal with locality while maintaining some type of global addressing in a way that can be mapped efficiently by compilers and run-time systems onto diverse hardware architectures. For lack of alternatives, many supercomputing applications are written in Fortran 90 and C. The use of High-Performance Fortran (HPF) on the Earth Simulator is one of only a few examples of using higher level programming languages with better support for parallelism. More versatile, higher-level languages would need to exploit architectures efficiently in order to attract a critical mass of followers that would sustain the language and its further development. In regard to memory access beyond an individual processor, most communication between and even within nodes uses MPI and sometimes OpenMP, again because of the lack of other choices. Many of the application areas are hampered by the software overheads of existing methods and would benefit significantly from more efficient tools to maximize parallel utilization with minimal programming effort. Chapter 5 discusses the hardware and software issues from a technology perspective.

5

Today's Supercomputing Technology

The preceding chapter summarized some of the application areas in which supercomputing is important. Supercomputers are used to reduce overall time to solution—the time between initiating the use of computing and producing answers. An important aspect of their use is the cost of solution—including the (incremental) costs of owning the computer. Usually, the more the time to solution is reduced (e.g., by using more powerful supercomputers) the more the cost of solution is increased. Solutions have a higher utility if provided earlier: A weather forecast is much less valuable after the storm starts. The aggressiveness of the effort to advance supercomputing technology depends on how much added utility and how much added cost come from solving the problem faster. The utility and cost of a solution may depend on factors other than time taken—for instance, on accuracy or trustworthiness. Determining the trade-off among these factors is a critical task. The calculation depends on many things—the algorithms that are used, the hardware and software platforms, the software that realizes the application and that communicates the results to users, the availability of sufficient computing in a timely fashion, and the available human expertise. The design of the algorithms, the computing platform, and the software environment governs performance and sometimes the feasibility of getting a solution. The committee discusses these technologies and metrics for evaluating their performance in this chapter. Other aspects of time to solution are discussed later.

SUPERCOMPUTER ARCHITECTURE

A supercomputer is composed of processors, memory, I/O system, and an interconnect. The processors fetch and execute program instructions. This execution involves performing arithmetic and logical calculations, initiating memory accesses, and controlling the flow of program execution. The memory system stores the current state of a computation. A processor or a group of processors (an SMP) and a block of memory are typically packaged together as a node of a computer. A modern supercomputer has hundreds to tens of thousands of nodes. The interconnect provides communication among the nodes of the computer, enabling these nodes to collaborate on the solution of a single large problem. The interconnect also connects the nodes to I/O devices, including disk storage and network interfaces. The I/O system supports the peripheral subsystem, which includes tape, disk, and networking. All of these subsystems are needed to provide the overall system. Another aspect of providing an overall system is power consumption. Contemporary supercomputer systems, especially those in the top 10 of the TOP500, consume in excess of 5 megawatts. This necessitates the construction of a new generation of supercomputer facilities (e.g., for the Japanese Earth Simulator, the Los Alamos National Laboratory, and the Lawrence Livermore National Laboratory). Next-generation petaflops systems must consider power consumption in the overall design.

Scaling of Technology

As semiconductor and packaging technology improves, different aspects of a supercomputer (or of any computer system) improve at different rates. In particular, the arithmetic performance increases much faster than the local and global bandwidth of the system. Latency to local memory or to a remote node is decreasing only very slowly. When expressed in terms of instructions executed in the time it takes to communicate to local memory or to a remote node, this latency is increasing rapidly. This nonuniform scaling of technology poses a number of challenges for supercomputer architecture, particularly for those applications that demand high local or global bandwidth.

Figure 5.1 shows how floating-point performance of commodity microprocessors, as measured by the SPECfp benchmark suite, has scaled over time.[1] The trend line shows that the floating-point performance of

---

[1]Material for this figure was provided by Mark Horowitz (Stanford University) and Steven Woo (Rambus). Most of the data were originally published in *Microprocessor Report*.

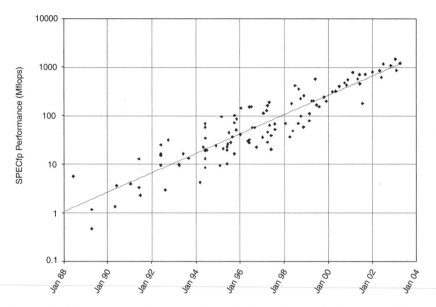

FIGURE 5.1 Processor performance (SPECfp Mflops) vs. calendar year of introduction.

microprocessors improved by 59 percent per year over the 16-year period from 1988 to 2004. The overall improvement is roughly 1,000-fold, from about 1 Mflops in 1988 to more than 1 Gflops in 2004.

This trend in processor performance is expected to continue, but at a reduced rate. The increase in performance is the product of three factors: circuit speed (picoseconds per gate), pipeline depth (gates per clock cycle), and instruction-level parallelism (ILP) (clock cycles per instruction). Each of these factors has been improving exponentially over time.[2] However, increases in pipeline depth and ILP cannot be expected to be the source of further performance improvement, leaving circuit speed as the driver of much of future performance increases. Manufacturers are expected to compensate for this drop in the scaling of single-processor performance by placing several processors on a single chip. The aggregate performance of such chip multiprocessors is expected to scale at least as rapidly as the curve shown in Figure 5.1.

Figure 5.2 shows that memory bandwidth has been increasing at a

[2]W.J. Dally. 2001. *The Last Classical Computer*. Information Science and Technology (ISAT) Study Group, sponsored by the Institute for Defense Analyses and DARPA.

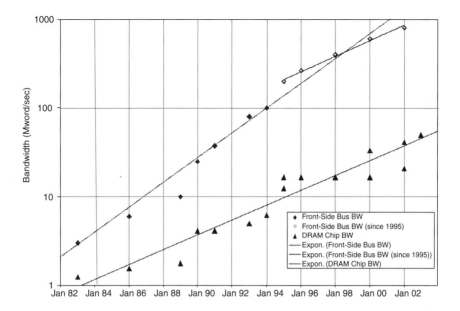

FIGURE 5.2 Bandwidth (Mword/sec) of commodity microprocessor memory interfaces and DRAM chips per calendar year.

much slower rate than processor performance. Over the entire period from 1982 to 2004, the bandwidth of commodity microprocessor memory systems (often called the front-side bus bandwidth) increased 38 percent per year. However, since 1995, the rate has slowed to only 23 percent per year. This slowing of memory bandwidth growth is caused by the processors becoming limited by the memory bandwidth of the DRAM chips. The lower line in Figure 5.2 shows that the bandwidth of a single commodity DRAM chip increased 25 percent per year from 1982 to 2004. Commodity processor memory system bandwidth increased at 38 percent per year until it reached about 16 times the DRAM chip bandwidth and has been scaling at approximately the same rate as DRAM chip bandwidth since that point. The figure gives bandwidth in megawords per second, where a word is 64 bits.

We are far from reaching any fundamental limit on the bandwidth of either the commodity microprocessor or the commodity DRAM chip. In 2001, chips were fabricated with over 1 Tbit/sec of pin bandwidth, over 26 times the 38 Gbit/sec of bandwidth for a microprocessor of the same year. Similarly, DRAM chips also could be manufactured with substantially higher pin bandwidth. (In fact, special GDDR DRAMs made for graphics systems have several times the bandwidth of the commodity chips shown here.) The trends seen here reflect not fundamental limits but market forces. These bandwidths are set to optimize cost/performance for the high-volume personal computer and enterprise server markets. Building a DRAM chip with much higher bandwidth is feasible technically but would be prohibitively expensive without a volume market to drive costs down.

The divergence of about 30 percent per year between processor performance and memory bandwidth, illustrated in Figure 5.3, poses a major challenge for computer architects. As processor performance increases, increasing memory bandwidth to maintain a constant ratio would require a prohibitively expensive number of memory chips. While this approach is taken by some high-bandwidth machines, a more common approach is to reduce the demand on memory bandwidth by adding larger, and often multilevel, cache memory systems. This approach works well for applications that exhibit large amounts of spatial and temporal locality. However, it makes application performance extremely sensitive to this locality. Applications that are unable to take advantage of the cache will scale in performance at the memory bandwidth rate, not the processor performance rate. As the gap between processor and memory performance continues to grow, more applications that now make good use of a cache will become limited by memory bandwidth.

The evolution of DRAM row access latency (total memory latency

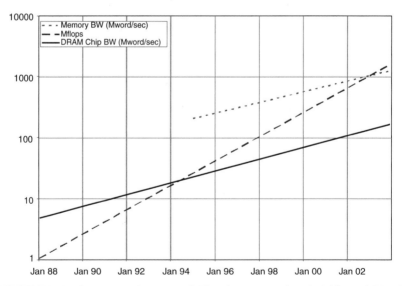

FIGURE 5.3 Arithmetic performance (Mflops), memory bandwidth, and DRAM chip bandwidth per calendar year.

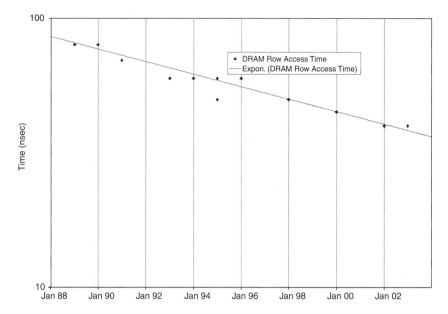

FIGURE 5.4 Decrease in memory latency (in nanoseconds) per calendar year.

is typically about twice this amount) is shown in Figure 5.4. Compared with processor performance (59 percent per year) or even DRAM chip bandwidth (25 percent per year), DRAM latency is improving quite slowly, decreasing by only 5.5 percent per year. This disparity results in a relative increase in DRAM latency when expressed in terms of instructions processed while waiting for a DRAM access or in terms of DRAM words accessed while waiting for a DRAM access.

The slow scaling of memory latency results in an increase in memory latency when measured in floating-point operations, as shown in Figure 5.5. In 1988, a single floating-point operation took six times as long as the memory latency. In 2004, by contrast, over 100 floating-point operations can be performed in the time required to access memory.

There is also an increase in memory latency when measured in memory bandwidth, as shown in Figure 5.6. This graph plots the frontside bus bandwidth of Figure 5.2 multiplied by the memory latency of Figure 5.4. The result is the number of memory words (64-bit) that must simultaneously be in process in the memory system to sustain the frontside bus bandwidth, according to Little's law.[3] Figure 5.6 highlights the

---

[3]Little's law states that the average number of items in a system is the product of the average rate of arrival (bandwidth) and the average holding time (latency).

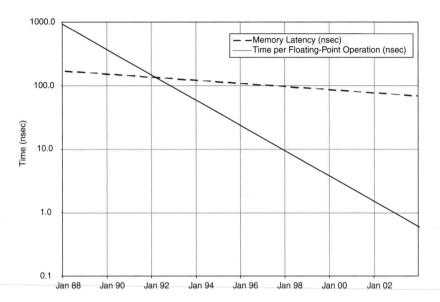

FIGURE 5.5 Decrease in DRAM latency and time per floating-point operation per calendar year.

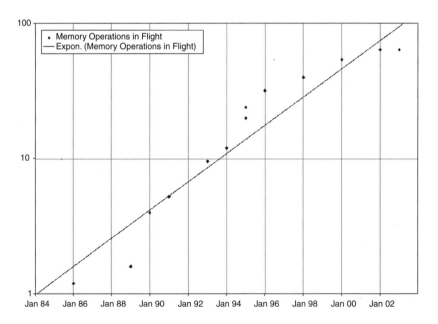

FIGURE 5.6 Increase in the number of simultaneous memory operations in flight needed to sustain front-side bus bandwidth.

need for latency tolerance. To sustain close to peak bandwidth on a modern commodity machine, over 100 64-bit words must be in transfer simultaneously. For a custom processor that may have 5 to 10 times the bandwidth of a commodity machine, the number of simultaneous operations needed to sustain close to peak bandwidth approaches 1,000.

Types of Supercomputers

Supercomputers can be classified by the degree to which they use custom components that are specialized for high-performance scientific computing as opposed to commodity components that are built for higher-volume computing applications. The committee considers three classifications—commodity, custom, and hybrid:

• A commodity supercomputer is built using off-the-shelf processors developed for workstations or commercial servers connected by an off-the-shelf network using the I/O interface of the processor. Such machines are often referred to as "clusters" because they are constructed by clustering workstations or servers. The Big Mac machine constructed at Virginia Tech is an example of a commodity (cluster) supercomputer. Commodity processors are manufactured in high volume and hence benefit from economies of scale. The high volume also justifies sophisticated engineering—for example, the full-custom circuits used to achieve clock rates of many gigahertz. However, because commodity processors are optimized for applications with memory access patterns different from those found in many scientific applications, they realize a small fraction of their nominal performance on scientific applications. Many of these scientific applications are important for national security. Also, the commodity I/O-connected network usually provides poor global bandwidth and high latency (compared with custom solutions). Bandwidth and latency issues are discussed in more detail below.

• A custom supercomputer uses processors that have been specialized for scientific computing. The interconnect is also specialized and typically provides high bandwidth via the processor-memory interface. The Cray X1 and the NEC Earth Simulator (SX-6) are examples of custom supercomputers. Custom supercomputers typically provide much higher bandwidth both to a processor's local memory (on the same node) and between nodes than do commodity machines. To prevent latency from idling this bandwidth, such processors almost always employ latency-hiding mechanisms. Because they are manufactured in low volumes, custom processors are expensive and use less advanced semiconductor technology than commodity processors (for example, they employ standard-cell design and static CMOS circuits rather than full-custom design and dynamic domino circuits). Consequently, they now achieve clock rates and sequential (scalar) performance only one quarter that of commodity processors implemented in comparable semiconductor technology.

• A hybrid supercomputer combines commodity processors with a custom high-bandwidth interconnect—often connected to the processor-memory interface rather than the I/O interface. Hybrid supercomputers often include custom components between the processor and the memory system to provide latency tolerance and improve memory bandwidth. Examples of hybrid machines include the Cray T3E and ASC Red Storm. Such machines offer a compromise between commodity and custom machines. They take advantage of the efficiency (cost/performance) of commodity processors while taking advantage of custom interconnect (and possibly a custom processor-memory interface) to overcome the global (and local) bandwidth problems of commodity supercomputers.

Custom interconnects have also traditionally supported more advanced communication mechanisms, such as direct access to remote memory with no involvement of a remote processor. Such mechanisms lead to lower communication latencies and provide better support for a global address space. However, with the advent of standard interconnects such as Infiniband[4] the "semantic gap" between custom interconnects and commodity interconnects has shrunk. Still, direct connection to a memory interface rather than an I/O bus can significantly enhance bandwidth and reduce latency.

The recently announced IBM Blue Gene/Light (BG/L) computer system is a hybrid supercomputer that reduces the cost and power per node by employing embedded systems technology and reducing the per-node memory. BG/L has a highly integrated node design that combines two embedded (IBM 440) PowerPC microprocessor cores, two floating-point units, a large cache, a memory controller, and network routers on a single chip. This BG/L chip, along with just 256 Mbyte of memory, forms a single processing node. (Future BG/L configurations may have more memory per node; the architecture is designed to support up to 2 Gbyte, although no currently planned system has proposed more than 512 Mbyte.) The node is compact, enabling 1,024 nodes to be packaged in a single cabinet (in comparison with 32 or 64 for a conventional cluster machine).

---

[4]See <http://www.infinibandta.org/home>.

BG/L is a unique machine for two reasons. First, while it employs a commodity processor (the IBM 440), it does not use a commodity processor chip but rather integrates this processor as part of a system on a chip. The processor used is almost three times less powerful than with single-chip commodity processors[5] (because it operates at a much lower clock rate and with little instruction-level parallelism), but it is very efficient in terms of chip area and power efficiency. By backing off on absolute single-thread processor performance, BG/L gains in efficiency. Second, by changing the ratio of memory to processor, BG/L is able to realize a compact and inexpensive node, enabling a much higher node count for a given cost. While custom supercomputers aim at achieving a given level of performance with the fewest processors, so as to be able to perform well on problems with modest amounts of parallelism, BG/L targets applications with massive amounts of parallelism and aims to achieve a given level of performance at the lowest power and area budget.

Performance Issues

The rate at which operands can be brought to the processor is the primary performance bottleneck for many scientific computing codes.[6,7] The three types of supercomputers differ primarily in the effective local and global memory bandwidth that they provide on different access patterns. Whether a machine has a vector processor, a scalar processor, or a multithreaded processor is a secondary issue. The main issue is whether it has high local and global memory bandwidth and the ability to hide memory latency so as to sustain this bandwidth. Vector processors typically have high memory bandwidth, and the vectors themselves provide a latency hiding mechanism. It is this ability to sustain high memory bandwidth that makes the more expensive vector processors perform better for many scientific computations.

A commodity processor includes much of its memory system (but little of its memory capacity) on the processor chip, and this memory system is adapted for applications with high spatial and temporal locality. A typical commodity processor chip includes the level 1 and level 2 caches

---

[5]A comparison of BG/L to the 3.06-GHz Pentium Xeon machine at NCSA yields a node performance ratio of 1:2.7 on the TPP benchmark.

[6]L. Carrington, A. Snavely, X. Gao, and N. Wolter. 2003. "A Performance Prediction Framework for Scientific Applications." International Conference on Computational Science Workshop on Performance Modeling and Analysis (PMA03). Melbourne, June.

[7]S. Goedecker and A. Hoisie. 2001. *Performance Optimization of Numerically Intensive Codes.* Philadelphia, Pa.: SIAM Press.

on the chip and an external memory interface that limits sustained local memory bandwidth and requires local memory accesses to be performed in units of cache lines (typically 64 to 128 bytes in length[8]). Scientific applications that have high spatial and temporal locality, and hence make most of their accesses from the cache, perform extremely well on commodity processors, and commodity cluster machines represent the most cost-effective platforms for such applications.

Scientific applications that make a substantial number of irregular accesses (owing, for instance, to sparse memory data organization that requires random access to noncontiguous memory words) and that have little data reuse are said to be scatter-gather codes. They perform poorly on commodity microprocessors, sustaining a small fraction of peak performance, for three reasons. First, commodity processors simply do not have sufficient memory bandwidth if operands are not in cache. For example, a 3.4-GHz Intel Xeon processor has a peak memory bandwidth of 6.4 Gbyte/sec, or 0.11 words per flops; in comparison, an 800-MHz Cray X1 processor has a peak memory bandwidth of 34.1 Gbyte/sec per processor, or 0.33 words per flops; and a 500-MHz NEC SX-6 has a peak memory bandwidth of 32 Gbyte/sec, or 0.5 words per flops. Second, fetching an entire cache line for each word requested from memory may waste 15/16 of the available memory bandwidth if no other word in that cache line is used—sixteen 8-byte words are fetched when only one is needed. Finally, such processors idle the memory system while waiting on long memory latencies because they lack latency-hiding mechanisms. Even though these processors execute instructions out of order, they are unable to find enough independent instructions to execute to keep busy while waiting hundreds of cycles for main memory to respond to a request. Note that low data reuse is the main impediment to performance on commodity processors: If data reuse is high, then the idle time due to cache misses can be tolerated, and scatter-gather can be performed in software, with acceptable overhead.

There are several known techniques that can in part overcome these three limitations of commodity memory systems. However, they are not employed on commodity processors because they do not improve cost/performance on the commercial applications for which these processors are optimized. For example, it is straightforward to build a wider interface to memory, increasing the total bandwidth, and to provide a short or sectored cache line, eliminating the cache line overhead for irregular accesses.

---

[8]The IBM Power 4 has a 512-byte level 3 cache line.

A latency-hiding mechanism is required to sustain high memory bandwidth, and hence high performance, on irregular applications. Such a mechanism allows the processor to initiate many memory references before the response to the first reference is received. In short, it allows the processor to fill the memory system pipeline. Without a latency-hiding mechanism, the processor idles waiting for a response from memory, and memory bandwidth is wasted, since no new requests are initiated during the idle period.

Common approaches to latency hiding, including multithreading and vectors (or streams), use parallelism to hide latency. A multithreaded processor uses thread-level parallelism to hide latency. When one thread needs to wait for a response from memory, the processor switches to another thread. While some commodity processors provide limited multithreading, they fall short of the tens to hundreds of threads needed to hide main memory latency—currently hundreds of cycles and growing. Vectors or streams use data parallelism[9] to hide latency. Each vector load instruction loads a vector (e.g., up to 64 words on the Cray X1), allowing a small number of instructions to initiate a large number of memory references, filling the memory pipeline.

Architectural organizations that enhance locality reduce bandwidth demand, complementing a high-bandwidth memory system. Two such organizations are currently being actively studied: processor-in-memory (PIM) and stream processing. A PIM machine integrates processors near or on the memory chips, allowing data to be operated on locally in memory. This approach is advantageous if there are large amounts of spatial locality—data can be operated on in place rather than having to be moved to and from a remote processor, reducing demand on bandwidth. Current research is focused on developing compilation techniques to exploit this type of spatial locality and on quantifying this locality advantage for programs of interest.

Stream processors exploit temporal locality by providing a large (100 kbyte or more) software-managed memory, the stream register file, and reordering programs so that intermediate results are stored in the stream register file and then immediately consumed without ever being written to memory. Short-circuiting intermediate results through this large register file greatly reduces demand on the memory system. There is some current software research on compilation techniques to take advantage of

---

[9]In data parallelism the same operation is applied to multiple elements of a data structure—usually a vector. This is less general than multithreading or control parallelism, where distinct threads can execute distinct sequences of instructions.

explicit data staging and on organizations to integrate software-managed memory with hardware-managed caches.

Global bandwidth issues are similar to local bandwidth issues but also involve the interconnection network and network interface. Because the cost of bandwidth increases with distance it is prohibitively expensive to provide flat memory bandwidth across a supercomputer. Even the best custom machines have a bandwidth taper with a local to global bandwidth ratio of about 10:1. Similarly, latency increases across a machine. In the past, well-designed custom machines exhibited global latencies that were only a few times local latency (e.g., 600 cycles to access global memory and 200 cycles to access local memory). Similar ratios will become harder to support in the future as the physical size of current systems increases and the absolute speed of light bounds global latency to be at least a few hundreds of nanoseconds.

Most commodity cluster machines employ off-the-shelf interconnect (such as Gigabit Ethernet) that is connected to the I/O buses of the processing nodes. This results in very low global bandwidth and high global latency (for instance, 10,000 cycles is not unusual). Moreover, software libraries are used to initiate message passing data transfers between processing nodes. The overhead of executing these library calls is sufficiently high that transfers must be aggregated into large units, often thousands of bytes, to amortize the overhead. This aggregation complicates the programming of these machines for programs where the natural transfer size is a few words.

As with local bandwidth, there are several known techniques to address global bandwidth and latency. These techniques are not typically employed in commodity interconnects but can be used in hybrid machines. Such machines cannot widen the memory interface of a commodity microprocessor. However, they can provide an external memory interface that has a wide path to the actual memory chips, supports efficient single-word access, and hides latency by allowing many remote accesses to be initiated in parallel (as with T3E E-registers). It is quite straightforward to interface the interconnection network to the processor-memory interface. The network interface can generate automatically a network request message for each memory access request to a remote address (global address space); it can process arriving requests and generate reply messages with no involvement from the main processor.

A wealth of technologies exists for building fast interconnection networks. High-speed electrical and optical signaling technology enables high raw bandwidth to be provided at reasonable cost. High-radix routers enable tens of thousands of nodes to be connected with just a few hops, resulting in both low cost and low latency. However, the software-driven, I/O-bus-connected interfaces of commodity cluster machines are unable to take advantage of the bandwidth and latency that can be provided by state-of-the-art networks.

The local and global memory bandwidth bottleneck is expected to become a more serious problem in the future due to the nonuniform scaling of technology, as explained in the preceding section. Memory latency hiding is becoming increasingly important as processor speed increases faster than memory access time. Global latency hiding is becoming increasingly important as global latency becomes constrained by the speed of light (see Table 5.1), while processor speeds continue to increase. The cost and power of providing bandwidth between chips, boards, and cabinets is decreasing more slowly than the cost and power of providing logic on chips, making the cost of systems bandwidth dominated by the cost of global bandwidth.

Another trend is the increased complexity of supercomputers and the increased variety of supercomputing platforms. A vector supercomputer will have at least three levels of parallelism: vector parallelism within a processor, thread parallelism across processors within an SMP, and internode parallelism. The synchronization and communication mechanisms will have very different performance and semantics at each level. Performance of commodity processors is affected by their cache hierarchy, which often includes three levels of caches, each with a different structure, as well as a translation lookaside buffer to cache page table entries. The processor performance is also affected by the performance of mechanisms such as branch prediction or cache prefetching, which attempt to hide various latencies. Many supercomputing applications stretch the capabilities of the underlying hardware, and bottlenecks may occur in many different parts of the system. As a result, small changes in the application

TABLE 5.1 Parallel Hardware Trends

	Annual change (%)	Typical value in 2004	Typical value in 2010	Typical value in 2020
No. of processors	20	4,000	12,000	74,000
General bandwidth (Mword/sec)	26	65 (= 0.03 word/flops)	260 (= 0.008 word/flops)	2,600 (= 0.0008 word/flops)
General latency (nsec)	(28)	2,000 (= 4,000 flops)	280 (= 9,000 flops)	200 (= 670,000 flops)
MPI bandwidth (Mword/sec)	26	65	260	2,600
MPI latency (nsec)	(28)	3,000	420	300

code can result in large changes in performance. Similarly, the same application code may exhibit a very different behavior on two fairly similar hardware platforms.

The largest supercomputers today include many thousands of processors, and systems with close to 100,000 processors are being built. Commodity processors are often designed to have a mean time to failure (MTTF) of a few years—there is no incentive to have the MTTF much longer than the average lifetime of a processor. Systems consisting of thousands of such processors have an MTTF that is measured in hours, so that long-running applications have to survive multiple failures of the underlying hardware. As hundreds of thousands of such processors are assembled in one supercomputer, there is a risk that the MTTF of a large supercomputer will be measured in minutes, creating a significant problem for a commodity supercomputer. Hardware mechanisms can be used to provide transparent recovery from such failures in custom supercomputers and, to a lesser extent, in hybrid supercomputers.

Trade-offs

It is important to understand the trade-offs among various supercomputer architectures. The use of custom processors with higher memory bandwidth and effective latency-hiding mechanisms leads to higher processor performance for the many scientific codes that have poor temporal and spatial locality. One can compensate for lower node performance in commodity systems by using more nodes. But the amount of parallelism available in a problem of a given size is limited; for example, in an iterative mesh algorithm, the level of parallelism is bounded by the number of points in the mesh. Furthermore, the parallel efficiency of computations decreases as one increases the number of processors used (each additional processor contributes slightly less).

One reason for decreasing returns from larger amounts of parallelism is Amdahl's law, which states that if a fraction s of a program's execution time is serial, then the maximum potential speedup is $1/s$. For example, if 1 percent of the code is serial, then there is very little gain from using more than 100 processors.

Another reason is that the relative overhead for communication between processors increases as more processors are used. Many computations proceed in alternating computation and communication phases; processors compute independently during the computation phase and synchronize and exchange data during the communication phase. As the number of processors is increased, the amount of computation done by each processor during a computation phase decreases, and the synchronization overhead becomes a higher fraction of the total execution time.

Many computations exhibit a surface-to-volume behavior that leads to relatively more data being exchanged when the computation is split among a larger number of processors. Thus, an iterative algorithm on a three-dimensional Cartesian mesh is parallelized by allocating to each processor a subcube; communication involves exchanges between grid points at the boundary of the subcubes. The number of points per subcube, hence the number of operations performed in a computation phase, decreases in proportion to the number p of processors used. But the surface of the subcubes, hence the amount of data exchanged between subcubes, decreases in proportion to $p^{2/3}$.

Load balance becomes more of an issue as the number of nodes is increased. As fewer data points are processed per node, the variance in execution time across nodes increases. This variance causes many nodes to idle while waiting for the most heavily loaded nodes to complete execution.

Other factors reduce the relative performance or increase the relative cost of very large clusters. Having more nodes often results in higher failure rates. To compensate, one needs more frequent checkpoints, which take time. More frequent checkpoints and restarts increase the relative overhead for error tolerance. The cost of some components of the system (in particular, the interconnect) increases faster than linearly with the number of nodes. The performance of various system services and tools may decrease: For example, it may take longer to load and start a job; debuggers and performance tools may not scale. Total power consumption may be higher, and the need for more floor space may be a practical obstacle.

Custom supercomputers are a good way to achieve lower time-to-solution performance for applications that have poor temporal and spatial locality and for applications that have limited amounts of parallelism or fast-decreasing parallel efficiency. Because of their limited volumes, custom processors are significantly more expensive than commodity processors. Thus, in many cases, the reduction in execution time is achieved at the expense of an increase in cost per solution.

The use of fewer, more powerful processors also typically reduces programming effort. Consider, for example, a weather code that simulates the atmosphere by discretizing the simulated atmosphere into cubic cells. If more processors are used, then each processor is allocated fewer cells. A code that partitions the cells in one dimension (longitude) is simpler than a code that partitions them in two dimensions (longitude and latitude), and such a code is simpler than a code that partitions cells in three dimensions (longitude, latitude, and altitude). If finer partitioning is needed, partitioning along more dimensions will be required. If it is acceptable to run the code only on a custom supercomputer, or to use a custom supercomputer for the more performance-demanding runs, then the programming time is reduced. (Weather codes are now adapted to run on each type of supercomputer platform; however, many codes run by intelligence agencies are customized to one platform.)

The advantages of a custom interconnect and custom interconnect interface can be understood in a similar way. If the interconnect has higher effective bandwidth and lower latency, then the synchronization and communication overheads are smaller, parallel efficiency increases, and it becomes possible to apply efficiently a greater number of processors on a problem of a given size in situations where performance does not scale well because of communication costs. One can more easily dynamically load balance a computation by allowing idle processors to process data points stored on other nodes. In addition, a custom interconnect simplifies programming because one need not aggregate communications into large messages: A custom interconnect and custom interface will typically provide better support for shared name space programming models, which are generally accepted to reduce programming overheads. (Here again, the reduction is most significant for codes that will only run on machines with custom interconnects.)

In summary,

• Commodity supercomputers have a cost advantage for many scientific computing applications; the advantage weakens or disappears for applications with poor temporal and spatial locality or for applications with stringent time-to-solution requirements, where custom supercomputers do better by reducing both programming time and execution time. As the memory gap continues to increase, the relative performance of commodity supercomputers will further erode.
• Many applications will scale up with better efficiency on hybrid supercomputers than on commodity supercomputers; hybrid supercomputers can also support a more convenient programming model.

The preceding discussion was processor-centric. A slightly different perspective is achieved by a memory-centric view of parallel computations. For codes where data caches are not effective, performance is determined by the rate at which operands are brought from memory. The main memory of custom processors has similar latency to the main memory of commodity processors; in order to achieve a given level of performance, both need to sustain the same number of concurrent memory accesses. From the memory perspective, custom architectures do not reduce the amount of parallelism needed to support a given level of performance but enable more memory parallelism per processor; interprocessor parallelism is replaced by intraprocessor parallelism, where one processor supports a larger number of concurrent memory operations. An important advantage is that synchronization and communication among operations executed on the same processor are much faster than synchronization and communication across processors. The faster synchronization and communication also enable finer-grained parallelism to be efficiently exploited, in effect exposing more parallelism than is available internode. Thus, the shift to custom processors can help speed up computations that have enough intrinsic parallelism (significantly more than the number of custom processors used) and that exhibit a surface-to-volume behavior so that most communications and synchronization are intranode. Another advantage is better utilization of the processor and memory bus on applications with low cache reuse.

The memory-centric discussion does not change the basic conclusions reached on the relative advantages of custom or hybrid supercomputers, but it introduces some caveats: To take advantage of custom supercomputers, one needs problems where the level of intrinsic parallelism available is much higher than the number of processors and where most communications are local. One often needs a multilevel problem decomposition and different mechanisms for extracting intranode and internode parallelism. Furthermore, vector processors support only a restricted form of intranode parallelism—namely, data parallelism where the same operation is applied to all the components of a vector. Codes need to be amenable to this form of parallelism in order to take advantage of intranode parallelism.

Trends in Supercomputer Architecture

Supercomputer evolution is driven by many forces.[10] Moore's law provides semiconductor components with exponentially increasing numbers of devices. As semiconductor technology evolves, commodity microprocessors improve in performance. The different scaling rates of components (e.g., processors improving faster than memory and interconnect bandwidth) create a need for novel architectures and software to compensate for the gap. At the same time, new applications drive demands for processing, global and local bandwidth, and I/O bandwidth.

Some evolution is parametric—that is, just a scaling of existing architecture and software. Replacing the processors in a machine with a new

---

[10]The time horizon in this subsection is 2020. The committee does not expect fundamentally new technologies, such as quantum computing, to be deployed in this time frame. Therefore, the discussion is based on an extrapolation of trends in current microelectronic technologies.

TABLE 5.2 Hardware Trends

	Annual change (%)	Typical value in 2004	Typical value in 2010	Typical value in 2020
Single-chip floating-point performance (Gflops)	59	2	32	3,300
Front-side bus bandwidth (Gword/sec)	23	1 (= 0.5 word/flops)	3.5 (= 0.11 word/flops)	27 (= 0.008 word/flops)
DRAM bandwidth (Mword/sec)	25	100 (= 0.05 word/flops)	380 (= 0.012 word/flops)	3,600 (= 0.0011 word/flops)
DRAM latency (nsec)	(5.5)	70 (= 140 flops or 70 loads)	50 (= 1,600 flops or 170 loads)	28 (= 94,000 flops or 780 loads)

generation of faster processors and the memories with a new generation of larger memories is an example of parametric evolution. This evolution is relatively simple (all that is required is integration), no new hardware or software technology needs to be developed, and old software runs with, at most, minor changes.

As different parts of the system scale at different rates, new bottlenecks appear. For example, if processor speed increases but the interconnect is not improved, then global communication may become a bottleneck. At some point, parametric evolution breaks down and qualitative changes to hardware and software are needed. For example, as memory latency (measured in processor cycles) increases, at some point a latency-hiding mechanism is needed to sustain reasonable performance on nonlocal applications. At this point, vectors, multithreading, or some other mechanism is added to the architecture. Such a change is complex, requiring a change in software, usually in both systems software (including compilers) and applications software. Similarly, increased latency may necessitate different software mechanisms, such as dynamic load balancing.

Table 5.2 shows expected parametric evolution of commodity components used in supercomputers—summarizing the trends shown earlier in Figure 5.1 through Figure 5.6.[11] As explained previously, the annual 59 percent improvement in single processor speed is expected to decrease in

[11]These extrapolations are for explanatory purposes only and do not represent detailed technology assessments. In particular, physical limits, such as the electromagnetic radiation that a 400 Gflops chip might emit, are not considered.

the future. However, the committee expects that processor chips will compensate for that by putting several processors on each chip to continue to scale the performance per chip at 59 percent annually. The numbers in Table 5.2 for 2010 and 2020 reflect this scaling of chip multiprocessors.

Table 5.2 highlights the divergence of memory speeds and computation speeds that will ultimately force an innovation in architecture. By 2010, 170 loads (memory reads) will need to be executed concurrently to keep memory bandwidth busy while waiting for memory latency, and 1,600 floating-point arithmetic operations can be performed during this time. By 2020, 780 loads must be in flight, and 94,000 arithmetic operations can be performed while waiting on memory. These numbers are not sustainable. It is clear that systems derived using simple parametric evolution are already greatly strained and will break down completely by 2020. Changes in architecture and/or programming systems are required either to enhance the locality of computations or to hide large amounts of latency with parallelism, or both.

It is not clear if commodity processors will provide the required innovations to overcome this "memory wall." While the PC and server applications for which commodity processors are tuned also suffer from the increased gap between arithmetic and memory performance, they exhibit sufficient spatial and temporal locality so that aggressive cache memory systems are largely sufficient to solve the problem. If commodity processors do not offer latency-hiding and/or locality-enhancing mechanisms, it is likely that a smaller fraction of scientific applications will be adequately addressed by these processors as the processor-memory performance gap grows.

Figure 5.7 shows the increase in the number of processors for high-end systems. At the high end, the number of processors is increasing approximately 20 percent per year. The committee sees no technology limits that would cause this trend to change. Extrapolating this trend to 2020 indicates a number of processors in the 100,000 range; since each of them will have significant amounts of concurrency for latency hiding, systems will run tens of millions of concurrent operations.

Figures 5.8 and 5.9 show measured latency (in microseconds) and bandwidth (in megabytes per second) for MPI programs between two nodes in a variety of commodity and hybrid supercomputer systems.[12]

---

[12]The numbers were collected by K. Yelick from the following sources: L. Oliker et al., In press, "Scientific Computations on Modern Parallel Vector Systems," *Supercomputing 2004*; C. Bell et al., 2003, "An Evaluation of Current High-Performance Networks," 17th International Parallel and Distributed Processing Symposium; D.E. Culler et al., 1996, "Performance Assessment of Faster Network Interfaces," *IEEE Micro*, February; and J. Dongarra and T. Dunigan, 1997, "Message-Passing Performance of Various Computers," *Concurrency: Practice and Experience* 9(10):915-926.

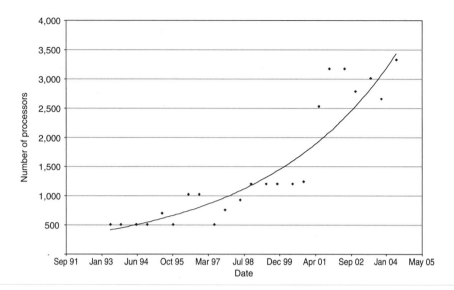

FIGURE 5.7 Median number of processors of the 10 leading TOP500 systems.

(The committee considers MPI measurements because the algorithmic models below are based on message passing programs.) Least-squares fits to the data show an annual improvement of 28 percent in latency and 29 percent in bandwidth, albeit with substantial variation. (R^2 values for the formulas are 0.83 and 0.54, respectively.) The improvement rates for lower-level communication systems (e.g., SHMEM on the Cray T3E) are similar—28 percent for latency and 26 percent for bandwidth.

The committee summarized the expected evolution of parallel systems in Table 5.1. A later section will discuss these extrapolations in more detail. For now, the committee simply points out that even if the individual components continue to improve parametrically, the overall system will see radical changes in how they are balanced. Parametric evolution of the system as a whole is unsustainable, and current machines arguably have already moved into a problematic region of the design space.

The numbers in Table 5.1 should be taken with a grain of salt, as they integrate factors such as software overheads and transmission delays that evolve at different rates. Furthermore, light traverses 60 m in 200 nsec, less than the diameter of the largest supercomputer installations; the decrease in general latency will slow down as one approaches this limit. However, even the numbers are grossly inaccurate; they clearly show that a parametric evolution of current communication architectures is not sustainable.

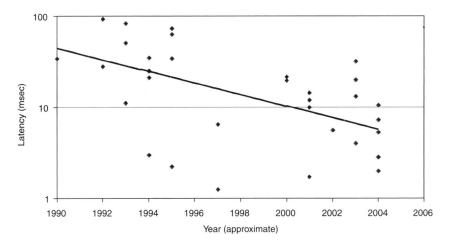

FIGURE 5.8 Latency.

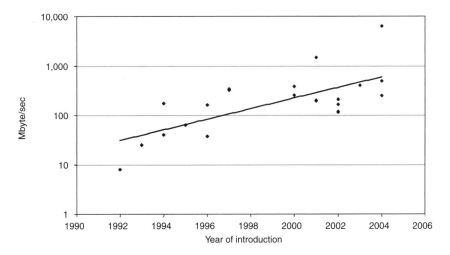

FIGURE 5.9 Bandwidth.

SUPERCOMPUTING ALGORITHMS

An algorithm is the sequence of basic operations (arithmetic, logic, branches, and memory accesses) that must be performed to solve the user's task. To be useful, an algorithm must solve the user's problem with sufficient accuracy and without using too much time or memory (exactly how much accuracy, time, or memory is enough depends on the application). Improvements in algorithms can sometimes improve performance as much as or more than improvements in hardware and software do. For example, algorithms for solving the ubiquitous linear system arising from the Poisson equation[13] on a regular three-dimensional grid with n grid points have improved over time from needing $O(n^{7/3})$ to $O(n)$ arithmetic operations.[14] Such algorithmic improvements can contribute as much to increased supercomputer performance as decades of hardware evolution,[15] even when the $O(n)$ algorithms run at a much lower fraction of peak machine speed than the older $O(n^{7/3})$ algorithms. While such dramatic breakthroughs are hard to predict, the rewards can be significant. Further research can lead to such breakthroughs in the many complicated domains to which supercomputers are applied.

There was considerable discussion of algorithms at the committee's applications workshop, as well as at site visits and in the recent reports of other study groups.[16] The presenters and reports concur that, although much is known about algorithms for solving scientific problems using supercomputing, a great deal more knowledge is needed. For some fields, the algorithms now in use will not solve the most challenging problems, even if they are run on the most capable systems expected to be available in a foreseeable future. For other fields, satisfactory algorithms of any kind remain to be developed. While these algorithmic needs arise from quite different application areas, they often have much in common.

The committee first describes the nature of the algorithms in common use, including their demands on the underlying hardware, and then summarizes some of their shortcomings and future challenges.

Solving Partial and Ordinary Differential Equations

Differential equations are the fundamental equations for many problems governed by the basic laws of physics and chemistry. Traditionally,

---

[13]A Poisson equation is an equation that arises in models of many physical systems, including heat flow, fluid flow, diffusion, electrostatics, and gravity.

[14]Note on $O(.)$ notation: We say that an algorithm uses $O(n)$ arithmetic operations, or runs in time $O(f(n))$, on a problem of size n if the number of arithmetic operations is bounded by some constant multiple of $f(n)$ or if it runs in a number of seconds bounded by some constant multiple of $f(n)$. An algorithm that runs in time $O(n^2)$ will be much slower than an algorithm that runs in time $O(n)$ once n is large enough, no matter what their respective constants are, which is why we use the $O(.)$ notation to compare the asymptotic speed of algorithms.

[15]DOE, Office of Science. 2003. "A Science-Based Case for Large-Scale Simulation." *Scales Workshop Report*, Vol. 1. July.

[16]For example, the HECRTF report, the *Scales Workshop Report*, Vol. 1, the IHEC Report, and the DOE Greenbook (DOE, NERSC, 2002, *The DOE Greenbook—Needs and Directions in High-Performance Computing for the Office of Science*, April).

much algorithmic research has been devoted to methods for their solution. These continuous equations are typically discretized by replacing them by algebraic equations for a (large) set of discrete variables corresponding to points or regions on a mesh approximating the physical and/or time domain of the continuous equations. (Alternatively, the solution could be represented by a collection of particles, vortices, or other discrete objects.) These equations arise, for example, in fusion, accelerator design, nuclear physics, weapons design, global climate change, reactive chemistry, astrophysics, nanotechnology, contaminant transport, material science, drug design, and related fields. A more recent variation on this theme is stochastic differential equations, where one or more of the terms represent a random process of some kind, like diffusion. In this case the goal is to compute certain statistics about the set of possible solutions. Included in this category of algorithms is work on new ways to discretize the equations and work on fast solution methods, such as multigrid and other multilevel methods, which use a hierarchy of meshes.

The demands these algorithms place on hardware depend both on the method and on the differential equation. Elliptic partial differential equations (PDEs), of which the aforementioned Poisson equation is the canonical example, have the property that the solution at every mesh point depends on data at every other mesh point, which in turn places demands on memory and network bandwidth. Their discretizations often use so-called "implicit difference schemes," which lead to large sparse systems of equations to be solved. On the other hand, the data at distant mesh points can often be compressed significantly without losing much accuracy, ameliorating bandwidth needs (a property exploited both by multigrid methods and by some of the fast transforms discussed below). In contrast to elliptic equations, time-dependent equations may (e.g., parabolic PDEs arising in diffusion or heat flow or their approximations by systems of ordinary differential equations [ODEs]) or may not (e.g., hyperbolic PDEs arising in electromagnetics or, again, some ODEs) have the same global dependence at every time step and corresponding bandwidth need. In the case without global dependence, often discretized using so-called "explicit difference schemes," communication only occurs between mesh points at processor boundaries, so that a surface-to-volume effect determines bandwidth needs. Some time-dependent equations (e.g., "stiff" ODEs) must be solved using communication-intensive implicit methods in order to avoid extremely small time steps. Even without global dependence, a time-dependent equation with a rapidly changing solution solved with a mesh that adapts to the solution may again have high bandwidth demands in order to support load balancing (see below). Finally, if the equation has a lot of "local physics" (e.g., as would a nuclear weapons simulation requiring the solution of complicated equations of state at each mesh point), then the correspondingly higher ratio of floating-point operations to memory operations makes performance less sensitive to bandwidth. This variety of behaviors can be found in many of the ASC codes.[17]

Long-standing open problems include overcoming the need for tiny (femtosecond) time steps in molecular dynamics simulations[18] and finding better anisotropic radiation transport algorithms than flux-limited diffusion, discrete ordinates (S_n), or Monte Carlo,[19] among many others. The desire to solve larger systems of equations describing more complicated phenomena (not all of which may be represented or discretized the same way) on more complicated domains spurs ongoing innovation in this area.

Mesh Generation

The committee considered both generating the above-mentioned initial mesh and adapting it during the solution phase. As for time to solution, it is often the process of generating the initial mesh that takes the most time. This is because it often requires a great deal of human intervention to create a suitable geometric model of a complicated physical system or object. Even when those models are available (as in the case of NASA's space shuttle), creating a mesh suitable for simulation may take months using traditional methods. The shuttle in particular has benefited from recent breakthroughs in mesh generation,[20] but many problems remain in producing three-dimensional meshes with guaranteed geometric and mathematical properties and in doing so efficiently in parallel or when memory is limited.

In addition to generating the initial mesh, hierarchies of meshes are needed for multigrid and multilevel methods, and producing these hierarchies in an automatic fashion so as to appropriately approximate the solution at each level of resolution is challenging. When the mesh represents a deforming material, algorithms are needed to deform the mesh as

---

[17]Based on excerpts from the white paper "Computational Challenges in Nuclear Weapons Simulation," by Charles F. McMillan et al., LLNL, prepared for the committee's Santa Fe, N.M., applications workshop, September 2003.

[18]Molecular dynamic simulations use time steps of a few femtoseconds; some phenomena, such as protein folding, take many milliseconds.

[19]Expert Group on 3D Radiation Transport Benchmarks, Nuclear Energy Agency of the Organisation for Economic Cooperation and Development (OECD), <http://www.nea.fr/html/science/eg3drtb>.

[20]NASA, Office of Aerospace Technology Commercial Technology Division. 2003. "Faster Aerodynamic Simulation with Cart3D." *Spinoff 2003*, p. 56.

well. Meshes are also sometimes adapted during the solution process to have higher resolution (more points) in regions where the solution is complicated and fewer points in simple regions. The complicated region can move during solution; an example is the intricate flame front between burnt and unburnt gas in an internal combustion engine.[21] Using a static mesh fine enough everywhere to resolve the solution would take orders of magnitude more work than using it only in complicated regions. Effective use of large numbers of parallel processors in these algorithms is an ongoing challenge, because the workload and load (im)balance changes unpredictably with the position of the complicated region.

Dense Linear Algebra

This class of algorithms for solving linear systems of equations, least squares problems, and eigenvalue problems in which all equations involve all or most variables, is epitomized by the Linpack benchmark discussed elsewhere in this report. These algorithms are among the least sensitive to memory and network bandwidth of any discussed here, provided the problems are large enough. Dense linear algebra still forms a significant fraction (but not majority) of the workload at some supercomputer centers. For example, NERSC reports that materials science applications representing 15 percent of their total cycles spend 90 percent of their time in dense linear algebra routines today.[22] Recent research has focused on exploiting structure, in effect finding and using sparse representations "hidden" inside certain dense problems. It is worth noting that even in this relatively mature field, only a relatively small fraction of the algorithms with good sequential software implementations have good parallel software implementations.

Sparse Linear Algebra

The discrete equations on a mesh arising in a discretized differential equation are typically sparse (i.e., most equations involve just a few variables). It is critical to exploit this mathematical structure to reduce memory and arithmetic operations, rather than using dense linear algebra. Ideal algorithms scale linearly—that is, they take time proportional to nnz/p,

---

[21]DOE, Office of Science. 2003. "A Science-Based Case for Large-Scale Simulation," *Scales Workshop Report*, Vol. 1. July.

[22]Based on presentations and discussions at the committee's site visit to DOE's National Energy Research Scientific Computing Center in Lawrence Berkeley National Laboratory in January 2004.

where *nnz* ("number of nonzeros") is the total number of appearances of variables in all equations and p is the number of processors. In other words, an ideal algorithm performs just a constant amount of work per nonzero and communicates very little. Whether in fact a reasonably efficient (let alone ideal) algorithm can be found depends strongly on the structure of the equations (namely, which variables appear and with what coefficients), so there is a large set of existing algorithms corresponding to the large variety of problem structures.[23] These algorithms are generally limited by memory and network bandwidth and are the bottlenecks in PDE solvers mentioned earlier, for PDEs where the solution at each point depends on data at all mesh points. General solution techniques (e.g., sparse Gaussian elimination) have been parallelized, but they are limited in scalability, especially for linear systems arising from three-dimensional PDEs. However, they remain in widespread use because of their reliability and ease of use. Iterative methods, which typically rely on the more scalable operation of matrix vector multiplication, can be much faster but often require careful problem-dependent design to converge in a reasonable number of iterations. As new exploitable problem structures arise and computer architectures change, algorithmic innovation is ongoing.

Discrete Algorithms

Discrete algorithms are distinguished from others in this summary by having few, if any, floating-point numbers required to define the inputs or outputs to the problem. Discrete algorithms can involve a wide array of combinatorial optimization problems arising in computational biology (for instance, looking for nearly matching sequences), the analysis of large data sets (finding clusters or other patterns in high-dimensional data sets), or even other parallel computing algorithms (balancing the workload or partitioning a sparse matrix among different parallel processors). Many of these problems are NP-hard (non-deterministic polynomial-time hard), meaning that an optimal solution would take impractically long to compute on any foreseeable computer, so that heuristic approximations are required. Again, the diversity of problems leads to a diversity of algorithms (perhaps involving floating point) and an ongoing potential for innovation.

---

[23]R. Barrett, M. Berry, T.F. Chan, J. Demmel, J. Donato, J. Dongarra, V. Eijkhout, R. Pozo, C. Romine, and H. van der Vorst. 1994. *Templates for the Solution of Linear Systems: Building Blocks for Iterative Methods*. Philadelphia, Pa.: SIAM Press; Zhaojun Bai, James Demmel, Jack Dongarra, Axel Ruhe, and Henk van der Vorst. 2000. *Templates for the Solution of Algebraic Eigenvalue Problems: A Practical Guide*. Philadelphia, Pa.: SIAM Press.

Other discrete algorithms involve number theory (arising in cryptanalysis), symbolic algorithms for exact solutions to algebraic equations (arising in the intelligence community and elsewhere), and discrete event simulation and agent-based modeling (arising in traffic, epidemiology, and related simulations). It appears that relatively little work (at least work that has been made public) has been done to parallelize symbolic algorithms.

Fast Transforms

There are a variety of widely used fast transform methods—such as the fast Fourier transform (FFT), wavelets, the fast multipole method, kernels arising in quantum chemistry, and their numerous variations—where a clever reformulation changes, for example, an $O(n^2)$ algorithm into an $O(n \log n)$ algorithm. These reformulations exploit the underlying mathematical or physical structure of the problem to represent intermediate results in compressed forms that are faster to compute and communicate. A recent big advance is $O(n)$ methods in electronic structures calculations. It is an ongoing challenge to adapt these methods to new problem structures and new computer architectures. Some of these algorithms (e.g., the fast multipole method) limit their bandwidth requirements by compressing and approximating distant data before sending them, whereas others (e.g., the FFT) need to communicate more intensively and so require more bandwidth to scale adequately. Fastest Fourier transform in the West (FFTW)[24] is a successful example of a system for automatically adapting an FFT algorithm to perform well on a particular problem size and a particular computer.

New Algorithmic Demands Arising from Supercomputing

In addition to opportunities to improve algorithms (as described above in the categories of differential equations, mesh generation, linear algebra, discrete algorithms, and fast transforms), there are new, cross-cutting algorithmic needs driven by supercomputing that are common to many application areas.

Disciplinary Needs

One reason for needing increased supercomputer performance is that many applications cannot be run using realistic parameter ranges of spa-

---

[24]See <http://www.fftw.org>.

tial resolution and time integration. For many such applications, applying more computer power with substantially the same algorithms can significantly increase simulation quality. For example, mesh resolution can be increased. But the need for higher-resolution analyses may also lead to the need for faster algorithms. For example, solving a problem 10 times larger than currently possible would require 10 times as powerful a machine using an algorithm with complexity $O(n)$ but 100 times as powerful a machine using an algorithm with complexity $O(n^2)$. It is sometimes possible to use physics-based algorithms (like the fast multipole method) or physics-based preconditioners that exploit particular properties of the equations being solved. One important area needing research is scalable adaptive methods, where the computational work adapts depending on the complexity of the physical solution, making load balancing difficult as the solution changes over time. But in other applications, increased mesh resolution may require the development of new physics or algorithms to resolve or approximate phenomena at tiny scales. In some cases, submodels of detailed processes may be required within a coarser mesh (e.g., cloud-resolving submodels embedded within a larger climate model grid). Sometimes completely different physical models may be required (e.g., particle models instead of continuum models), which in turn require different algorithms. In some problems (such as turbulence), physically unresolved processes at small length or time scales may have large effects on macroscopic phenomena, requiring approximations that differ from those for the resolved processes. A similar example arises in molecular dynamics, where the molecular motions at the shortest time scales must currently be computed at intervals of 10^{-15} seconds to resolve reactions that may take a second or more; a new algorithm is needed to avoid the current bottleneck of 10^{15} sequential steps.

Interdisciplinary Needs

Many real-world phenomena involve two or more coupled physical processes for which individual models and algorithms may be known (clouds, winds, ocean currents, heat flow inside and between the atmosphere and the ocean, atmospheric chemistry, and so on) but where the coupled system must be solved. Vastly differing time and length scales of the different disciplinary models frequently makes this coupled model much harder to solve. Emerging application areas also drive the need for new algorithms and applications. Bioinformatics, for example, is driving the need to couple equation-driven numerical computing with probabilistic and constraint-driven computing.

Synthesis, Sensitivity Analysis, and Optimization Replacing Analysis

After one has a model that can be used to analyze (predict) the behavior of a physical system (such as an aircraft or weapons system), it is often desirable to use that model to try to synthesize or optimize a system so that it has certain desired properties, or to discover how sensitive the behavior is to parameter changes. Such a problem can be much more challenging than analysis alone. As an example, a typical analysis computes, from the shape of an airplane wing, the lift resulting from airflow over the wing by solving a differential equation. The related optimization problem is to choose the wing shape that maximizes lift, incorporating the constraints that ensure that the wing can be manufactured. Solving that problem requires determining the direction of change in wing shape that causes the lift to increase, either by repeating the analysis as changes to shape are tried or by analytically computing the appropriate change in shape. Similar optimization problems can arise in any manufacturing process, as can parameter identification problems (e.g., reconstructing biological images or Earth's structure from measurements of scattered waves), finding stable molecular configurations, and optimizing control. This transition to synthesis, sensitivity analysis, and optimization requires improved algorithms in nonlinear solvers, mathematical optimization techniques, and methods for quantifying uncertainty.

Huge Data Sets

Many fields (e.g., biology) that previously had relatively few quantitative data to analyze now have very large amounts, often of varying type, meaning, and uncertainty. These data may be represented by a diversity of data structures, including tables of numbers, irregular graphs, adaptive meshes, relational databases, two- or three-dimensional images, text, or various combined representations. Extracting scientific meaning from these data requires coupling numerical, statistical, and logical modeling techniques in ways that are unique to each discipline.

Changing Machine Models

A machine model is the set of operations and their costs presented to the programmer by the underlying hardware and software. Algorithmic research has traditionally sought to minimize the number of arithmetic (or logical) operations. However, the most expensive operation on a machine is not arithmetic but, rather, fetching data from memory, especially remote memory. Furthermore, the relative costs of arithmetic and fetching data can change dramatically between machines and over time. This has profound implications for algorithm design. Sometimes this means that the fastest algorithm must compress data that are needed far away before communicating them; this compression often involves approximations (which one must carefully bound) that rely on the detailed physics or other mathematical structure of the problem. The fast multipole method and multigrid algorithms are celebrated and widely used examples of this technique. In these examples, reducing arithmetic and reducing data fetching go hand in hand. But there are yet other examples (e.g., certain sparse matrix algorithms) where one must increase the amount of arithmetic substantially from the obvious algorithm in order to reduce memory fetches and so speed up the algorithm.[25] As the machine model changes between technology generations or among contemporaneous platforms, an algorithm will probably have to be changed to maintain performance and scalability. This optimization process could involve adjusting a few parameters in the algorithm describing data layouts, running a combinatorial optimization scheme to rebalance the load, or using a completely different algorithm that trades off computation and communication in different ways. Successful tuning by hand is typically a tedious process requiring familiarity with everything from algorithms to compilers to hardware. Some success has been achieved in automating this process, but only for a few important algorithmic kernels, such as ATLAS[26] for matrix-matrix multiplication or FFTW for fast Fourier transforms. Work is needed on these adaptive algorithms to make them more broadly applicable and available to more users.

SUPERCOMPUTING SOFTWARE

The software used for computing in general and supercomputing in particular has multiple purposes. The system software—the operating system, the scheduler, the accounting system, for example—provide the infrastructure for using the machine, independently of the particular applications for which it is used. The programming languages and tools help the user in writing and debugging applications and in understanding their performance. The applications codes directly implement the application. The software system is sometimes described as a stack of abstractions, in the sense that the operating system is the lowest level, programming lan-

---

[25]Richard Vuduc, James W. Demmel, Katherine A. Yelick, Shoaib Kamil, Rajesh Nishtala, and Benjamin Lee. 2002. "Performance Optimizations and Bounds for Sparse Matrix Vector Multiply." *Proceedings of the ACM/IEEE SC2002*. November 16-22.
[26]See <http://math-atlas.sourceforge.net>.

guages and tools sit on top of the operating system, and the applications form the top layer. Each of the conceptual layers is important in the overall system, and each layer in a supercomputer system has special characteristics that distinguish it from the layers in other kinds of computing systems.

Supercomputing software has many requirements in common with software for other computing systems. Layered abstractions provide higher-level operations for most users, allowing them to reuse complex operations without needing the deep knowledge of the specialists writing the lower levels. Portability is essential, since many programs outlast their original platforms. In the supercomputing arena, a computer has a typical useful lifetime of 5 years, while many-decades-old applications codes are still in daily use. Execution efficiency is important in all areas, particularly for supercomputers, because of the high cost of the systems and the heavy demands of the applications. Ensuring correct results, a problem on all computers, is of course especially difficult on a large, complex system like a supercomputer.

Other issues are unique to supercomputer software. Foremost among these is the requirement for excellent scalability at all levels of the software. To benefit from parallel hardware, the software must provide enough concurrent operations to use all the hardware. For example, a supercomputer with a thousand processors needs many thousands of operations available for execution at all times—or many tens of thousands if custom processors are used. Today's largest systems typically have on the order of 10,000 processors to keep busy concurrently. Future systems may push this degree of concurrency to 100,000 or 1 million processors and beyond, and the concurrency level within each processor will need to increase in order to hide the larger memory latency. In addition to having a high level of concurrency, scalable software needs to avoid sequential bottlenecks so as not to suffer from the consequences of Amdahl's law, and it needs to manage the global communication and synchronization efficiently in order to reduce communication overheads.

Operating Systems and Management Software

Operating systems manage the basic resources of the system, such as the memory, the network interfaces, the processors, and the I/O devices. They provide services such as memory and process management to enable multiple executing programs to share the system and abstractions such as interfaces and file systems that both facilitate the programming layers above and reduce hardware dependence. Other key services they provide are security and protection, logging, and fault tolerance. Closely associated with those operating system roles is the management software that provides interfaces for servicing users. Key components include user accounts, queuing systems, system monitors, and configuration management.

In the operating system arena, virtually all supercomputers today use some variant of UNIX, including such systems as AIX (from IBM), IRIX (SGI), Linux (open source), SUPER-UX (NEC), Tru64 (Hewlett-Packard), UNICOS (Cray), and MacOS X (Apple). A few projects have created supercomputer-class clusters running versions of Microsoft Windows; a prominent example of such a system is at the Cornell Theory Center, 146th on the June 2004 TOP500 list.

Management software for supercomputing is quite varied. For example, just within the top 10 machines on the TOP500 list are found at least four batch job submission systems (LSF, Batch Priority Scheduler, Distributed Production Control System, and LoadLeveler). Even among sites that use the same management tools, the configurations—for instance, the number of queues and the policies that control them—differ substantially. Although there are open source versions of some of these tools, most production sites use proprietary management software even if they use open source software such as Linux for other software components. This is probably due to limitations of the open source tools. For example, Portable Batch System (OpenPBS) supports up to 32 processors, not nearly enough for supercomputing use. Management software for supercomputing typically uses straightforward extensions or improvements to software for smaller systems, together with policies tailored to their user community.

It is challenging to scale an operating system to a large number of processors. A modern operating system is a complex multithreaded application with asynchronous, event-driven logic, many sequential bottlenecks, and little data locality. It is hard to scale such an application, and even harder to do so while maintaining full compatibility with a broadly used commercial operating system such as Linux or Windows. Many of the operating system services (and the programming tools) need to scale as the number of concurrent threads that are created. Thus, custom systems that achieve a given level of performance with fewer concurrent threads facilitate the scaling of these subsystems.

Large supercomputers are typically managed by multiple operating system images, each controlling one node. A single-system image (common file space, single login, single administrative point of control, etc.) is provided by a set of distributed services that coordinate and integrate the multiple kernels into one system in a way that provides scalability and fault tolerance. This approach creates a fundamental mismatch between the virtual machine provided by the operating system, which is loosely coupled, and the application running atop this virtual machine, which is tightly coupled.

A key manifestation of this mismatch is the lack of concurrent scheduling. Most existing parallel programming models implicitly assume that the application controls a dedicated set of processors executing at the same speed. Thus, many parallel codes consist of an alternation of compute phases, where an equal amount of computation work is performed by each process and by global communication and synchronization phases. But a computation that frequently uses global synchronizations cannot tolerate nonsynchronized variations in computation speed that are due, for example, to asynchronous system activities (daemons, page misses, and so on). For example, suppose that each node spends 1 percent of its time handling system events and each event requires five times as long as it takes to execute a barrier (a synchronization of all active processes). If these system events occur simultaneously at all nodes, then the global loss of performance is 1 percent (as one might expect). However, if they occur at random times in a 100-node computation, then each barrier is statistically expected to be preceded by a system event, effectively raising the synchronization cost 500 percent. The effect is smaller on smaller systems, but still significant; for example, a 50-node system in the same circumstances would see a 250 percent synchronization cost increase. A programmer without detailed knowledge of the underlying operating system would be unable to design an appropriate program to compensate for this variation. Most supercomputer manufacturers (IBM, Hewlett-Packard, Cray) were surprised to encounter this problem on their systems, and most resolved it by various ad hoc means.

Some supercomputers run a microkernel on the compute nodes that reroutes many system functions to a service node running the full-function operating system. This approach reduces asynchronous system events on the compute nodes and also reduces the frequency of software failures. The implicit assumption in this approach is that page faults can be virtually eliminated.

The "crystalline" model of a parallel computer, where all processes execute the same quantity of work at the same speed, is harder and harder to maintain as the number of processors increases and low-probability events (in particular, recoverable failures) are more likely to disturb the smooth progress of individual processes. The model is increasingly inappropriate for complex, dynamic, heterogeneous applications. Changes in operating system structures to reduce asynchrony or in programming models to tolerate asynchrony (or, likely, both) will be required. Indeed, the more recent programming languages described in the next section tend to allow looser synchronization. However, it remains for applications and algorithms to utilize this freedom to improve their real-world performance.

Programming Models, Programming Languages, and Tools

A programming model is an abstract conceptual view of the structure and operation of a computing system. For example, a uniform shared memory (or a global addressing) model supports the abstraction that there is one uniformly addressable storage (even though there may be multiple physical memories being used). The use of a given programming model requires that the operating system, the programming languages, and the software tools provide the services that support that abstraction. In the context of this discussion, the programming languages at issue are the ones in which applications are written, not the ones in which the systems software is written (although the tools that support the applications programming language must provide appropriate interfacing with systems software). Programming tools provide a means to create and run programs. Key tools include compilers, interpreters, debuggers, and performance monitors.

The programming languages and tools for supercomputing are diverse. Many applications, in fact, use components written in more than one language. A useful taxonomy of languages might be based on the parts of the supercomputer under the control of language operations. Sequential imperative languages, such as C and Fortran, are commonly used to program individual processing elements (which may be single-processor nodes or threads in multithreaded systems). Nodes consisting of several processors with a shared memory are typically programmed using modest extensions to these languages, such as the OpenMP[27] extensions, which have bindings for C and Fortran. Collections of nodes (or processors) that do not share memory are programmed using calls to run-time system libraries for message passing, such as MPI, or other communications paradigms (for instance, one-sided communication). There has been some progress in the use of better-integrated parallel languages. As their names suggest, High-Performance Fortran (HPF)[28] and Co-Array Fortran[29] are parallel dialects of Fortran, and UPC[30] is a parallel version of C. There are also research languages based on Java, such as Titanium.[31]

---

[27]See <http://www.openmp.org>.
[28]See <http://dacnet.rice.edu/Depts/CRPC/HPFF/index.cfm>.
[29]See <http://www.co-array.org/>.
[30]See <http://upc.gwu.edu/>.
[31]See <http://www.cs.berkeley.edu/projects/titanium/>.

These languages support a shared memory model, in the sense that a single partitioned global name space allows all executing threads to access large shared data stored in shared (but distributed) arrays. At the full-system level, scripting languages (e.g., Python and Perl) are often used to link components written in all of the languages mentioned above. Object-oriented languages such as C++ and component frameworks such as Common Component Architecture (CCA)[32] and Cactus[33] are also used to provide a layer of abstraction on components written in lower-level languages. Of course, each language requires its own compiler and development tools. Some sharing of tools is possible in principle but less common in practice. One exception is the TotalView debugger,[34] which supports Fortran, C, OpenMP, and MPI.

Parallel programming languages and parallel programming models are necessarily compromises between conflicting requirements. Although many of the current compromises are deemed to be inadequate, it is not clear what a better solution should be. The use of dialects of Fortran and C stems, in part, from a desire to migrate legacy software and tools and to exploit existing user expertise. The ecosystem complexity described in Chapter 6 makes it difficult to experiment with new approaches.

To improve programmer productivity it would be desirable to have languages with a higher level of abstraction. A higher level of abstraction and/or a more restricted model of parallelism are essential in order to be able to comprehend the behavior of a large parallel code, debug it, and tune it. It is not possible to understand the behavior of 10,000 concurrent threads that may interact in unexpected ways. Although many bugs can be found on smaller runs, some problems only manifest themselves at large scales; therefore, the ASC program since at least 1998 has listed support for thousands of processors as one of its top requirements for parallel debuggers.[35] However, controlling concurrency and communication are essential activities in parallel algorithm design; a language that does not express parallelism and communication explicitly forces the programmer to reverse-engineer the implementation strategy used, so as to guess how much concurrency or how much communication will be generated by a given program. For example, a compiler for a sequential language that generates code for a vector machine may be very sensitive to exactly how the program is written, whereas a language with vector operations makes that form of parallelism explicit. Even if the compiler determines that a

---

[32]See <http://www.cca-forum.org/>.
[33]See <http://www.cactuscode.org/>.
[34]See <http://www.etnus.com/>.
[35]See <http://www.lanl.gov/projects/asci/PSE/ASCIdebug.html/>.

particular vector operation is not profitable (e.g., owing to short vector length), the notation may still help optimization (e.g., by improving the program analysis information available).

It is desirable to have portability across platforms. Portability is needed both to leverage the variety of platforms that a community may have access to at a given point in time and to handle hardware evolution. Supercomputer applications often outlive the hardware they were designed for: A typical application may be used for 20 years, while the useful life of a supercomputer is more often 5 years. (Currently, the oldest machine on the June 2004 TOP500 list is 7 years old.) By the same token, one wants good performance on each platform. Parallel platforms are distinguished not only by low-level details such as the precise instruction set of processors; they also may have very different performance characteristics, with numbers of processors ranging from just a few to 100,000, with global latency ranging from hundreds of cycles to more than 10,000 cycles, and so on. In some cases, different algorithms are needed to accommodate such large differences. In general, the more disparate the set of target platforms, the harder it is for a single computer program to be mapped efficiently onto all target platforms by compiler and run time; some user help is needed. In practice, supercomputer codes written to port to a multiplicity of platforms contain multiple versions tuned for different platforms. It is not clear how one improves this situation in general. Some research projects have attempted this in specific cases, including packages that generate tuned versions of library codes such as ATLAS[36] and FFTW,[37] domain-specific program generators such as the Tensor Contraction Engine[38] and Spiral,[39] and dynamic code generators such as tcc.[40]

Supercomputer platforms differ not only in the relative performance of their interconnects but also in the communication mechanisms sup-

---

[36]R. Clint Whaley, Antoine Petitet, and Jack Dongarra. 2001. "Automated Empirical Optimization of Software and the ATLAS Project." *Parallel Computing* 27(1-2):3-35.

[37]See <http://www.fftw.org/>.

[38]G. Baumgartner, A. Auer, D.E. Bernholdt, A. Bibireata, V. Choppella, D. Cociorva, X. Gao, R.J. Harrison, S. Hirata, S. Krishnamoorthy, S. Krishnan, C. Lam, M. Nooijen, R.M. Pitzer, J. Ramanujam, P. Sadayappan, and A. Sibiryakov. In press. "Synthesis of High-Performance Parallel Programs for a Class of Ab Initio Quantum Chemistry Models." *Proceedings of the IEEE.*

[39]Markus Püschel, Bryan Singer, Jianxin Xiong, José Moura, Jeremy Johnson, David Padua, Manuela Veloso, and Robert W. Johnson. 2004. "SPIRAL: A Generator for Platform-Adapted Libraries of Signal Processing Algorithms." *Journal of High Performance Computing and Applications* 18(1):21-45.

[40]Massimiliano Poletto, Wilson C. Hsieh, Dawson R. Engler, and M. Frans Kaashoek. 1999. "C and tcc: A Language and Compiler for Dynamic Code Generation." *ACM Transactions on Programming Languages and Systems* 21(2):324-369.

ported by their hardware. Clusters may not support direct access to remote memories; with no such hardware support, it is challenging to provide efficient support for a shared memory programming model. If support for shared memory is deemed important for good software productivity, then it may be necessary to forsake porting to clusters that use LAN interconnects.[41]

Different forms of parallelism operate not only on different supercomputers but at different levels within one supercomputer. For instance, the Earth Simulator uses vector parallelism on one processor, shared memory parallelism within one node, and message passing parallelism across nodes.[42] If each hardware mechanism is directly reflected by a similar software mechanism, then the user has to manage three different parallel programming models within one application and manage the interaction among these models, a difficult task. If, on the other hand, a common abstraction such as multithreading is used at all levels, then the mapping from user code to hardware may be less efficient. Two-level (or multilevel) problem decomposition is probably unavoidable, since on-chip parallelism will increasingly be the norm and on-chip communication will continue to be much faster than off-chip communication. Mechanisms for combining different programming models are not well understood and are a topic for research.

To the extent that on-chip or intrachip parallelism can be handled automatically by compilers, the need for distinct programming models can be reduced. Compilers have been fairly successful with automatic vectorization of code and reasonably successful with automatic parallelization in situations where there are relatively few implementation threads, where communication among implementation threads is very efficient, and where the application's dependences can be automatically analyzed (for instance, data parallelism, where the same operation is applied to multiple data items). Compilers have been less successful with automatic parallelization, where communication and synchronization among threads is relatively expensive or where data access is more irregular. Automatic parallelization is seldom, if ever, used to map sequential codes onto large supercomputers. It is still very much a research issue to find out the best division of labor between programmer, programming environment, and run time in managing parallelism at the different levels of a complex modern supercomputer.

---

[41]New emerging SAN interconnects, such as Infiniband, do support remote memory access (see, for example, the Infiniband Trade Association Web site at <http://www.infinibandta.org/specs>). However, it is not clear that they will do so with the low latency necessary for the efficient support of shared memory programming models.

[42]The design of the Earth Simulator system is summarized in Chapter 7.

Libraries

Since the earliest days of computing, software libraries have been developed to provide commonly used components in a convenient form to facilitate reuse by many programs. Indeed mathematical software libraries are a standard example of successful software reuse. Key examples used for supercomputing include mathematical libraries such as LAPACK[43] for linear algebra, templates such as C++ Standard Template Library,[44] run-time support such as MPI for message passing, and visualization packages such as the Visualization Tool Kit (VTK).[45]

The libraries of most interest to supercomputing involve mathematical functions, including linear algebra (e.g., LAPACK and its kin), Fourier transforms (e.g., FFTW and other packages), and basic functions. Owing to the needs of modern scientific software, advanced data structures (e.g., the C++ Standard Template Library), data management (e.g., HDF),[46] and visualization (e.g., VTK) are all vital for full application development as well. Both the mathematical and computer science libraries are typically required in both sequential and parallel form; sequential forms solve subproblems on a single processor, while the parallel variants are used for the global computation.

Applications Software

Applications software provides solutions to specific science and engineering problems. Such software is necessarily domain- or problem-specific and ranges from small codes maintained by a single researcher (for instance, a student's dissertation work) through large community codes serving a broad topic (for instance, MM5 for atmospheric research[47]) to commercial codes such as the NASTRAN structural engineering package.[48]

Large community codes can have hundreds of thousands of source lines; commercial packages can have many millions of lines, written over decades. Such codes are hard to port to new hardware platforms or new programming languages because of their size, the possible lack of struc-

---

[43]See <http://www.netlib.org/lapack/>.

[44]David R. Musser, Gillmer J. Derge, and Atul Saini. 2001. *STL Tutorial and Reference Guide, 2nd ed.: C++ Programming with the Standard Template Library*. Boston, Mass.: Addison-Wesley.

[45]See <http://public.kitware.com/VTK/index.php>.

[46]See <http://hdf.ncsa.uiuc.edu/>.

[47]See <http://www.mmm.ucar.edu/mm5/>.

[48]See <http://www.mscsoftware.com/products/products_detail.cfm?PI=7>.

ture due to repeated accretions, and the difficulty of verifying major changes. In the case of important codes such as NASTRAN, it is the platform that has to adapt to the application, not vice versa; compilers have to continue supporting obsolete language features, and obsolete architectures may continue having a market due to their support of important packages.[49] Thus, while the accelerated evolution of supercomputer architectures and programming environments satisfies important mission requirements of agencies and may accelerate scientific discovery, it also accelerates the obsolescence of important packages that cannot take advantage of the larger scale and improved cost/performance of new supercomputers.

Scalability of applications is a major challenge. One issue already discussed is that of appropriate programming languages and programming models for the development of supercomputing applications. Most application developers would like to focus their attention on the domain aspects of their applications. Although their understanding of the problem will help them in finding potential sources of concurrency, managing that concurrency in more detail is difficult and error prone. The problem is further compounded by the small size of the supercomputer market, the cost of large supercomputers, and the large variety of supercomputer applications and usage models. Because of the small size of the supercomputer market, commercial software vendors are unlikely to invest in state-of-the-art application development environments (ADEs) for parallel computing. Indeed, supercomputer users have to use ADEs that are less well integrated and less advanced than those used by commercial programmers. The high cost of supercomputers implies that achieving close to the best possible hardware performance is often paramount. Even on sequential processors one can often get a fivefold or better improvement in performance by playing close attention to hardware and system parameters (cache sizes, cache line sizes, page size, and so on) and tuning code for these parameters. The reward for platform-specific tuning on supercomputers can be much larger. But such code tuning is very laborious and not well supported by current ADEs. The variety of supercomputing applications implies that it is not sufficient to tune a few key subsystems and libraries: Most supercomputer programmers have to deal with performance issues. Finally, supercomputer applications range from codes with a few thousands of lines of source code that are developed in days by one person and run once, to codes with millions of

---

[49]This is, of course, true in the broad commercial market as well.

lines that are developed over many years by teams with tens of programmers and used over decades; it is not clear that the same programming languages and models can fit these very different situations.

Fortunately, software abstractions simplify these tasks and in some cases automate them. Data-parallel languages like HPF provide the ability to do the same (or very similar) operations on all (or many) elements of a data structure, with implicit synchronizations between these array operations. Other abstractions make the concurrency explicit but simplify and standardize the synchronization and communications. Languages with a loosely synchronous model of computation proceed in alternating, logically synchronized computation and communication steps. Most MPI programs follow this paradigm, although MPI does not require it. Similarly, many operating system operations encapsulate resources to avoid inappropriate concurrent operations.

All of these abstractions, however, represent trade-offs. For example, the global synchronizations used in a loosely synchronous model can cause onerous overheads. Alternatively, programs may allow more asynchrony between concurrent threads, but then the user has to understand the effect of arbitrary interleaved executions of interacting threads and use proper synchronization and communication, which is often complex. Compilers for data-parallel languages have had difficulty achieving good parallel efficiency owing to the difficulty of minimizing synchronization and communication from fine-grain operations. Successfully using any of these approaches on a large machine is a difficult intellectual exercise. Worse yet, the exercise must often be repeated on new machines, which often have radically different costs for the same operations or do not support some abstractions at all. Perhaps worst of all, even apparently minor inefficiencies in software implementation can have a devastating effect on scalability; hence, effectively programming these systems in a way that allows for software reuse is a key challenge.

Finally, implementation effort is a major consideration given the limited resources available for HPC software. One important reason that MPI is so successful is that simple MPI implementations can be created quickly by supplying device drivers for a public-domain MPI implementation like MPICH.[50] Moreover, that MPI implementation can be improved incrementally by improving those drivers and by tuning higher-level routines for the particular architecture. On the other hand, an efficient implementation of a full language like HPF may require many tens, if not hundreds,

---

[50]See <http://www-unix.mcs.anl.gov/mpi/mpich/>.

of person years. Development teams for HPF at various companies have been significantly larger than development teams for MPI; yet HPF implementations are not as mature as MPI implementations. Implementation cost and, hence, quality of implementation is also a big problem for tools and libraries: today's supercomputing tools frequently do not address the problems of interest to application programmers, do not function as advertised, and/or do not deliver a significant fraction of the performance available from the computer.

Reliability and Fault Tolerance

Another area where there is a complex interplay between hardware and software is reliability and fault tolerance. As systems become larger, the error rate increases and the mean time between failures (MTBF) decreases. This is true both of hardware failures and software failures. Hardware failures on some large ASC supercomputers are sufficiently frequent so as to cause 1,000 node computations to suffer about two unrecoverable failures a day. (This corresponds to an MTBF of about 3 years per node.) This problem is overcome by frequently checkpointing parallel applications and restarting from the last checkpoint after a failure occurred. At current failure rates, the fraction of performance loss due to checkpoints and restarts is modest. But, extrapolating today's failure rates to a machine with 100,000 processors suggests that such a machine will spend most of its time checkpointing and restarting. Worse yet, since many failures are heat related, the rates are likely to increase as processors consume more power. This will require new processor technologies to enable cooler-running chips, or even more support for fault tolerance.

There is little incentive to reduce failure rates of commodity processors to less than one error per few years of operations. Failure rates can be reduced using suitable fault-tolerant hardware in a custom processor or by using triplicated processors in hybrid supercomputers.

In many supercomputers the majority of failures are due to system software. Again, there is little incentive for commercial operating system producers to reduce failure rates to the level where a system with 100,000 copies of Linux or Windows will fail only once or twice a day. Failures can be reduced by using a specially designed operating system and, in particular, by using a reduced-function microkernel at the compute nodes.

Alternatively, higher error rates can be tolerated with better software that supports local rather than global fault recovery. This, however, may require more programmer effort and may require a shift in programming models—again toward a programming model that is more tolerant of asynchrony.

PERFORMANCE ESTIMATION

Most assertions about the performance of a supercomputer system or the performance of a particular implementation of an application are based on metrics—either measurements that are taken on an existing system or models that predict what those measurements would yield. Supercomputing metrics are used to evaluate existing systems for procurement or use, to discover opportunities for improvement of software at any level of the software stack, and to make projections about future sources of difficulty and thereby to guide investments. System measurement is typically done through the use of benchmark problems that provide a basis for comparison. The metrics used to evaluate systems are considerably less detailed than those used to find the performance bottlenecks in a particular application.

Ideally, the metrics used to evaluate systems would extend beyond performance metrics to consider such aspects of time to solution as program preparation and setup time (including algorithm design effort, debugging, and mesh generation), programming and debugging effort, system overheads (including time spent in batch queues, I/O time, time lost due to job scheduling inefficiencies, downtime and handling system background interrupts), and job postprocessing (including visualization and data analysis). The ability to estimate activities involving human effort, whether for supercomputing or for other software development tasks, is primitive at best. Metrics for system overhead can easily be determined retrospectively, but prediction is more difficult.

Performance Benchmarks

Performance benchmarks are used to measure performance on a given system, as an estimate of the time to solution (or its reciprocal, speed) of real applications. The limitations of current benchmarking approaches—for instance, the degree to which they are accurate representatives, the possibilities for tuning performance to the benchmarks, and so forth—are well recognized. The DARPA-funded High Productivity Computing Systems (HPCS) program is one current effort to improve the benchmarks in common use.

Industry performance benchmarks include Linpack, SPEC, NAS, and Stream, among many others.[51] By their nature they can only measure lim-

---

[51]See <http://www.netlib.org/benchweb>. Other industrial benchmark efforts include Real Applications on Parallel Systems (RAPS) (see <http://www.cnrm.meteo.fr/aladin/meetings/RAPS.html>) and MM5 (see <http://www.mmm.ucar.edu/mm5/mpp/helpdesk/20030923.html>).

ited aspects of system performance and cannot necessarily predict performance on rather different applications. For example, LAPACK, an implementation of the Linpack benchmark, produces a measure (R_{max}) that is relatively insensitive to memory and network bandwidth and so cannot accurately predict the performance of more irregular or sparse algorithms. Stream measures peak memory bandwidth, but slight changes in the memory access pattern might result in a far lower attained bandwidth in a particular application due to poor spatial locality. In addition to not predicting the behavior of different applications, benchmarks are limited in their ability to predict performance on variant systems—they can at best predict the performance of slightly different computer systems or perhaps of somewhat larger versions of the one being used, but not of significantly different or larger future systems. There is an effort to develop a new benchmark, called the HPC Challenge benchmark, which will address some of these limitations.[52]

As an alternative to standard benchmarks, a set of application-specific codes is sometimes prepared and optimized for a particular system, particularly when making procurement decisions. The codes can range from full-scale applications that test end-to-end performance, including I/O and scheduling, to kernels that are small parts of the full application but take a large fraction of the run time. The level of effort required for this technique can be much larger than the effort needed to use industry standard benchmarking, requiring (at a minimum) porting of a large code, detailed tuning, rerunning and retuning to improve performance, and rewriting certain kernels, perhaps using different algorithms more suited to the particular architecture. Some work has been done in benchmarking system-level efficiency in order to measure features like the job scheduler, job launch times, and effectiveness of rebooting.[53] The DARPA HPCS program is attempting to develop metrics and benchmarks to measure aspects such as ease of programming. Decisions on platform acquisition

---

[52]The HPC Challenge benchmark consists of seven benchmarks: Linpack, Matrix Multiply, Stream, RandomAccess, PTRANS, Latency/Bandwidth, and FFT. The Linpack and Matrix Multiply tests stress the floating-point performance of a system. Stream is a benchmark that measures sustainable memory bandwidth (in Gbytes/sec), RandomAccess measures the rate of random updates of memory. PTRANS measures the rate of transfer for large arrays of data from the multiprocessor's memory. Latency/Bandwidth measures (as the name suggests) latency and bandwidth of communication patterns of increasing complexity between as many nodes as is timewise feasible. FFTs stress low spatial and high temporal locality. See <http://icl.cs.utk.edu/hpcc> for more information.

[53]Adrian T. Wong, Leonid Oliker, William T.C. Kramer, Teresa L. Kaltz and David H. Bailey. 2000. "ESP: A System Utilization Benchmark." *Proceedings of the ACM/IEEE SC2000.* November 4-10.

have to balance the productivity achieved by a platform against the total cost of ownership for that platform. Both are hard to estimate.[54]

Performance Monitoring

The execution time of a large application depends on complicated interactions among the processors, memory systems, and interconnection network, making it challenging to identify and fix performance bottlenecks. To aid this process, a number of hardware and software tools have been developed. Many manufacturers supply hardware performance monitors that automatically measure critical events like the number of floating-point operations, hits and misses at different levels in the memory hierarchy, and so on. Hardware support for this kind of instrumentation is critical because for many of these events there is no way (short of very careful and slow simulation, discussed below) to measure them without possibly changing them entirely (a Heisenberg effect). In addition, some software tools exist to help collect and analyze the possibly large amount of data produced, but those tools require ongoing maintenance and development. One example of such a tool is PAPI.[55] Other software tools have been developed to collect and visualize interprocessor communication and synchronization data, but they need to be made easier to use to have the desired impact.

The limitation of these tools is that they provide low-level, system-specific information. It is sometimes difficult for the application programmer to relate the results to source code and to understand how to use the monitoring information to improve performance.

Performance Modeling and Simulation

There has been a great deal of interest recently in mathematically modeling the performance of an application with enough accuracy to predict its behavior either on a rather different problem size or a rather different computer system, typically much larger than now available. Performance modeling is a mixture of the empirical (measuring the performance of certain kernels for different problem sizes and using curve fitting to predict performance for other problem sizes) and the analytical

---

[54]See, for example, Larry Davis, 2004, "Making HPC System Acquisition Decisions Is an HPC Application," *Supercomputing*.

[55]S. Browne, J. Dongarra, G. Ho, N. Garner, and P. Mucci. 2000. "A Portable Programming Interface for Performance Evaluation on Modern Processors." *International Journal of High Performance Computing Applications*: 189-204.

(developing formulas that characterize performance as a function of system and application parameters). The intent is that once the characteristics of a system have been specified, a detailed enough model can be used to identify performance bottlenecks, either in a current application or a future one, and so suggest either alternative solutions or the need for research to create them.

Among the significant activities in this area are the performance models that have been developed for several full applications from the ASC workload[56,57,58] and a similar model that was used in the procurement process for the ASC Purple system, predicting the performance of the SAGE code on several of the systems in a recent competition.[59] Alternative modeling strategies have been used to model the NAS parallel benchmarks, several small PETSc applications, and the applications Parallel Ocean Program, Navy Layered Ocean Model, and Cobal60, across multiple compute platforms (IBM Power 3 and Power 4 systems, a Compaq Alpha server, and a Cray T3E-600).[60,61] These models are very accurate across a range of processors (from 2 to 128), with errors ranging from 1 percent to 16 percent.

Performance modeling holds out of the hope of making a performance prediction of a system before it is procured, but currently modeling has only been done for a few codes by experts who have devoted a great deal of effort to understanding the code. To have a wider impact on the procurement process it will be necessary to simplify and automate the modeling process to make it accessible to nonexperts to use on more codes.

[56]A. Hoisie, O. Lubeck, and H. Wasserman. 2000. "Performance and Scalability Analysis of Teraflop-Scale Parallel Architectures Using Multidimensional Wavefront Applications." *The International Journal of High Performance Computing Applications* 14(4).

[57]D.J. Kerbyson, H. Alme, A. Hoisie, F. Petrini, H. Wasserman, and M. Gittings. 2001. "Predictive Performance and Scalability Modeling of a Large-Scale Application." *Proceedings of the ACM/IEEE SC2001*, IEEE. November.

[58]M. Mathis, D. Kerbyson, and A. Hoisie. 2003. "A Performance Model of Non-Deterministic Particle Transport on Large-Scale Systems." Workshop on Performance Modeling and Analysis, 2003 ICCS. Melbourne, June.

[59]A. Jacquet, V. Janot, R. Govindarajan, C. Leung, G. Gao, and T. Sterling. 2003. "An Executable Analytical Performance Evaluation Approach for Early Performance Prediction." *Proceedings of IPDPS'03*.

[60]L. Carrington, A. Snavely, N. Wolter, and X. Gao. 2003. "A Performance Prediction Framework for Scientific Applications." Workshop on Performance Modeling and Analysis, 2003 ICCS. Melbourne, June.

[61]A. Snavely, L. Carrington, N. Wolter, J. Labarta, R. Badia, and A. Purkayastha. 2002. "A Framework for Performance Modeling and Prediction." *Proceedings of the ACM/IEEE SC2002*, November.

Ultimately, performance modeling should become an integrative part of verification and validation for high-performance applications.

Supercomputers are used to simulate large physical, biological, or even social systems whose behavior is too hard to otherwise understand or predict. A supercomputer itself is one of these hard-to-understand systems. Some simulation tools, in particular for the performance of proposed network designs, have been developed,[62] and computer vendors have shown significant interest.

Measuring performance on existing systems can certainly identify current bottlenecks, but it not adequate to guide investments to solve future problems. For example, current hardware trends are for processor speeds to increasingly outstrip local memory bandwidth (the memory wall[63]), which in turn will increasingly outstrip network bandwidth. Therefore, an application that runs efficiently on today's machines may develop a serious bottleneck in a few years either because of memory bandwidth or because of network performance. Performance modeling, perhaps combined with simulation, holds the most promise of identifying these future bottlenecks, because an application (or its model) can be combined with the hardware specifications of a future system. Fixing these bottlenecks could require investments in hardware, software, or algorithms. However, neither performance modeling nor simulation are yet robust enough and widely enough used to serve this purpose, and both need further development. The same comments apply to software engineering, where it is even more difficult to predict the impact on software productivity of new languages and tools. But since software makes up such a large fraction of total system cost, it is important to develop more precise metrics and to use them to guide investments.

Performance Estimation and the Procurement Process

The outcome of a performance estimation process on a set of current and/or future platforms is a set of alternative solution approaches, each with an associated speed and cost. Cost may include not just the cost of the machine but the total cost of ownership, including programming, floor space, power, maintenance, staffing, and so on.[64] At any given time, there

---

[62]See <http://simos.stanford.edu>.

[63]Wm. A. Wulf and S.A. McKee. 1995. "Hitting the Wall: Implications of the Obvious." *Computer Architecture News* 23(1):20-24.

[64]National Coordination Office for Information Technology Research and Development. 2004. *Federal Plan for High-End Computing: Report of the High-End Computing Revitalization Task Force (HECRTF)*. May.

will be a variety of low-cost, low-speed approaches based on COTS architectures and software, as well as high-cost, high-speed solutions based on custom architectures and software. In principle, one could then apply principles of operations research to select the optimal system—for example, the cheapest solution that computed a solution within a hard deadline in the case of intelligence processing, or the solution that computed the most solutions per dollar for a less time-critical industrial application, or the number of satisfied users per dollar, or any other utility function.[65]

The most significant advantage of commodity supercomputers is their purchase cost; less significant is their total cost of ownership, because of the higher programming and maintenance costs associated with commodity supercomputers. Lower purchase cost may bias the supercomputing market toward commodity supercomputers if organizations do not account properly for the total cost of ownership and are more sensitive to hardware cost.

THE IMPERATIVE TO INNOVATE AND BARRIERS TO INNOVATION

Systems Issues

The committee summarizes trends in parallel hardware in Table 5.1. The table uses historical data to project future trends showing that innovation will be needed. First, for the median number of processor chips to reach 13,000 in 2010 and 86,000 in 2020, significant advances will be required in both software scalability and reliability. The scalability problem is complicated by the fact that by 2010 each processor chip is likely to be a chip multiprocessor (CMP) with four to eight processors, and each of these processors is likely to be 2- to 16-way multithreaded. (By 2020 these numbers will be significantly higher: 64 to 128 processors per chip, each 16- to 128-way multithreaded.) Hence, many more parallel threads will need to be employed to sustain performance on these machines. Increasing the number of threads by this magnitude will require innovation in architecture, programming systems, and applications.

A machine of the scale forecast for 2010 is expected to have a raw failure rate of several failures per hour. By 2020 the rate would be several failures per minute. The problem is complicated because there are both more processors to fail and because the failure rate per processor is expected to increase as integrated circuit dimensions decrease, making cir-

---

[65]Marc Snir and David A. Bader. 2003. *A Framework for Measuring Supercomputer Productivity*. Technical Report. October.

cuitry more vulnerable to energetic particle strikes. In the near future, soft errors will occur not just in memory but also in logic circuits. Such failure rates require innovation in both fault detection and fault handling to give the user the illusion of a fault-free machine.

The growing gap between processor performance and global bandwidth and latency is also expected to force innovation. By 2010 global bandwidth would fall to 0.008 words/flops, and a processor would need to execute 8,700 flops in the time it takes for one communication to occur. These numbers are problematic for all but the most local of applications. To overcome this global communication gap requires innovation in architecture to provide more bandwidth and lower latency and in programming systems and applications to improve locality.

Both locally (within a single processor chip) and globally (across a machine), innovation is required to overcome the gaps generated by non-uniform scaling of arithmetic local bandwidth and latency, and global bandwidth and latency. Significant investments in both basic and applied research are needed now to lay the groundwork for the innovations that will be required over the next 15 years to ensure the viability of high-end systems. Low-end systems will be able, for a while, to exploit on-chip parallelism and tolerate increasing relative latencies by leveraging techniques currently used on high-end systems, but they, too, will eventually run out of steam without such investments.

Innovations, or nonparametric evolution, of architecture, programming systems, and applications take a very long time to mature. This is due to the systems nature of the changes being made and the long time required for software to mature. The introduction of vector processing is a good example. Vectors were introduced in the early 1970s in the Texas Instruments ASC and CDC Star. However, it took until 1977 for a commercially successful vector machine, the Cray-1, to be developed. The lagging balance between scalar performance and memory performance prevented the earlier machines from seeing widespread use. One could even argue that the systems issues were not completely solved until the introduction of gather-and-scatter instructions on the Cray XMP and the Convex and Alliant mini-supercomputers in the 1980s. Even after the systems issues were solved, it took additional years for the software to mature. Vectorizing compilers with advanced dependence analysis did not emerge until the mid 1980s. Several compilers, including the Convex and the Fujitsu Fortran Compilers, permitted applications that were written in standard Fortran 77 to be vectorized. Applications software took a similar amount of time to be adapted to vector machines (for example, by restructuring loops and adding directives to facilitate automatic vectorization of the code by the compiler).

A major change in architecture or programming has far-reaching effects and usually requires a number of technologies to be successful. Introducing vectors, for example, required the development of vectorizing compilers; pipelined, banked memory systems; and masked operations. Without the supporting technologies, the main new technology (in this case, vectors) is not useful. The main and supporting technologies are typically developed via research projects in advance of a first full-scale system deployment. Full-scale systems integrate technologies but rarely pioneer them. The parallel computers of the early 1990s, for example, drew on research dating back to the 1960s on parallel architecture, programming systems, compilers, and interconnection networks. Chapter 6 discusses the need for coupled development in more detail.

Issues for Algorithms

A common feature of algorithms research is that progress is tied to exploiting the mathematical or physical structure of the application. General-purpose solution methods are often too inefficient to use. Thus, progress often depends on forming interdisciplinary teams of applications scientists, mathematicians, and computer scientists to identify and exploit this structure. Part of the technology challenge is to facilitate the ability of these teams to address simultaneously the requirements imposed by the applications and the requirements imposed by the supercomputer system.

A fundamental difficulty is the intrinsic complexity of understanding and describing the algorithm. From the application perspective, a concise high-level description in which the mathematical structure is apparent is important. Many applications scientists use Matlab[66] and frameworks such as PETSc[67] to rapidly prototype and communicate complicated algorithms. Yet while parallelism and communication are essential issues in the design of parallel algorithms, they find no expression in a high-level language such as Matlab. At present, there is no high-level programming model that exposes essential performance characteristics of parallel algorithms. Consequently, much of the transfer of such knowledge is done by personal relationships, a mechanism that does not scale and that cannot reach a large enough user community. There is a need to bridge this gap so that parallel algorithms can be described at a high level.

It is both infeasible and inappropriate to use the full generality of a complex application in the process of designing algorithms for a portion of the overall solution. Consequently the cycle of prototyping, evaluating,

---

[66]<http://www.mathworks.com/products/matlab/>.
[67]<http://www-unix.mcs.anl.gov/petsc/petsc-2/>.

and revising an algorithm is best done initially by using benchmark problems. It is critical to have a suitable set of test problems easily available to stimulate algorithms research. For example, the collection of sparse matrices arising in real applications and made available by Harwell and Boeing many years ago spawned a generation of research in sparse matrix algorithms. Yet often there is a dearth of good benchmarks with which to work.[68] Such test sets are rare and must be constantly updated as problem sizes grow.

An Example from Computational Fluid Dynamics

As part of the committee's applications workshop, Phillip Colella explained some of the challenges in making algorithmic progress. He wrote as follows:[69]

> Success in computational fluid dynamics [CFD] has been the result of a combination of mathematical algorithm design, physical reasoning, and numerical experimentation. The continued success of this methodology is at risk in the present supercomputing environment, due to the vastly increased complexity of the undertaking. The number of lines of code required to implement the modern CFD methods such as those described above is far greater than that required to implement typical CFD software used twenty years ago. This is a consequence of the increased complexity of both the models, the algorithms, and the high-performance computers. While the advent of languages such as C++ and Java with more powerful abstraction mechanisms has permitted us to manage software complexity somewhat more easily, it has not provided a complete solution. Low-level programming constructs such as MPI for parallel communication and callbacks to Fortran kernels to obtain serial performance lead to code that is difficult to understand and modify. The net result is the stifling of innovation. The development of state-of-the-art high-performance CFD codes can be done only by large groups. Even in that case, the development cycle of design-implement-test is much more unwieldy and can be performed less often. This leads to a conservatism on the part of developers of CFD simulation codes: they will make do with less-than-optimal methods, simply because the cost of trying out improved algorithms is too high. In order to change this state of affairs, a combination of technical innovations and institutional changes are needed.

---

[68]DOE. 2003. *DOE Science Networking Challenge: Roadmap to 2008.* Report of the June 3-5 Science Networking Workshop, conducted by the Energy Sciences Network Steering Committee at the request of the Office of Advanced Scientific Computing Research of the DOE Office of Science.

[69] From the white paper "Computational Fluid Dynamics for Multiphysics and Multiscale Problems," by Phillip Colella, LBNL, prepared for the committee's Santa Fe, N.M., applications workshop, September 2003.

As Dr. Colella's discussion suggests, in addition to the technical challenges, there are a variety of nontechnical barriers to progress in algorithms. These topics are discussed in subsequent chapters.

Software Issues

In extrapolating technology trends, it is easy to forget that the primary purpose of improved supercomputers is to solve important problems better. That is, the goal is to improve the productivity of users, including scientists, engineers, and other nonspecialists in supercomputing. To this end, supercomputing software development should emphasize time to solution, the major metric of value to high-end computing users. Time to solution includes time to cast the physical problem into algorithms suitable for high-end computing; time to write and debug the computer code that expresses those algorithms; time to optimize the code for the computer platforms being used; time to compute the desired results; time to analyze those results; and time to refine the analysis into an improved understanding of the original problem that will enable scientific or engineering advances. There are good reasons to believe that lack of adequate software is today a major impediment to reducing time to solution and that more emphasis on investments in software research and development (as recommended by previous committees, in particular, PITAC) is justified. The main expense in large supercomputing programs such as ASC is software related: In FY 2004, 40 percent of the ASC budget was allocated for application development; in addition, a significant fraction of the acquisition budget also goes, directly or indirectly, to software purchase.[70] A significant fraction of the time to solution is spent developing, tuning, verifying, and validating codes. This is especially true in the NSA environment, where new, relatively short HPC codes are frequently developed to solve new emerging problems and are run once. As computing platforms become more complex, and as codes become much larger and more complex, the difficulty of delivering efficient and robust codes in a timely fashion increases. For example, several large ASC code projects, each involving tens of programmers, hundreds of thousands of lines of code, and investments from $50 million to $100 million had early milestones that proved to be too aggressive.[71] Many supercomputer users feel

---

[70]Advanced Simulation and Computing Program Plan, August 2003.

[71]See Douglass Post, 2004, "The Coming Crisis in Computational Sciences," Workshop on Productivity and Performance in High-End Computing, February; and D. Post and R. Kendall, 2003, "Software Project Management and Quality Engineering Practices for Complex, Coupled Multi-Physics, Massively Parallel Computation Simulations: Lessons Learned from ASCI," DOE Software Quality Forum, March.

that they are hampered by the difficulty of developing new HPC software. The programming languages, libraries, and application development environments used in HPC are generally less advanced than those used by the broad software industry, even though the problems are much harder. A software engineering discipline geared to the unique needs of technical computing and high-performance computing is yet to emerge. In addition, a common software environment for scientific computation encompassing desktop to high-end systems will enhance productivity gains by promoting ease of use and manageability of systems.

Extrapolating current trends in supercomputer software, it is hard to see whether there will be any major changes in the software stack used for supercomputers in the coming years. Languages such as UPC, CAF, and Titanium are likely to be increasingly used. However, UPC and CAF do not support object orientation well, and all three languages have a static view of parallelism (the crystalline model) and give good support to only some application paradigms. The DARPA HPCS effort emphasizes software productivity, but it is vendor driven and hardware focused and has not generated a broad, coordinated community effort for new programming models. Meanwhile, larger and more complex hardware systems continue to be put in production, and larger and more complex application packages are developed. In short, there is an oncoming crisis in HPC software created by barely adequate current capabilities, increasing requirements, and limited investment in solutions.

In addition to the need for software research, there is a need for software development. Enhanced mechanisms are needed to turn prototype tools into well-developed tools with a broad user base. The core set of tools available on supercomputers—operating systems, compilers, debuggers, performance analysis tools—is not up to the standards of robustness and performance expected for commercial computers. Tools are nonexistent or, even worse, do not work. Parallel debuggers are an often-cited example. Parallel math libraries are thought to be almost as bad, although math libraries are essential for building a mature application software base for parallel computing. Third-party commercial and public domain sources have tried to fill the gaps left by the computer vendors but have had varying levels of success. Many active research projects are also producing potentially useful tools, but the tools are available only in prototype form or are fragmented and buried inside various application efforts. The supercomputer user community desperately needs better means to develop these technologies into effective tools.

Although the foregoing discussion addresses the need for technical innovation and the technical barriers to progress, there are significant policy issues that are essential to achieving that progress. These topics are taken up in subsequent chapters.

6

Supercomputing
Infrastructures and Institutions

Supercomputing is not only about technologies, metrics, and economics; it is also about the people, organizations, and institutions that are key to the further progress of these technologies and about the complex web that connects people, organizations, products, and technologies. To understand supercomputing, one needs to understand the structure of the supercomputing community and the structure of the supercomputing landscape of concepts and technologies. Such a structuralist approach to supercomputing is necessarily less quantitative, more subjective, and more speculative than approaches that are more congenial to economists or engineers. However, it provides a necessary corrective for a study that might otherwise measure the trees but might not view the forest. The committee presents such an approach to supercomputing in this chapter.

It is useful to think of supercomputing infrastructure as an ecosystem. The Encarta dictionary defines an ecosystem as "a localized group of interdependent organisms together with the environment that they inhabit and depend on." A supercomputer ecosystem is a continuum of computing platforms, system software, and the people who know how to exploit them to solve supercomputing applications such as those discussed in Chapter 4.

In supercomputing ecosystems, the "organisms" are the technologies that mutually reinforce one another and are mutually interdependent. Examples include the following:

- Vector architectures, vectorizing compilers, and applications tuned for the use of vector hardware;
- Shared memory architectures, scalable operating systems, OpenMP-compliant compilers and run-time systems, and applications that can take advantage of shared memory; and
- Message passing architectures, parallel software tools and libraries, and applications that are designed to use this programming model.

The organism space tends to group according to the architecture class, the programming language and models used on the system, the algorithms, the set of applications and how the code is being tuned (e.g., vector version versus cache version), what application program packages are available, and so on. The success of supercomputer architectures is highly dependent on the organisms that form around them.

The architecture and the balance among its key configuration parameters (such as number of processors or memory size) are the dominant factors in determining the nature of the technologies in the ecosystem. For example, early supercomputers such as the CDC 7600 had rather small memories compared with their computing speed and the requirements of the applications that users wanted to run. That characteristic led to the development of system tools to reuse memory during execution (overlay management software) and to the use of different algorithms in certain cases, and it excluded certain classes of applications, together with a part of the user community. A second example is the speed of I/O to local disk, which can have a major impact on the design of application programs. For example, in a number of chemistry applications, if the ratio of I/O speed to computation performance is below a certain (well-understood) level, the application will run faster by recomputing certain quantities instead of computing them once, writing them to disk, and then reading them in subsequent phases of the job. Some widely used chemistry programs use this recompute strategy. Another common example of the impact of system performance characteristics on programming is that a message passing programming style is most often used when shared memory performance is below some threshold, even if shared memory programming tools are provided.

Because all current supercomputers have highly parallel architectures, the system software and the algorithms used have to be designed or adapted to function on such machines. As discussed in Chapter 5, the characteristics of the processors and the interconnection network (latency and bandwidth of access to memories, local and remote) are key features and determine to a large extent the algorithms and classes of applications that will execute efficiently on a given machine. Low latency and high-bandwidth access to memory not only yield higher performance—much

higher on some applications—but enable the use of less complex algorithms and ease the programming task. However, these features also lead
to higher hardware costs and are typically available on systems that use
less advanced device technology and run at a slower clock rate. Even for
machines with such hardware features, software tools or compiler directives are often needed to achieve high fractions of peak speed. In short,
the micro- and macro-architecture of a supercomputer determine to a
large extent the complexities of the other technologies in its ecosystem.
Grid computing environments may provide a way to integrate many components of the supercomputing ecosystem. But they will also create even
more complex ecosystems.

Without software, the hardware is useless; hence, another important
part of the ecosystem is the system software. By system software is meant
the operating system components as well as tools such as compilers,
schedulers, run-time libraries, monitoring software, debuggers, file systems, and visualization tools. But in supercomputing ecosystems, the existence of software with certain functionality is not sufficient. Unlike the
situation with PCs, almost all of which use the same type of processor, in
supercomputing environments the mere existence of system software is
not enough to create an effective supercomputing ecosystem. For example,
if the supercomputer configuration has thousands of processors but the
operating system is designed for systems with only a few processors,
many operating system tasks will run unacceptably slowly or even fail to
execute. This inadequacy was observed for computers from several different vendors, and until those gross inefficiencies were removed, the systems saw little use. Additional examples of software technology that may
be required for a supercomputing ecosystem to be effective are global
parallel file systems and fault tolerance.

Libraries are also part of the ecosystem. Examples include message
passing libraries (e.g., MPI) and numerical libraries that embody algorithms that are efficient on the supercomputer's architecture and that are
implemented appropriately (e.g., PETSc and ScaLAPACK).

To enable effective use of a supercomputer, the system software and
libraries must be tailored to the particular supercomputer that is the focus
of the ecosystem. As pointed out above, some of this software, such as
compilers and run-time libraries, may require extensive customization,
while others, such as networking software, might require relatively little.
The nature of the user's interface to the system—for example, the programming languages or the job scheduler—is also part of the ecosystem.

If the technologies that make up a supercomputing ecosystem constitute the "organism," the environment that they inhabit and depend on
includes people with the relevant skills (such as expertise in parallel algorithms) and projects with certain requirements (for instance, research

whose conduct requires supercomputers). The people with the expertise to produce the software, design the algorithms, and/or use the supercomputer are determinants of the scope (or sphere of influence) of the ecosystem associated with that supercomputer.[1]

Many industrial users depend on commercial software packages such as MSC NASTRAN or Gaussian. If those packages run poorly or not at all on a given supercomputer, the industrial users will be missing from the ecosystem, reducing the financial viability of that supercomputer. On the other hand, at national laboratories and research universities, almost all application programs are developed by individual research teams that do not depend on the availability of commercial software packages. As a result, a given installation may become favored by users of one or a few application classes, creating an ecosystem that is essentially a "topical center" because of the expertise, libraries, configuration details (such as storage and I/O), and visualization capabilities that are suitable for that class of applications. Expertise and sharing of methodologies might be as big a factor in creating the topical ecosystem as the use of the same software package by many projects.

Ecosystems are stable over several generations of a computer family, sometimes for one or two decades. As supercomputing hardware has become more complex, the barriers to creating a new ecosystem have risen, mostly due to the large effort required to develop a robust and full-featured software environment for complex architectures. Hence, creating a new ecosystem requires a significant, protracted effort and often also research and development of new software technologies. Vectorizing compilers took decades to mature and relied on the results of many academic research projects. Parallelizing compilers are still in their infancy more than 20 years after parallel computers came into use. The cost and time—and research and development in many different areas (compiler technology, operating system scalability, hardware, etc.)—make it very difficult to mount projects to introduce supercomputers with novel architectural features, especially if they require new programming paradigms for their efficient use.

Among the challenges in introducing new architectural features is finding ways to make them usable through languages and concepts that users can easily relate to familiar tools. If the learning curve for using a new system is too steep, there will be little development of system software and especially of applications, and users will simply not attempt to modify their applications to run on it. This is why programming languages persist for decades. For instance, Fortran 77 (a modest evolution of Fortran 66) is still heavily used 27 years after it first became a standard.

---

[1]The workforce portion of the supercomputer ecosystem is discussed later in this chapter.

The large cost in human effort and time to adopt new programming languages and programming paradigms raises barriers that further stabilize the ecosystem. Many supercomputer applications are very complex, entail hundreds of thousands of lines of code, and require multidisciplinary teams with tens of people. Like supertankers, they cannot change direction quickly.

Another factor that contributes to the stability of ecosystems is that different technologies have different lifetimes and different starting points. It is almost never the case that one is afforded a clean-sheet starting point, where hardware, software, applications, and interfaces can all be designed from scratch. This reality calls for long-term ecosystem planning: Application packages have to be ported and maintained, new systems have to interoperate with old ones, the same people have to operate the new and the old systems, and so on. A lack of continuity in platforms and a lack of platform independence in software raise the costs of hiring and retaining appropriate personnel. Long-term planning is also needed because buildings cost money and can often account for a substantial portion of the total costs of procurement. To amortize that investment, it is desirable that a given facility be designed to serve for several ecosystem generations.

SUPERCOMPUTING ECOSYSTEM CREATION AND MAINTENANCE

Supercomputing system evolution is not all that different from generic computing system evolution, with the same patterns of horizontally integrated ecosystems (for example, the Wintel ecosystem) and vertically integrated ecosystems (such as the ecosystem created by IBM mainframes) and with the same high cost of change. From this process point of view, there is very little difference between supercomputing systems and generic computing systems except that, since the architectural platform differences are so radical, it can be much more expensive to port applications in the supercomputing ecosystem than in the generic ecosystem. That expense, coupled with the very small number of supercomputers sold, greatly inhibits the development and porting of commercial software packages to supercomputer platforms.

Designing, developing, and deploying a truly radical new computing platform is a very difficult and expensive project. An example of the height of the barriers is illustrated by the IBM Blue Gene (BG) project.[2] The BG/

---

[2]See <http://www.research.ibm.com/bluegene/index.html>. The 8,192-processor BG/L prototype at IBM Rochester was 4th on the June 2004 TOP500 list, while the 4,096 prototype at IBM Watson was 8th.

L system that is currently being developed and built is substantially less innovative than the initial BG concept. The instruction set architecture is a known one, so that compilers, many parts of the operating system, and many software tools do not have to be written ab initio and so that users will find a somewhat familiar environment. Even so, for BG/L a large consortium is being formed of academic groups and research laboratories that are users and developers of very high end applications to build a community around this class of HPC architectures, which, in its largest configurations, will have an order-of-magnitude more nodes than previous multiple instruction, multiple data (MIMD) systems. The consortium is being formed to provide additional human capital to study the new architecture in the context of many applications, to develop some of the software tools or to migrate existing open source tools, and to provide input on hardware and software improvements that should be made for future generations of the Blue Gene family. The forming of a consortium reflects the fact that even a very large and profitable company like IBM does not have enough in-house expertise in all the necessary areas and cannot justify the investments needed to hire such experts. It is further evidence of the complexity of current supercomputer environments compared with those of only 20 years ago. Formation of the consortium is also an explicit attempt to quickly create an ecosystem around the Blue Gene platforms.

How Ecosystems Get Established

Traditionally, supercomputing ecosystems have grown up around a particular computer vendor's family of products, e.g., the Cray Research family of vector computers, starting with the Cray-1 and culminating in the T-90, and the IBM SP family of parallel computers. While a given model's lifetime is but a few years, the similarity of the architecture of various generations of hardware provides an opportunity for systems and application software to be developed and to mature. Cray-1 serial number one was delivered in 1976 with no compiler and an extremely primitive operating system. Twenty years later, there were good vectorizing compilers, reliable and efficient operating systems, and thick books that catalogued the hundreds of commercial application software packages available on the Cray vector machines.

The excellent access to memory of such high-bandwidth systems and the availability of good optimizing compilers and reliable libraries tuned to the system's architecture can yield much higher performance (by a factor of as much as 30) on some applications—and with less programming effort—than can commodity clusters. Even though less programming effort may be required, expertise is still quite important. People who were proficient in the efficient use of Cray vector computers became valued members of projects that used those systems, and small consulting firms were established to sell such expertise to groups that did not have it. The existence of a cadre of people with the expertise to use a particular supercomputer family further strengthens the corresponding ecosystem and adds to its longevity.

One can see the benefits of these two ecosystems in the more recent Earth Simulator. As the committee observed in Chapter 5, the Earth Simulator has three kinds of parallelism, requiring multiple programming models to be used in an application. However, once the applications developer does multilevel problem decomposition, there is an HPF compiler that performs vectorization, shared-memory parallelization, and distributed-memory communication, thus partially shielding the application programmer from those issues.

More recently, commodity cluster systems that use open, de facto software standards have become a significant component of the high-end computing scene, and modest ecosystems are forming around them. In many cases, cluster hardware is based on microprocessors that use the Intel x86 instruction set, providing some stability for the hardware and node architecture. Open source software suited to large clusters and high-end computing is becoming available, such as versions of the Linux operating system, parallel file systems such as PVFS, message-passing libraries such as MPICH, and visualization toolkits such as VTK. Reinforcing the trend toward clusters are factors such as these:

- The low entry cost, which enables even small university groups to acquire them;
- Their proliferation, which provides a training ground for many people, some of whom will use them as a development platform for software tools, libraries, and application programs, thus adding technologies to the ecosystem;
- The local control that a group has over its cluster, which simplifies management and accounting;
- The relative ease of upgrades to new processor and interconnection technologies; and
- Their cost effectiveness for many classes of applications.

Software challenges remain for the nascent cluster ecosystem. Since communication is more expensive on clusters, minimizing communication plays a big role in achieving good performance. The distribution of data and computation across nodes has to be planned carefully, as part of algorithm design, particularly because there is no hardware support for remote data access and because load balancing is more expensive. Tasks that are done by hardware in a high-bandwidth system have to be done in software in a cluster. Current vector systems further reduce programming effort because they have high-quality compilers available, facilitating the immediate use of legacy codes. Compilers for clusters have a much shorter history of development and are much less mature, even when they use vectorization technology.

The computer industry has shifted over the last decades from a model of vertically integrated systems to one of horizontally integrated systems. In a vertically integrated model, vendors develop the technology required across most of the layers of the system. Thus, IBM designed and manufactured almost everything associated with a mainframe: It designed and manufactured the chips and their package, the disks, the operating system, the compilers and tools, the databases, and many other specialized applications. The same was largely true of supercomputing manufacturers such as Cray. Today the dominant model is that of horizontal integration. Thus, Intel designs and manufactures chips, Microsoft develops operating systems and applications running on those and other chips, and Dell integrates both into one system. The same evolution has happened with high-end systems. Cray is still responsible for the design of most hardware and software components of the Cray X1; most of the value of such a product is produced by Cray. On the other hand, cluster systems are based on integration of technologies provided by many vendors, and the cluster integrators contribute only a small fraction of the product value.

A vertically integrated, vendor-driven ecosystem has the advantages that there are fewer variables to contend with and that there is centralized control of the hardware architecture and most of the software architecture. If the supercomputer vendor is successful financially, then commercial applications software is likely to emerge, lowering the barriers for use. On the other hand, a vertically integrated ecosystem might become fragile if the vendor encounters financial difficulties, switches to a new hardware architecture, or abandons its own proprietary operating system as a result of increasingly high costs. The tight integration that (1) ensured smooth functioning of the software on the hardware and (2) enabled the development of proprietary features that application developers and users came to rely on will now make it much more expensive to transition to another system, either from the same vendor or a different one.

Horizontal integration can provide a less arduous migration path from one supercomputer platform to another and thus a longer-lived, though less tightly coupled, ecosystem. Those advantages are gained through the use of portable software environments and less reliance on the highly specific characteristics of the hardware or proprietary vendor software. Such portability has its cost—a smaller fraction of the potential performance will be achieved, perhaps much smaller. A second disadvantage of the horizontal integration approach is that the various software components will not have been designed to be used in concert with one another; independently designed and implemented components will be less compatible and the integration less cohesive and more fragile. The fragility results from the independence of the efforts that produce each component; changes may be made to one component without considering whether the new version will still interface with other software in the ecosystem.

In a horizontal market, the role of integrators that assemble the various technologies into a coherent product becomes more important. Such integrators (for example, Linux Netwox[3]) have appeared in the cluster market, but their small size relative to that of the makers of the components they assemble implies that they have little clout in ensuring that these components fit well together. Furthermore, an integrator may not have the scope to provide the kind of ongoing customer support that was available from vertically integrated companies.

An example of a vertically integrated ecosystem that did not survive for very long is the Thinking Machines CM-5, a product of Thinking Machines Corporation (TMC). The CM-5 had a unique proprietary architecture and a software environment with highly regarded components: languages, compilers, mathematical software libraries, debuggers, and so forth. The largest CM-5 configuration was world-leading for a while. When TMC went out of business, users had to migrate to different systems that had less sophisticated software as well as different hardware architecture. One component of the ecosystem that adapted quickly to different systems was the group of highly skilled TMC employees. Many of the people who produced the CM-5 software environment were hired en masse by other computer companies because of their expertise, although their new employers have not attempted to produce as sophisticated an environment for their own systems.

Message passing libraries are an example of software technology that can stimulate the evolution of an ecosystem around an architecture family, in this case, processor-memory nodes connected by a network of some sort. Message passing has been the dominant programming model for parallel computers with distributed memory since the mid-1980s. Clusters fall into this class of computers. While the functionality provided in different systems was similar, the syntax and semantics were not. As early as the mid-1980s there were attempts to develop de facto standards for

---

[3]See <http://www.laurentconstantin.com/en/netw/netwox/>.

message passing libraries, but it was not until the MPI effort in 1993-1994 that a standard was developed and was widely adopted. It is worth noting that Argonne National Laboratory's MPICH was the first available implementation of the MPI standard and served as the basis for almost all MPI libraries produced by computer manufacturers. The wide availability of robust, open source MPI implementations was an important factor in the rapid and widespread proliferation of the commodity cluster supercomputer.

Potential Barriers for New Ecosystems

Each ecosystem has a critical mass below which it cannot survive; if it is too close to the critical mass, there is a high risk that a catastrophic event may wipe it out. A supercomputing ecosystem that is too small is not economically viable and cannot evolve fast enough to compete. Even if it is viable, but barely so, a few wrong decisions by company managers or national policy makers may destroy it. The demise of companies such as TMC or Kendall Square Research and the near demise of Cray clearly illustrate these points.

There are good reasons to believe that the critical mass needed to sustain a computer ecosystem has increased over the last decades. Computer systems have become more complex, so they are more expensive to develop. This complexity arises at all levels of current systems. It has been asserted that the development cost of Intel microprocessors has increased by a factor of 200 from the Intel 8080 to the Intel P6. Operating systems, compilers, and libraries are larger and more complex—the code size of operating systems has grown by two orders of magnitude in two decades. Application codes are larger and more complex, in part because of the complexity of the platforms on which they sit, but mostly because of the increased sophistication of the applications themselves. The increases can be explained, in large part, by the growth of the computer industry, which can support and justify larger investments in computer technologies. A small supercomputing niche will not be able to support the development of complex hardware and software and will be handicapped by a lack of performance or function relative to commodity computer products. As a result the critical mass of a viable supercomputing ecosystem is greater than it once was. This is an obstacle to the establishment of new supercomputing ecosystems.

Horizontal integration is another obstacle to the establishment of new ecosystems. It is not only that small agile vessels have been replaced by large supertankers that are hard to steer; they have been replaced by flotillas of supertankers that sail in tight formation and that all need to be steered in a new direction in order to achieve change.

Horizontal integration admits more specialization and provides a larger market for each component maker, thus allowing more R&D investments and faster technology evolution. This has clearly benefited the mainstream computer industry, in which vertically integrated servers, such as IBM mainframes, have become an anomaly. On the other hand, horizontal integration solidifies the boundaries across components and technologies provided by different vendors. System-level changes that require coordinated changes of multiple components provided by multiple vendors are less likely to occur. In other words, one trades off faster progress within a paradigm (the paradigm defined by agreed-upon interfaces at the various layers) against more frequent changes of the paradigm.

There are many examples of the difficulty of effecting such coordinated changes. For example, software-controlled cache prefetching is a well-known, useful mechanism for hiding memory latency. The instruction sets of several modern microprocessors have been modified to support a prefetch instruction. However, to take advantage of software controlled prefetching, one needs significant changes in compilers and libraries, and perhaps also application codes. As long as prefetch instructions are unavailable on the large majority of microprocessors, compiler writers and, a fortiori, application writers have limited incentives to change their code so as to take advantage of prefetching. As long as software and applications do not take advantage of prefetch instructions, such instructions add to hardware complexity but bring no benefit. Therefore, these instructions have been allowed, in one or more cases, to wither into a no-op implementation (i.e., the instructions have no effect), since that simplifies the microprocessor design and does not affect perceived performance. Software controlled prefetching did not catch on, because one could not coordinate multiple microprocessor designers and multiple compiler providers.

There are clear historical precedents for vertically integrated firms successfully introducing a new design (for instance, the introduction of the Cray), as well as many examples of such ambitions failing (which are amply documented in this report). In the present horizontal environment it is difficult for entrepreneurs with the ambition to effect radical changes to coordinate the changes across many areas of computing. Instead, today's supercomputing entrepreneurs tend to accept many component designs as given and try to improve in their own niche. Thus, a particular type of innovative design that might benefit supercomputing users does not get done. It is conceivable that the benefit of faster progress on each component technology (e.g., faster progress on commodity microprocessors) more than compensates for the lack of coordinated changes across a spectrum of technologies. However, it is also conceivable that supercomputing is stuck in a local optimum and is unable to move out of it because of the high costs and high risks and the small size of the market (and hence the small size of the reward even if a better global design point can be reached).

The biggest barrier to the evolution of a supercomputing ecosystem around a new computing platform is the effort and time required to develop the necessary software (for performance especially, but also for functionality). New software does not get used until it is refined to the point of actual productivity. (Fortran 90, for example, may not yet have reached that point. Some widely used applications still use Fortran 77, even though F90 compilers are widely available, because there are still vendors with significant market share whose F90 compilers produce significantly slower executables than their F77 compilers.) The generated code must be efficient for supercomputing applications; achieving that efficiency requires large investments and years of evolution as experience is gained.

If a new language is involved, the barrier is even higher. Adoption will be slow not only until there are reliable compilers that produce efficient code but also until that language is available on systems from a number of vendors. Until the new language is widely adopted there is little incentive for vendors to support it, thus creating a chicken-and-egg problem. This is another instance of the barriers introduced by standardized interfaces, this time the interface between application designers and the system on which they run their application. For example, while the limitations of MPI as a programming model are widely acknowledged, the ASC program leadership has expressed little enthusiasm for architectural improvements that would require forfeiting the use of MPI, because of the large existing investment in MPI codes and the likelihood that MPI will continue to be needed on many of the ASC platforms.

The barriers to acceptance extend to algorithms as well. Users are often justifiably wary about replacing a known and trusted, if suboptimal, algorithm with a new one. There need to be better quality vetting and communication mechanisms for users to discover and evaluate new algorithms.

Users resist migrating to a new system, either hardware or software, that may survive only a few years; most supercomputing application programs evolve and are used over decades. In other words, another barrier to be surmounted is the need to guarantee longevity. Computers with different architectures from sources new to supercomputing may not be successful in the marketplace and thus will no longer be available. This can be true even for new models from established vendors. The effort required to adapt most supercomputer application programs to new environments is substantial. Therefore, code developers are reluctant to invest the effort to migrate to different systems, even when they are likely to deliver a better than twofold increase in absolute performance or in cost/performance. Codes will run for decades, so developers are risk averse.

The effort required to port applications to new systems is a major barrier as well. Few supercomputer users can afford to halt their primary activity for months in order to move their application software to a new environment. They need to finish their papers or their Ph.D. dissertations or to produce a result for their mission within a fixed time frame. The cost to the end user of introducing new systems must be reduced. That is quite difficult to accomplish while preserving high performance.

Wider use of technologies for more automated code generation and tuning will also facilitate migration between ecosystems. A vision of the future is to develop supercomputing ecosystems that are broader and more general, so that they can support a variety of supercomputers with different characteristics. This would have the advantages of economy of scale, more years for system software and tools to mature, and a larger base of installations to pay for the continued enhancement of the software. Users of new supercomputers that fit into one of those ecosystems would also benefit by not having to learn everything new (although new machines will always have differences from previous generations of machines that affect their use and performance). Open source software that can be ported to a variety of systems might be able to engender those more general supercomputing ecosystems. In this scenario, many aspects of the operating system and tools could be made to improve monotonically over time, and much of the software could be reused in new machines. Parallel file systems are a case in point. Projects to develop them require specialized expertise and take years to complete. Open source attempts such as PFVS[4] and Lustre[5] to develop an open, fairly portable parallel file system may eventually reduce the effort required to provide a parallel file system for new platforms.

Similarly, one can envision strategies for application programs that would lower the barriers for new supercomputing ecosystems to evolve. An example is the relatively new type of application programs known as community codes. These programs address a particular class of applications such as chemical reactions (NWChem)[6] or climate modeling (CCSM).[7] Because community codes are implemented by large teams, often at different institutions and having complementary expertise, they are

---

[4]See <http://www.parl.clemson.edu/pvfs/>.
[5]See < http://www.lustre.org/>.
[6]See <http://www.emsl.pnl.gov/docs/nwchem/nwchem.html>.
[7]See <http://www.ccsm.ucar.edu/>.

carefully designed for modularity (so that better models and algorithms can be inserted with moderate effort) and portability (so that porting them to new systems is not too onerous). Their modularity promises to reduce the effort to migrate the code to different platforms, since relatively few modules may need to be redesigned to use different algorithms or reimplemented to exploit new hardware features. Designing and developing such programs is still a challenging research topic, but there are success stories (NWChem, CCSM, SIERRA,[8] PYRE,[9] and others).

A related approach is to develop higher level codes or parameterized codes that can run well on a broader range of platforms, codes that are programmed for performance portability. Such codes would adapt to the changes in hardware parameters that result from different exponents in the rate of change of different technologies, such as the much faster increase in processor speeds than in memory speeds. The ratios of hardware component speeds determine to a large extent the performance that is achieved. Automated library tuning and domain-specific code generators are discussed in Chapter 5. Although this is a good research topic, it is hard (it has been around for some time). We do not yet do a good enough job mapping higher-level programming languages onto one single-target platform; it is even more difficult to map them well onto a broad range of platforms.

ECOSYSTEM WORKFORCE

As has already been stated, one of a supercomputing ecosystem's most important investments is its investment in people. The technology is maintained, exploited, and enhanced by the collective know-how of a relatively small population of supercomputing professionals—from those who design and build the hardware and system software to those who develop the algorithms and write the applications programs. Their expertise is the product of years of experience. As supercomputing becomes a smaller fraction of research and development in information technology, there is a greater chance that those professionals will move out of supercomputing-related employment into more lucrative jobs. (For example, their systems skills could be reused at Google[10] and their applications/algorithms skills would be useful on Wall Street.) In companies such

---

[8]See <http://www.sandia.gov/ASCI/apps/SIERRA.html>.

[9]See <http://www.cacr.caltech.edu/projects/pyre/>.

[10]Google has been aggressively recruiting computer science graduates with advanced degrees and advertising openings at top conferences, such as the International Symposium on Computer Architectures, the top computer architecture conference.

as IBM, Hewlett-Packard, and Sun, which design and build not only supercomputers but also other commercial systems, people with unique skills could migrate to those other parts of the company in response to changes in company priorities or in pursuit of personal opportunities. If the funding stream of an academic or national laboratory's supercomputer center is unstable (e.g., NASA or NSF's Partnerships for Advanced Computational Infrastructure (PACI)), their professionals will seek greener, more stable pastures elsewhere, often outside supercomputing. As senior professionals move out of supercomputing, it becomes harder to maintain the knowledge and skill levels that come from years of experience.

At the other end of the people pipeline are the graduate students who will eventually become the next generation of senior supercomputing researchers and practitioners. According to the 2001-2002 Taulbee Survey of the Computing Research Association (the most recent survey available), a total of 849 Ph.D. degrees were awarded in 2002 by the 182 responding computer science and computer engineering departments, the lowest number since 1989. Of the 678 reporting a specialty area, only 35 were in scientific computing, the smallest total for any specialty area. (The next smallest group was 46, in programming languages/compilers, while the largest was 147, in artificial intelligence/robotics.) A review of research grants and publications in computer architecture shows a steady decrease in the number of grants and publications related to parallel architectures, leading to a decrease in the number of Ph.D. dissertations in computer architecture research that is relevant to HPC. For example, while NSF CISE funded about 80 grants a year in areas related to parallel processing in the mid-1990s, that number had shrunk to about 20 a year at the beginning of the 2000s.[11] During the same period, the number of papers containing terms such as "supercomputer," "parallel computing," "high-performance computing," and "parallel architecture" shrank by a factor of 2 or more.[12]

Of course, many of the new Ph.D.'s entering the supercomputing employment market receive degrees from departments other than computer science and computer engineering departments (for example, aerospace engineering, mechanical engineering, chemistry, physics, molecular biology, and applied mathematics), so the true number of new people entering the field is difficult to know. There are a handful of interdisciplinary graduate or certificate programs targeted specifically at educating the next-generation supercomputing professional, for example Princeton's

---

[11]Number of new grants matching the keyword "parallel" and funded by CISE.
[12]Based on a search of the INSPEC publication index.

Program in Integrative Information, Computer and Application Sciences (PICASso) (http://www.cs.princeton.edu/picasso) and the Computational Science and Engineering Program at the University of California, Santa Barbara (http://www.cse.ucsb.edu/index.html), both of which are funded, in part, by NSF IGERT's Computational Science and Engineering Graduate Option Program at the University of Illinois at Urbana-Champaign (http://www.cse.uiuc.edu/) and Pennsylvania State University's graduate minor in computational science and engineering (http://www.psu.edu/dept/ihpca). Such programs are typically open to interested graduate students from a wide range of science and engineering majors.[13] DOE's Computational Science Graduate Fellowship and High Performance Computer Science Fellowship programs support approximately 80 graduate students a year (http://www.krellinst.org/work/workhome.html). These programs promise to help increase the supply of new supercomputing professionals, although the committee believes that some faculty members, like faculty in other interdisciplinary fields, may have concerns about their career paths. (The academic value system often fails to reward "mere" code developers with tenure even if they are critical to a project and have made important computational or computer science advances.) Even with these programs, the supply of new people well educated in computational science is rather small and may be below the replacement rate for the current population.

To maintain knowledge and skills at the senior level, it is important to make sure that incentives are provided to keep the senior professionals in the field. The first step is to determine the key institutions (from academia, industry, and the national laboratories) that are the repositories of this institutional memory. Often the software is built by a team of academic researchers, national laboratory employees, and government agency staff. Next, strategies must be developed that provide these institutions with the mission and the stability necessary to retain supercomputing professionals. Also important is enough flexibility in the supercomputing ecosystem so that people can move within it as the money moves.

The key institutions in academia have been the NSF centers and partnerships (currently with leading-edge sites at Illinois, San Diego, and Pittsburgh and with partners at many universities) that together provide a national, high-end computational infrastructure for academic super-

---

[13]More information on computational science and engineering graduate programs can be found in SIAM's Working Group on CSE Education, at <http://epubs.siam.org/sam-bin/dbq/article/37974>. Information on the elements that make up computational science and engineering education can be found at <http://epubs.siam.org/sam-bin/dbq/article/40807>.

computing researchers and for advanced education in supercomputing. The PACI program evolved out of the NSF Supercomputing Program. Through these programs NSF has provided a reasonably stable funding base for academic supercomputing infrastructure (equipment and professionals) for over 15 years. The centers have brought together computer scientists, computational scientists, and scientists from a broad array of disciplines that use computer simulations, together with their research students, promoting fertile interdisciplinary interaction. However, NSF funding for the PACI program stayed flat despite major increases in NSF's budget. The PACI program ended in September 2004, and the form and level of future support are uncertain. A recent report from the NSF Advisory Panel on Cyberinfrastructure[14] makes numerous recommendations for ways to continue to provide supercomputing infrastructure for the academic community. For instance, the report says, "Subject to appropriate review, we anticipate that they [the PACIs] will play a continuing but evolving substantial role in the greatly enlarged activity we propose." However, funding for NSF's Cyberinfrastructure Program is pending. The leading-edge sites will receive some funding for the next 3 years, but no plans for technology refresh have been announced, and funding for the partners at other sites has been discontinued. Both the partnerships and the leading-edge sites are already in danger of losing key senior professionals.

Industrial institutions that have had the most success in keeping their professional employees are those that are specialized and physically located where there is little or no competition (for instance, Cray). Keeping their supercomputing professionals is easiest for those national laboratories and institutions (for instance, LANL or the Institute for Defense Analyses (IDA)) that have a long-term commitment to particular applications for which they have unique or near-unique responsibility—that is, those laboratories and institutions whose "mission" is protected. However, even in those organizations, uncertainties surrounding funding can cause professional employees to look elsewhere for perceived job security.

While it is important to keep senior professionals in the field, it is also important to continue to produce next-generation professionals. Funding models that encourage and support the education of the next generation, as well as those that provide the supercomputing infrastructure needed

---

[14]Daniel E. Atkins. 2003. *Revolutionizing Science and Engineering Through Cyberinfrastructure: Report of the National Science Foundation Blue-Ribbon Advisory Panel on Cyberinfrastructure.* January.

for their education, are necessary. It is also important that students preparing for a career in high-performance computing have confidence that attractive employment opportunities will continue to exist.

CONSUMER INSTITUTIONS

Consumers of supercomputers can be roughly divided into national laboratory and academic researchers and commercial users. Supercomputing "centers" have evolved for the use of national lab and academic researchers. These centers provide access to supercomputers and support (so-called cycle shops), or they can offer a fuller complement of services, including advancing the state of the art in supercomputing software and workforce infrastructure. Some (e.g., NCAR or the DOE weapons laboratories) are targeted at a single application domain; others (e.g., NSF's PACI and DOE's NERSC) serve multiple domains. Supercomputing exists in for-profit companies when it can give them a competitive advantage.[15]

Supercomputing Centers

Supercomputing centers provide a community of users, sometimes from the same organization and sometimes not, with shared access to one or more supercomputers. A center normally employs professional staff to help run the installation as well as to help users run and improve their application codes to best effect. Supercomputing centers are typically housed in special-purpose facilities that provide the needed physical plant, notably floor space, structural support, cooling, and power. They also provide working space for the operational staff. Thanks to the Internet, users normally need not be physically present.

The computing infrastructure provided by a center includes more than computing hardware. Typically, the users also share access to licensed or purchased software and, increasingly, to very large quantities of archival data. Thus a supercomputing center leverages its investment by gaining enough users to keep the system in constant use, by using the system well, and by sharing essential software, data, and expertise that facilitate the applications. Most centers also provide expertise on effective use of the supercomputers and software packages they support, through consulting and training services and occasionally by loaning programmers with relevant expertise to the application projects.

The primary organizations that provide supercomputing centers are government mission agencies such as the Department of Energy and the

---

[15]Cf. Chapter 4.

Department of Defense, and the National Science Foundation. Some centers are sponsored directly by universities; some are managed by companies. The main purpose of a mission agency center is to support the computing related to its mission. The users that support that mission sometimes come from outside the agency—for example, from academia or from companies that contract with the agency.

In most instances, a supercomputing center is part of a larger organization that includes researchers who use the computational facilities, computational science software developers, and education and training groups. Having local users provides continuing dialogue for improving the center's offerings and provides the justification for the host institution to house the facility. Having in-house software developers also facilitates better use of these systems.

The committee met with center directors from both NSF and DOE (see Appendix B). The center directors described a variety of difficulties they have had in planning supercomputing procurements, in ensuring that users can take full advantage of capability systems, and in balancing present-day needs against future demands.

- Centers are often under pressure to raise funds to cover both operating costs and technology refresh. Center directors find it difficult to do long-range planning in light of the year-to-year uncertainties that surround both capital and operating budgets.
- Centers are under pressure to use capability systems for capacity computing: (1) to respond to required measures of usage (such as having large numbers of jobs run and servicing large numbers of distinct users), (2) to satisfy influential users with noncapability needs, and (3) to make up for the lack of adequate capacity availability. Such use is increasingly hard to justify, in an era where capacity can be provisioned using cheap departmental clusters. Supercomputing centers have attempted to lessen the severity of this problem by developing software that facilitates the establishment and maintenance of departmental clusters. Suitably used grid computing infrastructure should further facilitate this shift.
- NSF centers in particular have experienced mission creep—they are expected to move into new areas such as very high capacity networking, grid computing, and so on without adequate additional funding or adequate consideration of the effect on their capability computing responsibilities. The expectations come both from users and from external program reviewers.
- Procurement is both very expensive and somewhat prolonged. Because of the time lags, it is speculative, in the sense that the delivered system may not meet expectations or requirements. (It is also expensive and difficult for the suppliers.) Procurement overheads cannot be amor-

tized over multiple platform acquisitions, and current processes do not facilitate the creation of long-term relationships with a vendor.

Industrial Supercomputing

In the context of this report, industrial supercomputing refers to the purchase and use of a supercomputer by a for-profit corporation. Supercomputers give commercial users capabilities similar to those that they give to defense and other government researchers. They enable scientists and engineers to study phenomena that are not readily observable such as the transient dynamics of semiconductor switching. Commercial supercomputers allow relatively inexpensive simulations to replace costly experiments, saving both time and money. An example is the crash testing of automobiles. Another driver for the commercial use of supercomputers is government regulations. Examples include the structural analysis of airplane frames, NO_x/SO_x analysis for combustion engines, and electromagnetic radiation for electronic devices.

Supercomputers can offer companies a competitive advantage by, for instance, enabling the discovery of new drugs or other technologies, resulting in lucrative intellectual property rights. Accurately modeling the yield of an oil field can impact lease prices by hundreds of millions of dollars. Engineering analysis can also allow reducing the cost of prototyping new products and reducing the time to market.

Many of today's commercial supercomputer applications were pioneered by scientists and engineers working on problems of great national importance. Over time, the technology they developed was transitioned to other uses (e.g., NASTRAN,[16] KIVA[17]). As Moore's law steadily reduced the cost and increased the performance of computers, a problem that was first only tractable as a critical national-scale problem then became approachable for a large corporation, then for an engineering department, and eventually for anyone with a desktop computer. This is not to suggest that industry no longer needs supercomputers. As pointed out in Chapter 4, industrial users not only are making more extensive use of high-performance computing than ever before, but they are also making more use of low-end supercomputers than ever before. Just as in defense and science, new problems arise that require increasingly higher fidelity and shorter turnaround times. John Hallquist, for one, contends that a 10^7 increase in

---

[16]See <http://www.mscsoftware.com/products/products_detail.cfm?PI=7>.

[17]See <http://www.eere.energy.gov/vehiclesandfuels/pdfs/success/model_of_comb_process_mar_2001.pdf>.

delivered computing power could be used for crash testing. However, it seems that the rate at which new codes are being developed or existing codes are being scaled up has slowed down. One way to help understand supercomputing use by the commercial sector is to partition it according to the application/industry sector. Another way is to partition it by market sector—consumer or capital equipment or government/defense industry. There are users in many fields who have applications that they would like to run on larger data sets, with less turnaround time. These users constitute the potential commercial market for supercomputers.

Figure 6.1 shows the relative share of the various sectors of the technical computing market in 1998-2003, the importance of the scientific research and classified defense sectors, the relative growth of new sectors such as biosciences, and the relative stability of sectors such as mechanical engineering. It also shows that no market is so large as to dominate all

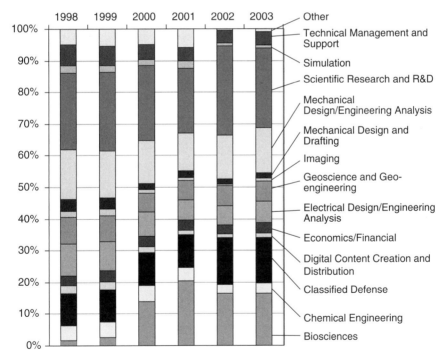

FIGURE 6.1 Revenue share of industry/applications segments, 1998-2003. SOURCE: Earl Joseph, Program Vice President, High-Performance Systems, IDC; e-mail exchanges, phone conversations, and in-person briefings from December 2003 to October 2004.

others. As a result, large computer manufacturers have to develop systems that perform well on a very broad range of problems. This maximizes the potential return on investment when developing a product but has the unfortunate effect of delivering suboptimal performance to the different end users.

Figures 6.2 and 6.3 show the evolution of the worldwide technical computing market from 1998 to 2003. They indicate that the overall size of the market is about $5 billion, with less than $1 billion being spent on capability systems. The market exhibits significant fluctuations; the capability segment has been moving 10 or 20 percent up or down almost every year. Supercomputing vendors are hampered both by the small size of the high-end market and by the large year-to-year variations. The charts also indicate the significant impact of public acquisitions on this market—over 50 percent of the HPC market is in the public sector, as is over 80 percent of the capability market. Public sector purchases are very volatile, with large changes from year to year.

Industrial use is changing, and for reasons of competitive advantage, that industrial use is often not revealed. In fact, the ability of small groups

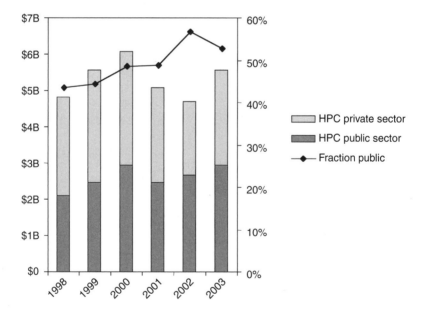

FIGURE 6.2 Worldwide HPC market. SOURCE: Earl Joseph, Program Vice President, High-Performance Systems, IDC; e-mail exchanges, phone conversations, and in-person briefings from December 2003 to October 2004.

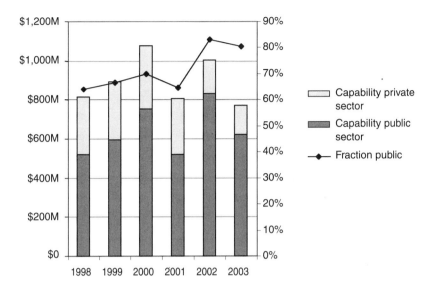

FIGURE 6.3 Worldwide capability markets. SOURCE: Earl Joseph, Program Vice President, High-Performance Systems, IDC; e-mail exchanges, phone conversations, and in-person briefings from December 2003 to October 2004.

to assemble PC clusters from existing office equipment means that today, managers of large commercial enterprises are often unaware of the supercomputers within their own companies. The overall decline in the technical computing market indicated by these charts may be due to this effect.

7

Supercomputing Abroad

T he committee devoted most of its attention to supercomputing in the United States. A subcommittee made a visit to Japan in March 2004, but there were no visits to other countries. However, most committee members have significant contact with supercomputing experts in other countries, and there is considerable literature about supercomputing activities abroad. A very useful source is a recent survey by the Organisation Associative du Parallelisme (ORAP)[1] in France. The committee drew on all those sources when it considered the state of supercomputing and its future abroad.

Supercomputing is an international endeavor and the research community is international. Many countries have significant supercomputing installations in support of science and engineering, and there is a significant exchange of people and technology. However, the United States clearly dominates the field. Of the TOP500 systems in June 2004, 255, or 51 percent, are installed in the United States, which also has 56 percent of the total compute power of the systems on that list. The next country, Japan, has 7 percent of the systems and 9 percent of the total compute power. As Figure 7.1 shows,[2] this situation has not changed significantly in the last

---

[1]ORAP. 2004. *Promouvoir le Calcul Haute Performance 1994-2004.*

[2]In contrast to the data presented in Chapter 3, Figure 3.7, which are based on manufacturer, the data in Figure 7.1 present the percent of worldwide supercomputing systems that are installed in a given country regardless of manufacturer. This figure was generated at the TOP500 Web site.

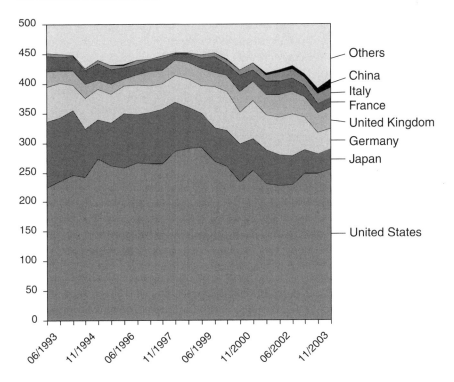

FIGURE 7.1 TOP500 by country.

decade: No particular trend emerges, except the progressive broadening of the "other" category, indicating the progressive democratization of supercomputing, attributable to the advent of relatively low cost commodity clusters.

The dominance is even more striking when one looks at manufacturers: 91 percent of the TOP500 systems are manufactured in the United States (see Figure 3.7). Many of the remaining systems use U.S.-manufactured commodity parts. The software stack of supercomputing systems used worldwide (operating systems, compilers, tools, libraries, application codes, etc.) was also largely developed in the United States, with significant contributions from researchers in other countries.

However, this is no reason for complacency. Since late 2001, the system that heads the TOP500 list has been the Earth Simulator (ES), installed in Japan. Even more important than being the most powerful system, the ES, because of its use of custom vector processors, achieves higher sustained performance on application codes of interest than many of the other top-performing machines. While the ES is likely to lose its top position on the TOP500 list soon,[3] it is likely to continue providing significantly better performance than competing systems on climate codes and the other applications it runs. (At present, the ES is 5 to 25 times faster than large U.S. systems on the various components of climate models used at NCAR.) IDC estimates that in the last few years, the North America, Europe, and the Asian-Pacific regions each purchased about one-third of the total dollar value of the capability systems sold. Another trend that has been much in evidence in recent years is the ability of many countries to build top-performing systems using commodity parts that are widely available. This reduces the usefulness of export restrictions and enables many countries to reduce their dependence on the United States and its allies for supercomputing technology. China is vigorously pursuing a policy of self-sufficiency in supercomputing.

Next, the committee presents highlights of supercomputing activities in various countries.

JAPAN

The committee found both similarities and differences in supercomputing in Japan and in the United States.[4]

Similarities

In many areas the issues and concerns about HPC are broadly similar in Japan and in the United States. HPC continues to be critical for many scientific and engineering pursuits. Many are common to the United States and Japan, for example, climate modeling, earthquake simulation, and biosystems. However, Japan does not have the kind of defense missions, such as stockpile stewardship, that have historically been drivers for U.S. supercomputing.

The HPC community is small in both countries relative to the science and engineering community overall and may not have achieved a critical mass—in both countries it is hard to attract top young researchers with the needed skills in simulation and high-performance computing. The

---

[3]On September 29, 2004, IBM announced that the Blue Gene/L system, which is being assembled for LLNL, had surpassed the performance of the Earth Simulator according to the standard Linpack benchmark. On October 26, 2004, Silicon Graphics announced that the Columbia system installed at NASA Ames had surpassed the Earth Simulator. As a result, it is expected that the Earth Simulator will lose the top spot on the November 2004 TOP500 list.

[4]The subcommittee participated in a 1-day joint NAE–Engineering Academy of Japan forum and visited six supercomputing sites in Japan (see Appendix B for a complete list of sites and participants).

committee had a lively technical exchange at the 1-day joint forum, where its members learned of several Japanese research projects with which they had not been familiar. More international collaboration on research would clearly be beneficial to both countries.

The commercial viability of traditional supercomputing architectures with vector processors and high-bandwidth memory subsystems is problematic. Commodity clusters are increasingly replacing such traditional systems and shrinking their market. It has become harder to identify attractive payoffs for investments in the development of vector architectures. The large investments needed to continue progress on custom HPC systems, as well as the opportunity costs, are increasingly difficult to justify. However, at least one large company in Japan (NEC) continues to be committed to traditional vector architectures.

Continuity is a problem in both countries. The ES project was officially proposed in 1996 and started in 1997,[5] at a time when Japan's economy and politics were different. In the current Japanese economic and political climate, it has become harder to allocate significant funds on a continuous basis for large, innovative projects in HPC. Similar pressures exist in the United States.

HPC usage is also constrained in both countries by the lack of suitable software and by the difficulty of using less expensive machines with lower memory bandwidth.

Differences

There were some notable differences between the United States and Japan. Traditional supercomputer architectures (vector, pseudo vector, etc.) play a larger role in Japan. Top NEC, Fujitsu, and Hitachi machines are still the mainstay of academic supercomputing centers and national laboratories. As a result, there is more reliance on vendor-provided software than on third-party or open source software, which is less available. However, the trend is toward increased use of clusters and open source software. Also, since Japan does not have a military rationale for HPC, it has to be justified on the basis of its ultimate economic and societal benefits for a civil society.

The Earth Simulator

The Earth Simulator was developed as a national project by three government agencies: the National Space Development Agency of Japan

---

[5]See <http://www.es.jamstec.go.jp/esc/eng/ES/birth.html>.

FIGURE 7.2 Earth Simulator Center. This figure is available at the Earth Simulator Web site, <http://www.es.jamstec.go.jp/esc/eng/ES/hardware.html>.

(NASDA), the Japan Atomic Energy Research Institute (JAERI), and the Japan Marine Science and Technology Center (JAMSTEC). The ES (see Figure 7.2) is housed in a specially designed facility, the Earth Simulator Center (approximately 50 m × 65 m × 17 m). The fabrication and installation of the ES at the Earth Simulator Center of JAMSTEC was completed at the end of February 2002. The ES is now managed by JAMSTEC, under the Ministry of Education, Culture, Sports, Science and Technology (MEXT).

The system consists of 640 processor nodes, connected by a 640 by 640 single-stage crossbar switch. Each node is a shared memory multiprocessor with eight vector processors, each with a peak performance of 8 Gflops. Thus, the total system has 5,120 vector processors and a peak performance of 40 Tflops. Most codes are written using MPI for global communication and OpenMP or microtasking for intranode parallelism. Some codes use HPF for global parallelism. As shown in Figure 7.3, the sustained performance achieved by application codes is impressive: The ES achieved 26.58 Tflops on a global atmospheric code; 14.9 Tflops on a three-dimensional fluid simulation code for fusion written in HPF; and 16.4 Tflops on a turbulence code.

The ES, with its focus on earth sciences, was one of the first mission-oriented projects of the Science and Technology Agency.[6] Although the

---

[6]MEXT took over the ES after the merger of the Ministry of Education and the Science and Technology Agency.

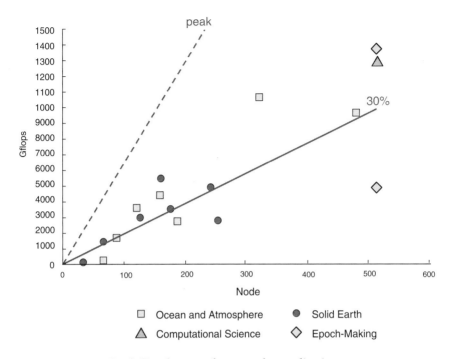

FIGURE 7.3 2002 Earth Simulator performance by application group.

U.S. NCAR is also mission-oriented for earth sciences, it is perceived that in the United States "mission-oriented" usually implies "national security." The ES also might turn out to be a singular event: MEXT officials with whom the committee met stated that as of March 2004 there were no plans to build topical supercomputing centers in support of Japanese priority science areas (biotechnology, nanotechnology, the environment, and IT), nor were there plans to build a second ES. Tetsuya Sato, Director-General of the Earth Simulator Center, has plans for another very powerful system and is trying to marshal the necessary support for it. Plans for research on technology for an ES successor with 25 times the performance of the ES were recently announced.[7]

The launch of the Earth Simulator created a substantial amount of concern in the United States that this country had lost its lead in high-

---

[7]According to an article in the August 27, 2004, issue of the newspaper *Nihon Keizai*, MEXT will request ¥2 billion (about $20 million) in FY 2005 to fund an industry-university-government collaboration on low-power CPU, optical interconnect, and operating system. Participants include NEC, Toshiba, and Hitachi.

performance computing. While there is certainly a loss of national pride because a supercomputer in the United States is not first on a list of the world's fastest supercomputers, it is important to understand the set of issues that surround that loss of first place. The development of the ES required a large investment (approximately $500 million, including the cost of a special facility to house the system) and a commitment over a long period of time. The United States made an even larger investment in HPC under the ASC program, but the money was not spent on a single platform. Other important differences are these:

- The ES was developed for basic research and is shared internationally, whereas the ASC program is driven by national defense and may be used only for domestic missions.
- A large part of the ES investment supported NEC's development of its SX-6 technology. The ASC program has made only modest investments in industrial R&D.
- ES uses custom vector processors; the ASC systems use commodity processors.
- The ES software technology largely comes from abroad, although it is often modified and enhanced in Japan. For example, a significant number of ES codes were developed using a Japanese-enhanced version of HPF. Virtually all software used in the ASC program has been developed in the United States.

Surprisingly, the Earth Simulator's number one ranking on the TOP500 list is not a matter of national pride in Japan. In fact, there is considerable resentment of the Earth Simulator in some sectors of the research community in Japan. Some Japanese researchers feel that the ES is too expensive and drains critical resources from other science and technology projects. Owing to the continued economic crisis in Japan and the large budget deficits, it is becoming more difficult to justify government projects of this kind.

Computing time on the Earth Simulator is allocated quite differently from the way it is done by NSF in the U.S. supercomputer centers. Most projects are sponsored by large consortia of scientists, who jointly decide which projects are of most interest to the science community. The director has a discretionary allocation of up to 20 percent that can be used, for example, to bring in new user communities such as industry or to support international users. Japanese private sector companies are permitted to use the resources of the government-funded supercomputer. (For example, auto manufacturers recently signed a memorandum of understanding for use of the ES.)

The machine cannot be accessed remotely, although that policy may change within Japan. Collaborators must be on site to run on the ES. They may not use the machine unless they can demonstrate on a small subsystem that their codes scale to achieve a significant fraction of peak performance. Because of the custom high-bandwidth processors used in ES and the user selection policy, the codes running on the ES achieve, on average, a sustained performance that is 30 percent of the peak. Thus the system is used to advantage as a capability machine, but at the political cost of alienating scientists who are unable to exploit that capability. There are several international collaborations being conducted at the ES, including a joint effort between NCAR and the Central Research Institute of the Electric Power Industry (CRIEPI), which involves porting and running the NCAR CCSM on the ES, and a joint research effort with scientists from the California Institute of Technology in earthquake simulation.[8]

Other Japanese Centers

Other large supercomputer installations in Japan are found in university supercomputer centers, in national laboratories, and in industry. In the June 2004 TOP500 list, Japan appears again in 7th place with a Fujitsu system at the Institute of Physical and Chemical Research (RIKEN); in 19th place with an Opteron cluster at the Grid Technology Research center at the National Institute of Advanced Industrial Science and Technology (AIST); in 22nd place with a Fujitsu system at the National Aerospace Laboratory (JAXA); and also further down the list. Japanese manufacturers are heavily represented. Commodity clusters are becoming more prevalent.

The university supercomputer centers were until recently directly funded by the government. Funding was very stable, and each center had a long-term relationship with a vendor. The centers have been managed mostly as "cycle-shops" (i.e., centers that do not advance the state of the art but, rather, maintain the status quo) in support of a research user community. For example, at the University of Tokyo center, the main applications are climate modeling and earthquake modeling. There appear to be less software development and less user support than the NSF centers provide in our country.

Since April 1, 2004, universities in Japan have been granted greater financial autonomy. Funds will be given to a university, which will decide how to spend the money. Universities are being encouraged to emulate the American model of seeking support from and fostering collabora-

---

[8]See <http://www.es.jamstec.go.jp/esc/images/journal200404/index.html> for more information on the Caltech research project at the ES.

tion with industry. This change could have a dramatic effect on existing university supercomputing centers because the government will no longer earmark money for the supercomputer centers.

There is widespread concern on the part of many in Japan regarding the quality of students. Both industry and government agencies (such as JAXA) expressed concern that students have no practical experience. Universities have been encouraged to provide more practical training and decrease the emphasis on academic study. JAXA has a comprehensive 2- to 3-year program to train graduate students before hiring them; a constraint to participation is that the students are not paid while training.

CHINA

China is making significant efforts to be self-sufficient in the area of high-performance computing. Its strategy is based on the use of commodity systems, enhanced with home-brewed technology, in an effort to reduce its dependence on technologies that may be embargoed. China had little or no representation on the TOP500 list until recently. It reached 51st place in June 2003, 14th in November 2003, and 10th in June 2004. The accumulated TOP500 performance has been growing by a factor of 3 every 6 months since June 2003. Today, China has a cumulative performance roughly equal to that of France, making it the fifth largest performer.

The top-listed Chinese system has a peak performance of 11 Tflops. It is a cluster of 2,560 Opteron multiprocessors (640 four-way nodes) connected by a Myrinet switch. The system was assembled and installed at the Shanghai Supercomputing Center by the Chinese Dawning company.[9] This company markets server and workstation technologies developed by the Chinese Academy of Science (CAS-ICT), the National Research Center for Intelligent Computing Systems (NCIC), and the National Research Center for High Performance Computers.

Another top-ranked system (in 26th place) is the DeepComp 6800, a 1,024-processor Itanium cluster with a Quadrics QsNet interconnect that is used by the CAS-ICT. The system was assembled by the Chinese Lenovo Group Limited.[10] CAS-ICT is the main shareholder of Lenovo, an important PC manufacturer.

China is also developing its own microprocessor technology: The Dragon Godson microprocessor is a low-power, MIPS-like chip; the God-

[9]See <http://www.dawning.com.cn>.
[10]See <http://www.legendgrp.com>.

son-II runs at 500 MHz and consumes 5 W. Dawning has announced plans to build clusters using this microprocessor.

EUROPE

Collectively, the European Union countries had 113 of the TOP500 systems as of June 2004; this amounts to 23 percent of the TOP500 listed systems and 19 percent of their total compute power. However, it is not clear that one should treat the European Union as a single entity. In the past, the European Union made significant coordinated investments in HPC research: The 1995-1998 Fourth EU Framework Program for Research and Technological Development[11] included €248 million for high-performance computing and networking (HPCN). However, HPC is not identified as a separate area in the Fifth or Sixth Framework Programs.[12] The thematic areas are life sciences, information technology, nanotechnology, aeronautics and space, food quality and safety, sustainable development, and citizens and governance. While some of the funding under these headings supports the use of supercomputing systems, it is quite clear that HPC is driven in Europe by national policies rather than EU initiatives.

United Kingdom

The United Kingdom is the largest European supercomputer user, with two large academic centers—the Edinburgh Parallel Computing Center (EPCC) and the CSAR consortium at Manchester. Recently, it announced a large e-science initiative with a total budget of £213 million. The budget funds a national center at Edinburgh, nine regional centers, and seven centers of excellence. The e-science vision promoted by this initiative is similar to the cyberinfrastructure vision promoted by the Atkins report;[13] it includes significant funding for supercomputers as part of a grid infrastructure.

Some U.K. users have recently moved from vector systems to commodity-based systems. The European Center for Medium-Range Weather Forecasts, which was a major Fujitsu user, now has an IBM Power 4-based

---

[11]The Fourth Framework Program is available online at <http://europa.eu.int/comm/research/fp4.html>.

[12]The Sixth Framework Program, the current program, is available online at <http://europa.eu.int/comm/research/fp6/pdf/how-to-participate_en.pdf>.

[13]Daniel E. Atkins. 2003. *Revolutionizing Science and Engineering Through Cyberinfrastructure: Report of the National Science Foundation Blue-Ribbon Advisory Panel on Cyberinfrastructure.* January.

system that was ranked 6th on the June 2004 TOP500 list. The center's operational forecasts are carried out in ensembles of up to 100 simultaneous runs, which require large computing capacity rather than capability. (NCAR in the United States has also moved to an IBM system, but unwillingly, as a result of the antidumping case against NEC; see Box 8.1.) On the other hand, many weather and climate centers, including the U.K. Meteorology Office and DKRZ, the German HPC Center for Climate and Earth System Research, prefer to use custom SX-6 systems with 120 and 192 processors, respectively. EPCC was a heavy Cray T3E user and now hosts the 18th place system (owned by the HPCx consortium); also, Power 4-based CSAR deploys large shared memory machines with Origin and Altix processors.

An interesting aspect of U.K. HPC is the use of long-term contracts for procurements. Both EPCC and CSAR have 6-year service contracts with their platform suppliers that include an initial platform delivery and a 3-year refresh. Plans are made to allow such contracts to be extensible for up to 10 years, with periodic hardware refresh; 2-year extensions can be granted subject to a "comprehensive and rigorous review."[14]

Germany

Germany has almost as many listed supercomputers as the United Kingdom. Many of the systems are hosted in regional centers that are locally funded by provincial authorities and by federal programs. There are three national centers: HLRS at Stuttgart, NIC at Jülich, and LRZ at Munich. The centers at Stuttgart and Munich host several large custom systems: a 48-processor NEC SX-6 at Stuttgart and a 1,344-processor Hitachi SR8000-F1 and a 52-processor Fujitsu VPP700/52 vector supercomputer at Munich.

France

France has fallen behind Germany and the United Kingdom in supercomputing. The largest French supercomputer is operated by the French Atomic Energy Commission (CEA-DAM) and is 28th on the TOP500 list. It supports the French equivalent of the ASC program and is similar to (but smaller than) the ASC-Q system at LANL. Unlike the DOE

---

[14]U.K. Engineering and Physical Sciences Research Council. 2004. *A Strategic Framework for High-End Computing*, May, <http://www.epsrc.ac.uk/Content/Publications/Other/AStrategicFrameworkForHighEndComputing.htm>.

centers, the French center is partly open and supports a collaboration with French industrial partners and other agencies (power, EDF; space, ONERA; engines, SNECMA; and turbines, TURBOMECA). France's next two largest systems are industrial and commercial (petroleum, Total-Fina ELF; and banking, Société Générale). France has two academic supercomputing centers: CINES (55 people, yearly budget of about €10 million) and IDRIS (44 people, yearly budget of about €1 million).

Spain

Spain recently announced its plan to build a 40-Tflops cluster system in Barcelona using IBM Power G5 technology. The Spanish government will invest €70 million in the National Centre for Supercomputing over 4 years. This will significantly enhance the compute power available in that country.

APPLICATION SOFTWARE

Generally, the type of research performed in these various centers is similar to the research performed in the United States; similar software is being used, and there is significant sharing of technology. However, both in Japan and in Europe there seem to be more targeted efforts to develop high-performance application software to support industry. Japan's Frontier Simulation Software Project for Industrial Science is a 5-year program to develop parallel software in support of industrial applications, funded at about $11 million per year. The expectation is that the program, once primed, will be able to support itself from revenues produced by commercial software use. In joint university/industry projects, it is anticipated that university-developed software will be available through open source licensing, although industry-developed software will probably be proprietary. Various European countries, in particular France, have significant programs with industrial participation for the development of engineering codes. For example, the French SALOME project aims at the development of a large open source framework for CAD and numeric simulation; currently available code is distributed and maintained by the French Open Cascade company. EDF, EADS (aerospace) and other French companies are partners in the project. DARPA invested in similar projects as part of the SCI program, but that support seems to have disappeared. Furthermore, from the committee's visits to DOE sites, members got the clear impression that there are no incentives for the transfer of codes developed at those sites to industrial use and no significant funding to facilitate the transfer.

8

A Policy Framework

In this chapter the committee discusses a policy framework for government activities in supercomputing. It does so in general terms, without going into the specifics of current or proposed policies. Concrete government policies in supercomputing in areas such as acquisitions, research funding, and support of industrial R&D are discussed in Chapter 9.

The federal government has been involved in the development and advancement of supercomputing since the advent of computers. Although the mechanisms and levels of support have varied over time, there has been a long-standing federal commitment to encourage technical progress and the diffusion of high-performance computing systems. (Key aspects of this history are summarized in Chapter 3.) Effective policy must be premised on a clear understanding of the rationale for intervention and an analysis of how intervention might be tailored to adapt to a changing economic and technological environment. In the absence of a compelling rationale for intervention, economists are generally reluctant to see government intervene in highly competitive markets, where the costs of disruption to well-functioning and efficient private sector allocation mechanisms are likely to be high. However, there are two broad and widely accepted rationales for government involvement in supercomputing: (1) the government is the primary customer and (2) supercomputing technology is beneficial to the country as a whole.

THE GOVERNMENT AS THE LEADING USER AND PURCHASER
OF SUPERCOMPUTER TECHNOLOGY

Much technological innovation is, at least initially, directed to applications dominated by government involvement and purchasing. Most notably, defense and national security needs have often been the specific setting in which new technologies—including supercomputing—were first developed and applied. Even when commercial firms are the locus of research and development for new technology, governments are often the largest single customer for the resulting innovations.

Government demand for advanced information technology—including supercomputers—is not static. Historically, government demand has been quite responsive to current technological capabilities. As technical progress over time relaxes a given set of constraints, key government supercomputer purchasers have not simply taken advantage of a fixed level of performance at a lower cost; instead they spur continuing technical progress by demanding ever higher levels of technical performance.

The use of supercomputing allows mission-oriented government agencies to achieve their objectives more effectively, with the consequence that the federal government has a strong interest in ensuring a healthy rate of technological progress within supercomputing. The U.S. government remains the single largest purchaser of supercomputers in the world, and most federal supercomputer procurement is justified by the requirements of missions like national security and climate modeling.

For example, the justification for the original ASCI program was to promote supercomputing technology not for its own sake but for the sake of ensuring confidence in the nuclear stockpile in the absence of nuclear testing. DOE tried to achieve this objective by two means: The aggressive procurement of supercomputers throughout the 1990s and funding of the PathForward development program, which attempted to accelerate technical progress in the types of supercomputers used by the ASCI program.

Other defense and national security agencies have also been aggressive users of supercomputing technology. (See Chapter 4 for a description of specific applications.) For example, the timely calculation of areas of enemy territory where enemy radars are not able to spot our airplanes (such calculations were performed during the first Gulf war) can be crucial.[1] Design and refurbishment of nuclear weapons depends critically on supercomputing calculations, as does the design of next-generation armament for the Army's Future Combat System.

---

[1]William R. Swart. 1991. Keynote address. SC1991, Albuquerque, N.M., November 20.

It is likely that supercomputing will be increasingly important to homeland security. Examples include micrometeorology analysis to combat biological terrorism and computer forensic analysis in the wake of terrorist bombings. The federal government must be able to guarantee that such systems do what they are intended to do. Moreover, these programs must ensure that, while supercomputers are available to U.S. security agencies with no hindrance and with capabilities that satisfy their needs, other countries can be prevented from achieving key capabilities in supercomputing. To achieve this balancing act, the relevant federal agencies and research laboratories must often be closely involved in critical aspects of supercomputing R&D, even when the research and development are carried out in the private sector.

As the social custodian of well-defined government missions and the largest and most aggressive customer for new technology related to these missions, the government has an incentive to ensure appropriate and effective funding for innovative supercomputing investments so as to guarantee that the technology progresses at a rate and in a direction that serve the missions.

SUPERCOMPUTER TECHNOLOGY INVESTMENTS AS PUBLIC GOODS

The public goods nature of supercomputer investment is a second broad rationale for government intervention. In contrast to purely private goods (such as hot dogs or pencils, which only one person owns and consumes), public goods are nonrival (many consumers can take advantage of the good without diminishing the ability of other consumers to enjoy it) and nonexcludable (suppliers cannot prevent some people from using the good while allowing others to do so). National defense is an important example of a public good. Even though the national defense protects one person, it can still protect others (nonrival), and the national defense cannot protect some people without also protecting others (nonexcludable).

When a market involves goods that are both nonrival and nonexcludable, innovators are unable to capture the full value of their inventions, so the incentive for an individual firm to undertake investment is less than the socially optimal level of incentive. In the absence of government intervention or coordinated action, the underinvestment problem tends to be most serious for basic research, fundamental scientific discoveries, technologies that serve as stepping-stones for follow-on research by others, and software.

Both policymakers and economists have emphasized the public goods rationale for government intervention in areas like supercomputing technology. In large part, and as discussed in more detail in Chapter 3 (and elsewhere), a number of technologies and innovations first implemented in supercomputers played an important role in shaping the architecture and performance of mainstream computers today (from workstations to personal computers). Moreover, initiatives funded in the context of supercomputers have influenced the ability to commercialize innovations, from workstation architecture to the latest Intel processor. Algorithms and codes initially developed for supercomputers in areas such as computational fluid dynamics, solid modeling, or signal processing are now broadly used by industry. As well, many of the most important applications of supercomputing technology, such as national security and climate modeling, are themselves public goods. Given these conditions, it is not surprising that both policymakers and economists have long justified investments in supercomputing technology on the basis of their status as public goods.

Several perceived shortcomings of the environment for supercomputing may reflect the public goods problem. For example, supercomputer users suffer from a lack of accessible and well-maintained software. Moreover, the development of better programming interfaces would greatly enhance productivity. While such initiatives would benefit all supercomputer users, no individual programmer or team has sufficient incentives to develop such complementary software and interface technologies. Similar to the more comprehensive approach to software development that is being attempted in recent projects such as the Earth System Modeling Framework at multiple institutions, overcoming these deficiencies requires either government intervention to provide direct support for the development of these technologies or a mechanism for coordinated action across groups involved in supercomputing technology.[2]

POTENTIAL COSTS OF GOVERNMENT INTERVENTION

Because the federal government is the main purchaser of supercomputing technology, and supercomputer hardware and software development is a public good, the federal government has played a leading and crucial role in the development and procurement of supercomputing technology. As discussed in Chapter 3, the federal government is not simply a passive consumer in these markets but has actively sought to influence

---

[2]Some people have also attempted to justify government intervention on the grounds of international competitiveness. According to this argument, government intervention can ensure that U.S. products are superior and thus benefit U.S. economy. Most economists reject this type of argument, and the committee found no reason to endorse it for supercomputing.

the rate and precise direction of technological change, with consequences for both the supercomputer market and the evolution of computing more generally.

It is important to emphasize that federal intervention in a technologically dynamic industry can be costly and disruptive, substantially limiting the efficiency and incentives provided by competitive markets. Many economists question the desirability of government involvement in the development and commercialization of new technology; government intervention can often be a far from benign influence on the market for new technologies.[3] First, attempts to promote standardization through procurement can result in inadequate diversity, reducing the degree of technological experimentation. Inadequate experimentation with a variety of new technologies can be particularly costly in areas like supercomputing, where much of the realized value of a given technology is only realized over time through user experience and learning. Second, individual firms and vendors supporting specific supercomputer architectures may attempt to exert political influence over the procurement process itself. When such rent seeking occurs, government purchasing decisions may be based on the political influence of a firm rather than on its ability to meet the needs of government agencies in terms of performance and cost.

Given that government intervention may come with substantial costs, it is important to consider the types of interventions that the government can undertake and some of the key trade-offs that policymakers might consider as they develop and implement policy towards supercomputing.

ALTERNATIVE MODES FOR GOVERNMENT INTERVENTION

Almost by definition, government intervention in the supercomputer industry influences the allocation of resources toward supercomputing technology. However, the government has wide latitude in choosing the form of its intervention, and each type of intervention has its own costs and benefits. In large part, the government's optimal choice of intervention and involvement depends on the balance between the specific mission-oriented objectives of individual agencies and the broader goal of encouraging technological progress in supercomputing (and information technology more generally).

The government has two main avenues for increasing innovation in

---

[3]Linda Cohen and Roger Noll. 1991. *The Technology Pork Barrel*. Washington, D.C.: Brookings Institution Press.

supercomputers. It can either provide incentives to the nongovernment sector or it can conduct the research itself.

Government Incentives

Government policy can provide broad encouragement to private industry to develop and commercialize supercomputing technology and affect the broader information technology marketplace. The government can influence the private sector by providing incentives for innovation and development investments, including grants or other subsidies, tax incentives, and intellectual property protection.

The government may subsidize private R&D activities. For example, a pervasive form of federal support for scientific and engineering research is grant and research contract programs, ranging from the peer-reviewed grant systems maintained by the National Science Foundation and other institutions to research contracts awarded by mission agencies such as DARPA. Such programs are particularly effective when the government would like to encourage basic research in specific areas but has limited information or knowledge about the precise nature of the outputs from research in that area. For example, grants and subsidies to the supercomputer center at the University of Illinois during the early 1990s were the principal form of support underlying the development of the Mosaic browser technology, an enormously beneficial innovation whose precise form, features, or impact could not have been forecast prior to its invention.[4]

Alternatively, R&D tax credits can provide important incentives for innovative investment. R&D tax credit programs provide direct incentives to private firms at a relatively low administrative burden.[5] How-

---

[4]A somewhat similar approach is for the government, a nonprofit organization, or even a private firm to offer a prize. This approach has been tried throughout history with mixed results. For example, in 1795, the French Directory offered a prize of 12,000 francs "to any Frenchman who could devise a method of ensuring fresh, wholesome food for his armies and navies." The prize was awarded by Napoleon Bonaparte to Nicholas Appret, who invented a method for preservation by sealing foods in airtight bottles and immersing them in boiling water for varying periods, which led to modern-day canning. Sobel provides an extremely rich description of the deficiencies and politics of government-sponsored prizes in his history of a prize for longitude at sea (David Sobel, 1995, *Longitude: The True Story of a Lone Genius Who Solved the Greatest Scientific Problem of His Time*, New York, N.Y.: Walker and Company). Recent examples of prizes range from the efforts by U.S. electrical companies to encourage research on a refrigerator that runs on 25 percent less electricity to the Ansari X Prize, which awarded $10 million to the first privately sponsored spacecraft to reach 100 km above Earth's surface (www.xprize.org).

[5]The costs and delays in grant review are often cited as the reason private firms are unwilling to apply for government subsidy programs.

ever, tax credit programs have often been criticized for subsidizing private research that would have taken place even in the absence of a tax credit program.[6] Moreover, it is difficult to use tax credits to specifically encourage research in specialized technical areas such as supercomputing. While tax credit programs are an appropriate tool to achieve broad R&D investment objectives, they are often too blunt to influence the precise direction of technical advance.

Finally, the patent system provides an indirect incentive system to encourage the development and commercialization of new supercomputing technology. Underinvestment in research and development will occur if others can copy a new idea or invention. A patent for a new invention gives the inventor monopoly rights to the invention for a fixed period of time, currently 20 years, so that the inventor can capture a relatively large proportion of the gains from innovation.[7] Unlike fixed subsidies, patents lead to distortions from monopoly pricing; however, a principal rationale for the patent system is that the short-run loss from high prices is (hopefully) more than compensated for by the enhanced incentives for innovative investment. Perhaps the chief benefit of the patent system is its inherent flexibility: Rather than having the government determine in advance the types of innovations and discoveries to be encouraged, the patent system provides a market-based incentive available across a wide range of technologies and industries. However, the influence of the patent system on innovation incentives is subtle, and there is an ongoing debate about its use, particularly in areas of science and technology that might also benefit from subsidies or other mechanisms.[8]

Each of these mechanisms provides incentives for innovation but

---

[6]B. Hall and J. van Reenen. 2000. "How Effective Are Fiscal Incentives for R&D? A New Review of the Evidence." *Research Policy* 29(4-5):449-469.

[7]An alternative method whereby firms can avoid the problem of underinvestment is for the firms in an industry to engage in research joint ventures, where they agree to share the cost of development as well as the benefits. However, firms may fear that such joint research activity may lead to antitrust prosecutions. The National Cooperative Research Act of 1984 tried to reduce firms' fears of antitrust penalties by lowering the damages a joint venture must pay if it is convicted of an antitrust violation. International joint ventures are increasingly common. For example, in 1992, Toshiba, IBM, and Siemens announced they would collaborate in developing advanced memory chips, and on the same day, Fujitsu and Advanced Micro Devices said they would jointly manufacture flash memories, which are used for data storage instead of disk drives. From April 1991 to July 1992, at least seven technology alliances to produce memory chips were formed between U.S. and Japanese firms.

[8]See, for example, Nancy Gallini and Suzanne Scotchmer, 2002, "Intellectual Property: When Is It the Best Incentive Mechanism?" *Innovation Policy and the Economy*, Adam B. Jaffe, Josh Lerner, and Scott Stern, eds., Cambridge, Mass.: MIT Press.

places few restrictions on the ultimate output of the R&D investment or the use made of the technology and discoveries resulting from that investment. As such, these mechanisms will be inadequate when the government would like to maintain close control over the precise development of a technology or keep a given technology secret. When the government has clear technical objectives and an interest in maintaining precise control, the government can staff and fund intramural research and even implement prototyping and development programs.

Government Research

Since the beginning of the computer era, national laboratories and other government agencies have conducted supercomputer research and, in some cases, been responsible for building individual machines. A key benefit of internal development is that the government can maintain extensive control over the evolution of the technology and, when needed, maintain a high level of secrecy for the technology. Maintaining such control may be important in those cases where the technology is being developed for very specific government missions within very narrow parameters and where secrecy and continued control over the technology is much more important than cost or the ability to build on a diverse set of already existing technologies. The degree of control and secrecy that are feasible even under internal development should not be overstated. Government employees can move to private industry (or even start their own companies), and as long as individual components or subsystems are being procured from the private sector, it is difficult to maintain complete secrecy over the technology choices and capabilities of large government projects.

Most important, large intramural technology development projects are likely to be extremely costly, relative to what could be achieved through procurement from the private sector. Indeed, while overall government science and technology expenditures are predominantly funded through grants and tax credits, a high share of supercomputer investment is implemented through procurement contracts with private firms. Under ideal conditions, procurement allows the government to acquire specific types of advanced technology while taking advantage of competition between firms on the basis of cost and performance. The government can indeed take advantage of these benefits when it is a relatively small player in an otherwise competitive market. For example, over the past two decades, the government has been able to take advantage of the rapid pace of technical advance and the high level of competition in the market for personal computers as it acquires desktop PCs for nearly all government functions.

However, reaping the benefits of competition through a procurement system is more challenging when the government is the principal (or even sole) demander and the development requires substantial sunk investments. In this case, procurement decisions themselves shape the degree of competition in the marketplace. For example, the government can choose to deal with one, two, or more firms in the market over time. By committing to one firm, the government may be able to encourage the firm to make large sunk investments to take advantage of economies of scale and also maintain a relatively high level of secrecy. A single vendor captures a larger share of the benefits from innovation and customizing the software to work well with the hardware than would two vendors. The single firm gains from economies of scale in producing more units. However, a single vendor will exercise market power, setting a price above marginal cost and hence reducing demand for its product. By dealing with several firms over time, the procurement environment will be more competitive, leading to greater technological diversity, greater technological experimentation, and less risk. The probability of discovering a superior technology may be greater if more independent groups are involved. Because the government buys or funds most supercomputer purchases, its approach to procurement largely determines the degree of competition in this industry.

When a single government agency such as a single branch of the Department of Defense has faced this type of procurement environment, it often uses a "committed supplier" approach. When procuring technologies such as those for advanced fighter aircraft, the government chooses to engage (and commit) to a few firms (sometimes as few as two or three) over a relatively long horizon. By so doing, the government gives each firm a relatively strong incentive to make large investments, while maintaining at least a degree of flexibility and competition over time.[9] At the broadest level, committing to several firms would probably be effective for supercomputing if there were a single coordinated approach to supercomputing procurement across the government. However, in contrast to the environment facing the Department of Defense, government procurement of supercomputing is dispersed across multiple government agencies and facilities, many of which are engaged in (at least tacit) competition with one another. Since technology changes rapidly, it is not possible to specify deliverables in detail beyond a short horizon. Therefore,

---

[9]For a review of the literature related to government sourcing, see W.N. Washington, 1997, "A Review of the Literature: Competition Versus Sole Source Procurements," *Acquisition Review Quarterly* 10:173-187.

contracts are short term. In the current institutional structure, any given agency cannot commit to a long-term relation with a vendor. Doing so would require an accord and coordinated procurement across agencies and a different procurement model.

Finally, it is important to emphasize that government policy can, by itself, substantially limit the degree of competition available for future procurement. For example, if the U.S. government contracts with only one company, it virtually guarantees that there will be a monopoly (or at least a dominant firm) in the U.S. supercomputer market. In addition, by enacting trade barriers (see Box 8.1), the government may benefit a small number of domestic firms at the expense of government agencies and other consumers of supercomputers in the future, who may have to bear much higher prices or make do with inferior equipment.

COMPETING GOVERNMENT OBJECTIVES

Overall, optimal government policy toward supercomputing must therefore balance competing objectives, including serving the requirements of mission-oriented agencies and encouraging technological progress more broadly. As a practical matter, these objectives are balanced through the procurement process, which is discussed in detail in Chapter 9. In managing the procurement process, the government faces three key trade-offs: coordination versus diversification, commitment versus flexibility, and secrecy versus spillovers.

Coordination Versus Diversification

Government agencies can coordinate or they can act independently, obtaining diverse individual solutions. By coordinating (e.g., buying the same equipment and using common software), the agencies benefit from economies of scale. However, individual agencies would not necessarily obtain the best solution for their individual needs. A central planner (supercomputer czar) would be more likely to obtain the benefits of coordination at the expense of not fully satisfying the diverse needs of individual agencies. On the other hand, if each individual agency makes independent decisions, it probably will forgo the benefits from coordination (local versus global maximization).

Commitment Versus Flexibility

The government may commit or maintain flexibility. For example, the government may commit to a particular vendor (a particular piece of hardware or software) or a particular approach (parallel versus vector machines) for a given period of time. By so doing, it would benefit from economies of scale and leverage investments by others. However, it would lose flexibility. If the government backs the "wrong horse," the rate of future advances might be slowed.

At least in part, the trade-off between commitment and flexibility reflects mandates to maintain a procurement process with high integrity. The government intentionally layers the procurement process with enormous amounts of auditing (and other legal constraints) in order to eliminate corruption. While such mandates serve the purpose of avoiding favoritism, they inevitably slow down the process of acquiring a new system, adopting frontier technology, and coordinating across different bidding processes.[10] They may also make it harder to weigh intangibles such as a good, continued relation between government and a vendor.

Secrecy Versus Spillovers

Because the government has many missions that depend on secrecy, such as code breaking and weapons development, it often sacrifices spillover benefits. A national defense agency may develop superior hardware or software that would benefit other government agencies or other users around the world by allowing them to avoid "reinventing the wheel." However, to maintain secrecy for reasons of national security, the government does not share these innovations. Obviously there are many cases where secrecy is paramount, but there may be many cases at the margin, where the cost of reducing secrecy (at least to the degree of allowing government agencies to share information) would be justified by the spillover benefits to others.

Secrecy also reduces spillovers in the reverse direction. If much of the research on certain forms of supercomputing is done in a classified environment, then one creates two distinct supercomputing research communities; an academic one that is open to foreigners and a classified one. The two communities have a limited ability to interact, thus reducing the inflow of people and research ideas from universities to classified supercomputing. Such a separation is more hurtful in areas where technology changes rapidly.

Overall, managing each of these trade-offs requires a detailed understanding of the specific needs and requirements of different agencies and institutions, as well as the environment and infrastructure in which

---

[10]See, for example, Steven Kelman, 1990, *Procurement and Public Management: The Fear of Discretion and the Quality of Government Performance*, Washington, D.C.: American Enterprise Institute Press; Shane Greenstein, 1993, "Procedural Rules and Procurement Regulations: Complexity Creates Trade-offs," *Journal of Law, Economics, and Organizations*, pp. 159-180.

supercomputing technology will be developed and deployed. It requires a clear understanding of the critical points of control. For example, there is no practical way to prevent foreign countries from assembling powerful clusters out of commodity components, but it is practical to restrict access to critical application codes.

BOX 8.1 Trade Policies

Several U.S. government policies affect international trade, such as antidumping laws, subsidies for sales in third markets, restrictions on imports (quotas or tariffs, if allowed under international agreements), and exports (export restrictions). Using these policies, the United States has effectively banned Japanese supercomputers from the U.S. supercomputer market. The events leading up to this ban follow.

As summarized in Chapter 3, Japanese firms started manufacturing high-performance vector machines in the early 1980s. By the late 1980s, using vector designs based on high-performance custom processor chips, these manufacturers posed a substantial competitive threat to U.S. producers. They benefited substantially from procurement by the Japanese government and the educational system and also received direct government subsidies for related research and development. It has also been alleged that large Japanese private customers that received substantial government funding were under pressure to buy Japanese supercomputers. The U.S. government pressured Japan to open its markets. In 1996, NEC developed the SX-4, a fast and relatively inexpensive CMOS-based vector supercomputer.

On May 17, 1996, the federally funded University Corporation for Atmospheric Research (UCAR) decided to lease a supercomputer made by a Japanese company, the first such decision by a public entity.[1] It awarded a $35 million, 5-year leasing contract for a supercomputer to the U.S.-based integrator company Federal Computer Corporation (FCC), which had outbid two other finalists for the contract—Fujitsu America, Inc., and Cray Research of Eagan, Minnesota—to supply a supercomputer to the National Center for Atmospheric Research (NCAR) for modeling weather and climate. The heart of FCC's proposal was four NEC SX-4 machines, to be provided by HNSX Supercomputing, the U.S.-based subsidiary of NEC. Within 2 months, a domestic firm, SGI/Cray Research, which had submitted a bid to UCAR, filed an antidumping complaint.

Continued

BOX 8.1 Continued

In 1997, the International Trade Administration (ITA) of the Department of Commerce determined in "Notice of Final Determination of Sales at Less Than Fair Value: Vector Supercomputers from Japan" (A-588-841) that vector supercomputers from Japan were being sold in the United States at less than fair value. In its determination,[2] the ITA concluded that dumping had occurred and calculated dumping margins using relatively indirect evidence:

Manufacturer/producer exporter	Margin percentage
Fujitsu Ltd.	173.08
NEC	454.00
All others	313.54

On September 26, 1997, a second U.S. agency, the International Trade Commission, made the dumping charge final with its determination that Cray Research had suffered material injury, even though NCAR argued that the hardware Cray proposed did not meet its minimum specifications.[3]

The punitive tariffs of between 173 percent and 454 percent on all supercomputers imported from Japan established a barrier so high that it effectively prevented imports and excluded Japanese supercomputers from the U.S. market.[4] NEC and Fujitsu were, however, able to sell many supercomputers outside the United States.

NEC filed suit with the Court of International Trade (CIT) seeking suspension of the antidumping investigation. The suit, which was unsuccessful, alleged that the U.S. actions were politically motivated and reported that, prior to its findings, the Department of Commerce had arranged five meetings between it and government agencies, meetings that were attended by high-ranking officials.[5]

On May 3, 2001, the Commerce Department revoked the duties on vector supercomputers made by NEC and Fujitsu Ltd., retroactive to October 1, 2000. Ironically, Cray requested this action as part of Cray's distribution and service agreement with NEC, whereby Cray became the exclusive distributor of NEC's vector supercomputers in North America and a nonexclusive distributor in the rest of the world other than certain accounts in France. However, it has not yet sold any NEC SX-6 machines in the United States.

This U.S. policy has had adverse effects on U.S. scientific computing. For example, as a consequence of the initial CIT action, NCAR was unable to upgrade its supercomputing capability for almost 2 years and suffered a serious delay in research.[6] In addition, because the NCAR climate codes were heavily oriented toward a vector architecture-based supercomputer, they could easily have been ported to the powerful NEC system. Subsequent reprogramming of the major climate models to allow them to run on commodity equipment caused additional delays during which very little science could be undertaken.

The new CRAY T-90 vector supercomputer was generally considered to be overpriced. Many of the U.S. supercomputer users that would have preferred a Japanese vector machine turned instead to commodity microprocessor-based clusters from various vendors. Applications such as those at NCAR, which require high machine capability and broad memory access, were hampered by the small caches and slow interconnects of the commodity products. After a number of years of optimization efforts, the efficiency of the NCAR applications taken as a whole is only 4.5 percent on a large system of the 32-processor IBM Power 4 nodes and 5.7 percent on a large system of the 4-processor IBM Power 3 nodes.[7] Only recently, and with substantial U.S. development funding, has Cray Research successfully developed the X-1, a vector supercomputer comparable in power to those produced in Japan.

Commodity-based systems are now increasingly used for weather simulations, since the problem has become one of capacity. Many independent simulations are carried in an ensemble study and each can now be performed on a relatively modest number of nodes, even on a commodity system. While efficiency is low, these systems seem to offer good cost/performance. However, custom systems are still needed for climate simulations, since climate studies require that a few scenarios be simulated over long time periods, and scientists prefer to study scenarios one at a time. Commodity systems cannot complete the computation of one scenario in a reasonable time. The same consideration applies to large fluid problems such as the long global ocean integrations with 10-km or finer horizontal grids that will be needed as part of climate simulations—such problems require the scalability and capability of large systems that can only be provided by hybrid or fully custom architectures.

---

[1]Christopher M. Dumler. 1997. "Anti-dumping Laws Trash Supercomputer Competition." Cato Institute Briefing Paper No. 32. October 14.

[2]Federal Register, vol. 62, no. 167, August 28, 1997:45636.

[3]See <http://www.scd.ucar.edu/info/itc.html>.

[4]See <http://www.computingjapan.com/magazine/issues/1997/jun97/0697indnews.html>.

[5]Ibid.

[6]Bill Buzbee, Director of the Scientific Computing Division at NCAR during that antidumping investigation, argued in 1998 that the decision gave a significant computational advantage to all Earth system modelers outside the United States and that it would still be 1 to 2 years before U.S. commodity-based supercomputers were powerful enough to carry out the NCAR research simulations that could be done on the NEC system in 1996 (National Research Council, 1998, Capacity of U.S. Climate Modeling to Support Climate Change Assessment Activities, Washington, D.C.: National Academy Press).

[7]The underlying hardware reasons for these numbers are discussed in an online presentation by Rich Loft of NCAR, available at <http://www.scd.ucar.edu/dir/CAS2K3/CAS2K3%20 Presentations/Mon/ loft.ppt>.

9

Stewardship and Funding of Supercomputing

C hapters 1 through 8 of this report described in some detail the current state of supercomputing and provided some context based on history, policy considerations, and institutions. The situation we find ourselves in at the present time can be summarized as follows:

- In the United States, the government is the primary user of super-computing (directly or indirectly). Supercomputing is used for many public goods, including national defense, pollution remediation, improved transportation, and improved health care. It is used for government-sponsored basic research in many areas of science and engineering. Although U.S. industry uses supercomputing as well, companies report that there are major inhibitors to greater use.[1]
- Many of the most computationally demanding applications have great societal benefit. Health care, defense, climate and earthquake modeling, clean air, and fuel efficiency are examples of public goods that are facilitated by the applications discussed earlier.
- U.S. leadership in supercomputing is essential. Supercomputing plays a major role in stockpile stewardship, in intelligence collection and analysis, and in many areas of national defense. For those applications, the government cannot rely on external sources of technology and expertise. More broadly, leadership in science and engineering is a national

---

[1]Earl Joseph, Christopher G. Williard, and Allison Snell. 2004. *Council on Competitiveness Study of U.S. Industrial HPC Users*. International Data Corporation. July.

priority.[2] Leadership in supercomputing is an important component of overall leadership in science and engineering.

• By its very nature, supercomputing has always been characterized by higher performance than mainstream computing. However, as the price of computing has dropped, the cost/performance gap between mainstream computers and top-priced supercomputers has increased. The computer market has grown most vigorously at the bottom end (cheap PCs and low-end servers). The share of that market devoted to supercomputing has diminished, and its importance in economic terms to hardware and software vendors has decreased. Even within supercomputing, the relative weight of the most challenging systems, those based on custom components, has decreased as an increasing number of supercomputer users are having their needs met by high-end commodity systems. Yet some essential needs can only be met by custom components. Consequently, market forces are less and less natural drivers of advances in supercomputing-specific technologies.

• Supercomputer systems are highly complex. Supercomputing is, almost exclusively, parallel computing, in which parallelism is available at all hardware and software levels of the system and in all dimensions of the system. The coordination and exploitation of those aspects of parallelism is challenging; achieving balance among the aspects is even more challenging.

• Ecosystem creation is both long term and expensive. The amalgam of expertise, technology, artifacts, and infrastructure that constitutes a supercomputing ecosystem is developed over a significant period of time. To get all the necessary components in place, a lot of effort is required. The nurturing of human talent, the invention of new ideas and approaches, and the use of those ideas and approaches in hardware and software artifacts all require significant investment. Given the lead time needed, and the fact that a given ecosystem has a bounded lifetime, investment in future ecosystems is needed to sustain leadership.

Given that leadership in supercomputing is essential to the government, that supercomputing is expensive, and that market forces alone will not drive progress in supercomputing-directed technologies, it is the role of the government to ensure that supercomputing appropriate to our needs is available both now and in the future. That entails both having the necessary activities in place in an ongoing fashion and providing the funding to support those activities.

---

[2]National Coordination Office for Information Technology Research and Development. 2004. *Federal Plan for High-End Computing: Report of the High-End Computing Revitalization Task Force (HECRTF).* May.

The government needs to be concerned with both the producers of supercomputing—the researchers who create new technology, the hardware and software designers, the manufacturers and service organizations—and the consumers of supercomputing—the academic, government, and industrial users.

SATISFYING CURRENT SUPERCOMPUTING NEEDS

Virtually every group consulted by the committee had concerns about access to supercomputing. Supercomputer center directors in academic settings and in both unclassified and classified mission-oriented centers were concerned about two things: (1) the large amount of time and effort required for procurement decisions and (2) the long time (up to 3 years) between the initial decision to acquire a new system and its actual installation. The recent report by the JASONs[3] noted the need for increased capacity computing for the DOE/NNSA Stockpile Stewardship Program. (As pointed out previously, users of capability computing are also users of capacity computing.) Demand for time on NSF supercomputing center resources greatly exceeds supply;[4] at the same time, the performance gap between those resources and the highest capability systems is increasing.[5] Academic access to DOE/DoD mission-oriented centers is limited by the priority assigned to the mission and, in some cases, by the constraints on access by noncitizens.

At the same time, many users complained about the difficulties in using supercomputer systems to full advantage, the problems caused by moving to a new system, and the absence of supercomputing systems of sufficiently high performance to solve their problems. Those communities able to draw on hero programmers worry that the supply of such individuals is too small.

Some of these immediate needs can be satisfied by additional funding. Capacity computing is a commodity that can be purchased. Additional staffing could help with migration to new systems—higher salaries might help increase the supply of such staff. However, the difficulties of using current systems and the absence of more powerful systems are not fixed so quickly.

---

[3]JASON Program Office. 2003. *Requirements for ASCI.* July.

[4]The National Resource Allocations Committee (NRAC) awards access to the computational resources in the NSF PACI program. Information is available at <http://www.npaci.edu/Allocations/ alloc_txt.html>.

[5]See TOP500 rankings.

ENSURING FUTURE SUPERCOMPUTING LEADERSHIP

The Need for Hardware and Software Producers

The need for the government to ensure that there are suppliers to meet national needs is not unique to supercomputing. The committee's earlier discussion suggests some possible modes of government intervention. In the case of supercomputing, the discussion of ecosystems has illustrated the interdependency of hardware, system software, and applications software. Nevertheless, different forms of intervention might be possible in different cases.

In the committee's view, it is necessary that there be multiple suppliers of both hardware and software. As it discussed previously, different applications (and different problems within those applications) have different computational needs. There is no single architecture or architectural family that will satisfy all needs. In the foreseeable future, some of the needed architectures will come from systems built from custom processors. Among the possible hardware suppliers are vertically integrated supercomputer vendors, such as Cray used to be,[6] vertically integrated supercomputer product lines within larger companies such as IBM or Hewlett-Packard, and systems created from products of horizontal vendors that produce components (e.g., commodity microprocessors from Intel, AMD, and Apple/IBM and switches from LAN vendors, Myricom or Quadrics).

Vertically integrated companies usually provide system software as well as hardware. However, the committee also believes it is possible to have nonprofit software organizations that develop and maintain community codes, software tools, or system software. These organizations might have a single physical location, or they might be geographically distributed. Their products might be open source, or they might have other licensing agreements. They would likely draw on contributions from the larger research and development community, much as Linux efforts do today. They might be broad in scope or more narrowly specialized. Historically, supercomputing software has also been supplied by ISVs. However, participants in many such companies say that there is no longer a successful profit-making business model, in part because highly skilled software professionals are so attractive to larger companies. For example, many companies that were developing compilers, libraries, and tools for high-performance computing went out of business, were bought, or no

---

[6]The recent development of the X1 was largely vertically integrated, but the development of other Cray products such as Red Storm is not.

longer focus on high-performance computing (e.g., KAI, PGI, Pallas, APR, and Parasoft). No new companies have entered this field to replace those that left.

In all of these possible modes of intervention, one thing is clear. Success in creating the suppliers depends on long-term, stable, predictable acquisitions and on the fruits of long-term, government-funded R&D.

The Need for Stability

The committee heard repeatedly from people with whom members spoke about the difficulties and the disincentives caused by the lack of long-term planning and the lack of stability in government programs. In order to undertake ambitious projects, retain highly skilled people, achieve challenging goals, and create and maintain complex ecosystems, organizations of all kinds need to be able to depend on predictable government commitments—both to programs and to ongoing funding for those programs.[7] If that stability is absent, companies will go out of business or move in other directions, researchers will shift to other topics, new professionals will specialize in other skills, corporate memory is lost, and progress on hard problems slows or stops. Once interruptions occur, it may be difficult and expensive, or even impossible, to recover from lost opportunities or discarded activities.[8]

Ongoing commitments are not entitlements; the government should demand accountability and performance. However, priorities and long-term objectives need to be sufficiently clear that when funded efforts are performing well, they have stability.

The committee heard of many areas where stability has been lost. Following are a few examples.

---

[7]For example, approximately 80 percent of Cray's sales in 2003 were to the U.S. government. Cray's revenue dropped from over $100 million in 2003 to less than $20 million in 2004 due to a drop in a defense appropriation and a delay in DOE's Oak Ridge National Laboratory project (see Lawrence Carrel, 2004, "Crunch Time at Cray," available online at <http://yahoo.smartmoney.com/onedaywonder/index.cfm?story=20040727>).

[8]The same issue has been studied for other long-term government procurements. For example, a RAND study examined in 1993 the costs and benefits of postponing submarine production; even though no new submarines were needed until 2006, the cost of the lost of expertise was believed to outweigh the savings from postponing production by 10 years (J.L. Birkler, J. Schank, Giles K. Smith, F.S. Timson, James R. Chiesa, Marc D. Goldberg, Michael G. Mattock, and Malcolm Mackinnon, 1994, "The U.S. Submarine Production Base: An Analysis of Cost, Schedule, and Risk for Selected Force Structures," RAND document MR-456-OSD; summary at <http://www.rand.org/publications/RB/RB7102/>).

- *Architecture.* DARPA built up an impressive body of national expertise in supercomputer architecture in the 1980s and 1990s, which was
then allowed to languish and atrophy. DOE sponsored the acquisition
and evaluation of experimental architectures in the 1980s, but such experimentation has largely disappeared.
- *Software.* NASA actively supported the development and maintenance of libraries, benchmarks, and applications software, but support for
many projects and organizations that would have continuing value has
disappeared.
- *Collaborations.* The NSF Grand Challenge program of the early
1990s produced some strong collaborative interdisciplinary teams that had
no follow-on program in which to continue. More recently, the NSF ITR
program has again led to the creation of successful collaborations, but
their expertise seems destined to be lost.

It is difficult to achieve stability in the face of local decisions that have
an unpredictable collective effect. Each of the inauspicious outcomes mentioned above has an explanation. Some outcomes stem from the turnover
of government personnel and concomitant shifts in budget priorities. Others come from the near-universal desire to start something new without,
however, waiting to extract the best aspects of the previous programs.
Still others ensue when agencies decide to stop sponsoring an important
activity without finding other sponsorship. The net effect is that U.S. leadership in supercomputing suffers.

The Need for a Continuum from Research to Production

As the discussion in Chapter 5 makes clear, research in supercomputing has to overcome many hard, fundamental problems in order for
supercomputing to continue to progress. The dislocations caused by increasing local and remote memory latencies will require fundamental
changes in supercomputer architecture; the challenge of running computations with many millions of independent operations will require fundamental changes in programming models; the size of the machines and the
potential increase in error rates will require new approaches to fault-tol-
erance; and the increased complexity of supercomputing platforms and
the increased complexity of supercomputing applications will require new
approaches to the process of mapping an application to a platform and
new paradigms for programming languages, compilers, run-time systems,
and operating systems. Restoring a vigorous, effective research program
is imperative to address these challenges.

Research and development in an area such as supercomputing requires the interactions of many organizations and many modes of activity

(see Box 9.1 and Figure 9.1). It also requires its own instrumentation. Research in applications requires stable production platforms. In contrast, research in technologies requires experimental platforms that are not used for production. While production platforms for applications research are in short supply today, experimental platforms are largely absent.

To ensure that there will be new technologies to form the basis for supercomputing in the 5- to 15-year time frame (a typical interval between

---

BOX 9.1 The Research-to-Production Continuum

Basic research is generally done in small projects where many different ideas can be explored. The research can be integrated with graduate education if conducted in academia, thus ensuring a steady supply of professionals. Experimental systems research and applied research projects can further validate ideas emerging from basic research and will often (but not always) involve larger groups, whether in academia or in national or corporate research laboratories. Before a fundamentally new design can become a product, it is often necessary to develop a large "vertical" prototype that integrates multiple technologies (e.g., new architecture, a new operating system, new compilers) and validates the design by showing the interplay of these technologies. Such a prototype can lead to a vertical product, where one vendor develops and provides much of the hardware and software stack of a system. However, part of the supercomputing market is served by horizontal vendors that provide one layer of the system stack for many different systems—for example, companies such Myricom or Etnus produce, respectively, switches and debuggers for many platforms. To the same extent, some large applied research or prototyping efforts are best organized horizontally—for example, an effort where a group develops a new library to be widely available on many supercomputer platforms. The technology developed by such a group may migrate to a horizontal vendor or be adapted and turned into a product for a specific platform by a vertical vendor.

The free dissemination of ideas and technologies is essential for this research enterprise to succeed, because a relatively small group of people have to ensure rapid progress of complex technologies that have complex interactions. The model is not a simple pipeline or funnel model, where many ideas flourish at the basic research level, to be downselected into a few prototypes and one or two winning products. Rather, it is a spiral evolution with complex interactions whereby projects inspire one another; whereby ideas can sometimes migrate quickly from basic research to products and may sometimes require multiple iterations of applied research; and whereby failures are as important as successes in motivating new basic research and new products.

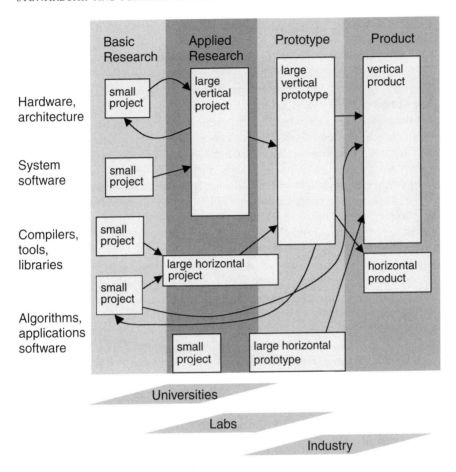

FIGURE 9.1 The research-to-production continuum.

research innovation and commercial deployment in the computer industry), a significant and continuous investment in basic research (hardware
architecture, software, and numerical methods) is required. Historically,
such an investment in basic research has returned large dividends in the
form of new technology. The need for basic research in supercomputing is
particularly acute. Although there has been basic research in general-purpose computing technologies with broad markets, and there has been significant expenditure in advanced development efforts such as the ASC
program and the TeraGrid, there has been relatively little investment in
basic research in supercomputing architecture and software over the past

decade, resulting in few innovations to be incorporated into today's supercomputer systems.

Our country has arrived at this point by a series of investment decisions. In the 1990s, HPCCI supported the development of several new computer systems. In retrospect, we did not recognize the critical importance of long-term, balanced investment in all of hardware, software, algorithms, and applications for achieving high performance on complex scientific applications. Instead, mission-oriented government agencies (including non-computer-science directorates of NSF) focused their investments on their mission applications and algorithms tailored for them rather than on broad-based improvements. This was noted in a 1999 PITAC report[9] and, more obliquely, in PITAC's review of the FY 2000 Information Technology for the 21st Century (IT[2]) budget initiative.[10] A recent report card on the PITAC implementation[11] listed "HPC software still not getting enough attention" as one of three top-level concerns.

Research in supercomputer architecture, systems software, programming models, algorithms, tools, mathematical methods, and so forth is not the same as research in using supercomputing to address challenging applications. Both kinds of research are important, but they require different kinds of expertise; they are, in general, done by different people, and it is a mistake to confuse them and to fail to support both.

Basic long-range research is the exploration of ideas. It is not the same as advanced development, although such development often ensues. Basic research projects should not be required to produce products or deliverables other than exposition, demonstration, and evaluation. A valuable benefit of basic research is that it can combine research and education—helping to create the next generation of supercomputing professionals. The benefits of that education outweigh the occasional delays in progress stemming from inexperience. An important attribute of well-run research projects is that they make room for serendipity. Many important discoveries arise from satisfying needs along the way to the main goal—an often-cited example is the NCSA Mosaic browser, which was an unintended consequence of NCSA's interest in Web access to scientific data. Performance tools are another example.

As the discussion in Chapter 5 made clear, supercomputing is headed

---

[9]President's Information Technology Advisory Committee (PITAC). 1999. *Information Technology Research: Investing in Our Future*. Report to the President. February. Available at <http://www.hpcc.gov/pitac/report/>.

[10]Available at <http://www.hpcc.gov/pitac/pitac_it2_review.pdf>.

[11]Ken Kennedy. 2004. "PITAC Recommendations: A Report Card." Presentation to the President's Information Technology Advisory Committee. June 17. Available at <http://www.hpcc.gov/pitac/meetings/2004/20040617/20040617_kennedy.pdf>.

for major problems as systems continue to scale up; it is not clear that incremental research will solve these problems. While incremental research has to be pursued so as to continue the flow of improvements in current platforms, there must also be room for outside-the-box thinking—that is, for projects that propose to solve the problems of supercomputing in an unorthodox manner.

An important stage in the transfer of research results to deployment and products is the creation and evaluation of prototypes. Not all basic research leads to prototypes, but prototypes are essential to migrating research results into practice. Prototyping provides an essential opportunity to explore the usefulness and the usability of approaches before committing to product development. For example, prototype systems serve to identify research issues associated with the integration of hardware and software and to address system-level problems such as system scalability and I/O performance in high-performance computing.

Ultimately, the purpose of the technology research is to facilitate the use of supercomputing. Prototyping is an appropriate stage at which to support technology and applications partnerships, in which applications researchers become early adopters of prototypes and evaluate them against their applications. Successful partnerships are those from which both the technology researchers and the applications researchers benefit—the technology researchers by getting feedback about the quality and utility of their results; the applications researchers by advancing their application solutions. As part of the transfer of research to production, prototyping activities should normally include industrial partners and partners from government national laboratories. The building of prototypes and hardening of software require the participation of professional staff—they cannot be done solely by researchers.

Prototypes may range from experimental research systems to more mature advanced development systems to early examples of potential products. Because both industry representatives and professional staff are involved, there is often considerable pressure for prototyping projects to yield products. That is not their purpose—the primary purpose is experience and evaluation. However, organizations sometimes find it difficult to take that view when there is strong pressure for short-term delivery of products or deliverables from users. Government investment to support prototyping is needed in all contributing sectors, including universities, national laboratories, and vendors.

Mechanisms are needed to create productive partnerships of this kind and to sustain them. Both the NSF Grand Challenge program and the NSF PACI program have stimulated such partnerships. The most successful partnerships are those organized around research problems, not around funding opportunities.

The Need for Money

Progress in supercomputing depends crucially on a sustained investment by the government in basic research, in prototype development, in procurement, and in ensuring the economic viability of suppliers. Erratic or insufficient funding stifles the flow of new ideas and cuts off technology transfer, inevitably increasing aggregate costs.

Basic research support requires a mix of small science projects and larger efforts that create significant experimental prototypes. Large numbers of small individual projects are often the best way of exploring new concepts. A smaller number of technology demonstration systems can draw on the successes of basic research in architecture, software, and applications concepts, demonstrate their interplay, and validate concepts ahead of their use in preproduction or production systems. These would typically be the sorts of projects centered at universities or research laboratories.

It is difficult to determine the U.S. government investment in supercomputing research at the present time, in terms of either money or the number of projects. The current Blue Book[12] has a category called High-End Computing Research and Development. (This annual publication is a supplement to the President's budget submitted to Congress that tracks coordinated IT research and development, including HPC, across the federal government.[13]) From the description of the programs in various agencies, one sees that the category includes efforts that are in development and research efforts, as well as research in topics outside the scope of this discussion (such as quantum computing or astronaut health monitoring). The recent HECRTF report[14] estimates 2004 funding for basic and applied research in high-end computing to be $42 million.

A search of the number of funded NSF projects with the word "parallel" in the title or abstract (admittedly an imperfect measure) shows that there were an average of 75 projects per year in the 1990s, but only 25 from 2000 to 2003.[15] The committee does not have numbers for other agencies, but its experience suggests that there were decreases at least as

---

[12]National Coordination Office for Information Technology Research and Development. 2004. *Advanced Foundations for American Innovation: Supplement to the President's Budget.* Available online at <http://www.hpcc.gov/pubs/blue04/>.

[13]An archive of these documents is at <http://www.hpcc.gov/pubs/bb.html>.

[14]NITRD High End Computing Revitalization Task Force (HECRTF). 2003. *Report of the Workshop on the Roadmap for the Revitalization of High-End Computing.* Daniel A. Reed, ed. June 16-20, Washington, D.C.

[15]These projects include some that entail only equipment or workshop sponsorship and a few that have nothing to do with supercomputing. On the other hand, there are undoubtedly supercomputing projects that have not been described using the word "parallel."

great at other agencies. Decreases in Ph.D. production and publication of supercomputing research papers are consistent with this falloff in support.

The committee estimates the necessary investment in these projects at approximately $140 million per year, with approximately 35 to 45 projects of 3- to 5-year duration initiated each year and funded at $300,000 to $600,000 per year and three or four technology demonstration projects averaging 5 years in length initiated each year, each at between $3 million and $5 million per year. Even the smaller projects need professional staff, which becomes more expensive as the number of staff members increases. The demonstration projects will likely involve larger, multidisciplinary teams and may require the manufacture of expensive hardware and the development of large, complex software systems. Both small and large projects will often require more expensive infrastructure and more extensive and expensive personnel than similar NSF-supported projects in computer science and computer engineering; the underlying platforms are large, complex, and expensive, and most of the difficult problems are at the integration level. The limited supercomputing industrial base precludes the industrial support—in particular, equipment donations—that often supplements federal research funding in other areas in computer science and computer engineering.

That estimate does not include support for applications research that uses supercomputing—it includes only support for research that directly enables advances in supercomputers themselves. Also, it does not include advanced development, testbeds, and prototyping activities that are closer to product creation (such as DARPA's HPCS program). The estimate is necessarily approximate but would bring us part of the way back to the level of effort in the 1990s. As one data point, to increase the number of Ph.D.'s to 50 a year would require approximately $15 million a year just for their direct support (assuming an average of $60,000 per year and 5 years per student), and that education would come only in the context of projects on which they worked. Not all projects are conducted in academia, and not all projects produce Ph.D. students in any given year.

Prototypes closer to production would normally be produced not by research groups but by companies and advanced development organizations (usually with research collaborators). The first two phases of the DARPA HPCS program are sponsoring activities of that kind, at a level of about $60 million per year. This level for the three projects seems reasonable.

By way of comparison, the Atkins report[16] (Chapter 6) proposes a

---

[16]Daniel E. Atkins. 2003. *Revolutionizing Science and Engineering Through Cyberinfrastructure: Report of the National Science Foundation Blue-Ribbon Advisory Panel on Cyberinfrastructure.* January.

yearly budget of $60 million for fundamental and applied research to advance cyberinfrastructure and a yearly budget of $100 million for "research into applications of information technology to advance science and engineering research." Taking into account the fact that cyberinfrastructure includes more than supercomputing and that the categories are different, the Atkins committee's estimate is similar to this committee's.

The sustained cost of providing a supply of production-quality software depends in part on the funding model that is assumed. The cost of a nonprofit software organization of the kind described earlier would be $10 million to $15 million per year, but such an organization would provide only a fraction of the needed software. A vertically integrated supercomputer vendor would provide some system software as part of the delivered system. The development cost for such a supplier is on the order of $70 million per year, some of which would come from the purchase of systems and some from direct investment in R&D.

These estimates do not include the cost of procuring capability supercomputers to satisfy government missions (except indirectly as customers of vendors). Assuming a cost of between $100 million and $150 million per procurement and six or seven procurements per year by organizations such as DOE (the National Nuclear Security Administration and the Office of Science), DoD (including NSA), NSF, NIH, NOAA, and NASA, the procurement cost for capability supercomputers would be approximately $800 million per year. This estimate does not include the cost of meeting capacity computing needs.

The Need for People

The report presented in Chapter 6 some results from the most recent Taulbee Survey, which showed that only 35 people earned Ph.D.'s in scientific computing in 2002. This is not an anomaly, as the chart in Figure 9.2 shows.[17] The average yearly number of Ph.D.'s awarded in scientific computing in the last 10 years was 36; on average, government laboratories hire only three of them a year. These numbers are extremely low.

While it is hard to collect accurate statistics, the same situation seems to hold for other areas of supercomputing. For example, few students study supercomputer architecture. Increased and stable research funding is needed not only to ensure a steady flow of new ideas into supercomputing but also, and perhaps more importantly, to ensure a steady flow of new people into supercomputing.

---

[17]Taulbee Survey data are available at <http://www.cra.org/statistics/>.

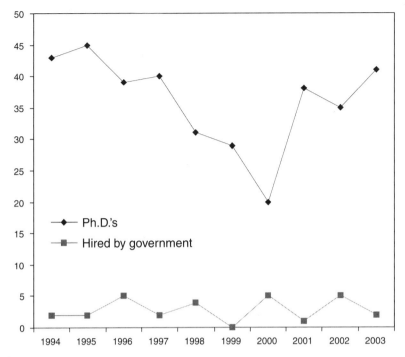

FIGURE 9.2 Number of Ph.D.'s in scientific computing and number hired by government laboratories.

The Need for Planning and Coordination

Given the long lead time that is needed to create an ecosystem, it seems obvious that planning for technological progress would be advisable. Given that there are commonalities in supercomputing systems used for many different purposes, it is equally obvious that coordination among government agencies, as well as within government agencies, would be a good thing. Not surprisingly, many previous studies have noted the benefits of planning and coordination and have made recommendations along those lines. There has also been legislation for that purpose. For instance, Finding 5 of the High-Performance Computing Act of 1991 stated as follows: "Several Federal agencies have ongoing high performance computing programs, but improved long-term interagency coordination, cooperation, and planning would enhance the effectiveness of these programs."[18] Among its provisions, the Act directed the President to "imple-

---

[18]The House-Senate compromise version of S. 272, the High-Performance Computing Act, passed the House on November 20, 1991, the Senate on November 22, 1991, and was signed by the President on December 9, 1991.

ment a National High-Performance Computing Program, which shall (A) establish the goals and priorities for Federal high-performance computing research, development, networking, and other activities; and (B) provide for interagency coordination of Federal high-performance computing research, development, networking, and other activities undertaken pursuant to the Program."

Yet the need for planning and coordination remains. The committee gave particular attention to two aspects of planning and coordination: What needs to be done? Who needs to take responsibility for it? A coordinated way to figure out what needs to be done would be to create and maintain a supercomputing roadmap. The issue of responsibility must satisfy the identified needs of hardware and software producers for stability over time, for a research-to-production continuum, and for the continuing allocation of adequate funding.

A Supercomputing Roadmap

Roadmaps are one kind of planning mechanism. A roadmap starts with a set of quantitative goals, such as the target time to solution for certain weapons simulations or the target cost per solution for certain climate simulations. It identifies the components required to achieve these goals, along with their quantitative properties, and describes how they will enable achievement of the final quantitative goals. For example, certain classes of technologies might enable certain processor and memory speeds. In order to evaluate progress, conduct rational short- and medium-term planning, and accommodate increasing scientific demands, the roadmap should specify not just a single performance goal (like petaflops) at a distant point in time but a sequence of intermediate milestones as well. The roadmap also identifies the activities (for instance, work on higher bandwidth networks or work on higher performance optimization tools) and the resources (such as widgets, money, or people) needed for each goal. A roadmap is periodically updated to reflect current progress and needs. The roadmap needs to be quantitative to allow rational investment decisions and instill confidence that the ultimate goal will be reached.

One well-known roadmap activity is that by the semiconductor industry,[19] which spends approximately $1 million per year on the effort.

---

[19]W.J. Spencer and T.E. Seidel. In press. "International Technology Roadmaps: The U.S. Semiconductor Experience." *Productivity and Cyclicality in Semiconductors: Trends, Implications, and Questions.* Dale W. Jorgenson and Charles W. Wessner, eds., Washington, D.C.: The National Academies Press.

Many recent supercomputing-related reports identify the need for roadmaps and attempt to provide them.[20] However, these reports only partially quantify their goals: They do not identify all the necessary components and almost universally do not quantitatively explain how the components will enable reaching the final goal. For this reason, they cannot yet be used for rational investment decisions.

In the case of the semiconductor industry roadmap, because the participants all share common economic goals and motivations, they are strongly motivated to cooperate. This is not the case in supercomputing, where the participants include (at least) the national security establishment, academic scientists, industrial users, and the computer industry. The computer industry's commercial goals of building cost-effective computers for popular commercial applications and the national security establishment's goal of weapons simulation may or may not be well aligned. The goals of climate modeling, weapons simulation, cryptography, and the like may all require somewhat different supercomputer systems for their attainment. But they will all share certain components, like scalable debuggers. So a supercomputing roadmap will necessarily be somewhat different from the semiconductor industry roadmap.

In particular, some components of the roadmap will be inputs from the computer industry, basically a set of different technology curves (such as for commercial processors and for custom interconnects) with associated performances and costs as functions of time. Other components will be application codes, along with benchmarks, performance models, and performance simulations that measure progress toward the final goals. Activities will include better software tools and algorithms, whose contribution is notoriously hard to quantify because of the difficulties of software engineering metrics and the unpredictability of algorithm breakthroughs but whose availability is nonetheless essential.

For each application, the roadmap will investigate a set of technological solutions (combinations of algorithms, hardware, and software) and for each one estimate as carefully as possible both the time to solution (or its reciprocal, speed) and the total cost of ownership. (These were both discussed in more detail in the section on metrics in Chapter 5.) Finally, given a utility function, which could be the cheapest solution that meets a certain hard deadline, or the maximum number of solutions per dollar, or whatever criteria are appropriate, it might be possible to choose the optimal technological solution.

---

[20]For example, the NITRD's HECRTF report, the ASC curves and barriers report ("ASCI Technology Prospectus," DOE/DP/ASC-ATP-001, July 2001), and NASA's Earth Science Enterprise report.

The above process is a typical rational industrial planning process. A unique feature of supercomputing that makes it difficult is the technical challenge of estimating the time to solution of a complicated problem on a future hardware and software platform that is only partially defined. Here are some possible outcomes of this roadmap process:

- Performance models will show that some applications scale on commodity-cluster technology curves to achieve their goals. For these applications, no special government intervention is needed.
- For other applications, it may be the case that the algorithms used in the application will not scale on commodity-cluster technology curves but that known alternative algorithms will scale. Supporting these applications may require investment in algorithms and software but not hardware.
- For yet other applications, commodity processors will be adequate, but only with custom interconnects. In this case, government investment in supercomputer interconnection network technology will be required, in addition to the investment in associated software and related costs.
- For some applications, only full-custom solutions will work. In this case long-term technology R&D and "submarine"-style procurement will be required.

It is likely that this roadmap process will identify certain common technologies that different applications can use, such as software tools, and it will be fortunate if this turns out to be so. Indeed, in order to leverage government investment, the roadmap process must be coordinated at the top in order to identify as many common solutions as possible.

Responsibility and Oversight

In response to the High-Performance Computing Act of 1991, the National Coordination Office for High Performance Computing and Communications (NCO/HPCC) was established in September 1992. (It has had several name changes subsequently.) That office has done an excellent job over the years of fostering information exchange among agencies, facilitating interagency working groups, and increasing human communication within the government concerning high-end computing. However, its role has been coordination, not long-range planning.

The High-Performance Computing Act of 1991 also directed the President to establish an advisory committee on high-performance computing. That committee, the President's Information Technology Advisory Committee (PITAC), which was not established until 1997 under a somewhat broader mandate, issued a report in February 1999, in which it recommended that a senior policy official be appointed and that a senior-level policy and coordination committee be established for strategic planning for information technology R&D.[21] Neither recommendation has been followed.

In May 2004, an interagency High End Computing Revitalization Task Force (HECRTF) report again recommended an interagency governance and management structure. The report suggests some forms that such a structure might take.[22] Legislation has been proposed to implement that recommendation.

The NSF is a primary sponsor of basic research in science and engineering and thus has the responsibility to support both the engineering research needed to drive progress in supercomputing as well as the infrastructure needs of those using supercomputing for their scientific research. However, a study of research grants in areas such as computer architecture shows a steady decrease in research focused on high-performance computing in the last decade: NSF has essentially ceased to support new HPC-motivated research in areas such as computer architecture or operating systems. In computational sciences, reduced NSF support for long-term basic research is not compensated for by an increase in DOE support through the SciDAC program, because the latter's 5-year project goals are relatively near term. The significant DARPA investment in the HPCS program has not extended to the support of basic research. There is at present a gap in basic research in key supercomputing technologies.

NSF supported supercomputing infrastructure through the PACI program, which ended in September 2004. There is some uncertainty about follow-on programs. Supercomputing infrastructure at NSF is the responsibility of the Division of Shared Cyberinfrastructure (SCI) within the Directorate for Computer and Information Science and Engineering (CISE); most of the users of this infrastructure are supported by other disciplinary directorates in NSF, or by NIH. The role of supercomputing in the larger cyberinfrastructure is not yet clear. This uncertainty continues to hurt supercomputing centers: It leads to a loss of talent as the more creative and entrepreneurial scientists move to areas that seem to offer more promising opportunities, and it leads to a conservative strategy of diversifying into many different directions and small projects to reduce risk,

---

[21]PITAC. 1999. *Report to the President: Information Technology Research: Investing in Our Future.* February.

[22]National Coordination Office for Information Technology Research and Development. 2004. *Federal Plan for High-End Computing: Report of the High-End Computing Revitalization Task Force (HECRTF).* May.

rather than placing a few large bets on projects that could have an important impact.

This chapter has focused on the tangible aspects of supercomputing and the actions needed to improve them. However, one should not neglect the intangible assets of the supercomputing enterprise. Supercomputing has attracted the brightest minds and drawn broad support because of the reality as well as the perception that it is a cutting-edge, world-changing endeavor. The reality has not changed. There are difficult fundamental computer science and engineering problems that need to be solved in order to continue pushing the performance of supercomputers at the current rate. Clearly, fundamental changes will be needed in the way supercomputers are built and programmed, to overcome these problems. Supercomputers are becoming essential to research in an ever-growing range of areas; they are solving fundamental scientific problems and are key to progress on an increasing range of societal issues. Computational science is becoming an increasingly challenging intellectual pursuit as the ad hoc use of numerical recipes is replaced by a deeper understanding of the relation between the physical world and its discrete representation. The reality is there, but, arguably, the perception has dimmed. As some uses of high-performance computing become easier and more common, it becomes easier to forget the incredibly difficult and immensely important challenges of supercomputing.

Initiatives to buttress the research on supercomputing technologies and the use of supercomputers in science and engineering should address the perception as well as the reality. It is important that research programs be perceived as addressing grand challenges: The grand engineering challenge of building systems of incredible complexity that are at the forefront of computer technology and the grand scientific challenges addressed by these supercomputers. It is also important that government agencies, supercomputing centers, and the broad supercomputing community do not neglect cultivating an image they may take too much for granted.

10

The Future of Supercomputing—
Conclusions and Recommendations

C hapters 1 through 9 describe a long and largely successful history of supercomputing, a present state of turmoil, and an uncertain future. In this chapter the committee summarizes what it has learned during this study and what it recommends be done.

CONCLUSIONS

Supercomputing has a proud history in the United States. Ever since the 1940s our nation has been a leader in supercomputing. Although early applications were primarily military ones, by the 1960s there was a growing supercomputer industry with many nonmilitary applications. The only serious competition for U.S. vendors has come from Japanese vendors. While Japan has enhanced vector-based supercomputing, culminating in the Earth Simulator, the United States has made major innovations in parallel supercomputing through the use of commodity components. Much of the software running on the Earth Simulator and on supercomputer platforms everywhere originates from research performed in the United States.

Conclusion: Since the inception of supercomputing, the United States has been a leader and an innovator in the field.

Ever since the 1960s, there have been differences between supercomputing and the broader, more mainstream computing market. One difference has been the higher performance demanded (and paid for) by supercomputer users. Another difference has been the emphasis of supercomputer users on the mathematical aspects of software and on the data structures and computations that are used in scientific simulations. However, there has always been interplay between advances in supercomputing (hardware and software) and advances in mainstream computing.

There has been enormous growth in the dissemination and use of computing in the United States and in the rest of the world since the 1940s. The growth in computing use overall has been significantly greater than the growth in the use of supercomputing. As computing power has increased, some former users of supercomputing have found that their needs are satisfied by computing systems closer to the mainstream.

Conclusion: Supercomputing has always been a specialized form at the cutting edge of computing. Its share of overall computing has decreased as computing has become ubiquitous.

Supercomputing has been of great importance throughout its history because it has been the enabler of important advances in crucial aspects of national defense, in scientific discovery, and in addressing problems of societal importance. At the present time, supercomputing is used to tackle challenging problems in stockpile stewardship, in defense intelligence, in climate prediction and earthquake modeling, in transportation, in manufacturing, in societal health and safety, and in virtually every area of basic science understanding. The role of supercomputing in all of these areas is becoming more important, and supercomputing is having an ever-greater influence on future progress. However, despite continuing increases in capability, supercomputer systems are still inadequate to meet the needs of these applications. Although it is hard to quantify in a precise manner the benefits of supercomputing, the committee believes that the returns on increased investments in supercomputing will greatly exceed the cost of these investments.

Conclusion: Supercomputing has played, and continues to play, an essential role in national security and in scientific discovery. The ability to address important scientific and engineering challenges depends on continued investments in supercomputing. Moreover, the increasing size and complexity of new applications will require the continued evolution of supercomputing for the foreseeable future.

Supercomputing benefits from many technologies and products developed for the broad computing market. Most of the TOP500 listed systems are clusters built of commodity processors. As commodity processors have increased in speed and decreased in price, clusters have benefited. There is no doubt that commodity-based supercomputing systems are cost effective in many applications, including some of the most demanding ones.

However, the design of commodity processors is driven by the needs of commercial data processing or personal computing; such processors are not optimized for scientific computing. The Linpack benchmark that is used to rank systems in the TOP500 list is representative of supercomputing applications that do not need high memory bandwidth (because caches work well) and do not need high global communication bandwidth. Such applications run well on commodity clusters. Many important applications need better local memory bandwidth and lower apparent latency (i.e., better latency hiding), as well as better global bandwidth and latency. Technologies for better bandwidth and latency exist. Better local memory bandwidth and latency are only available in custom processors. Better global bandwidth and latency are only available in custom interconnects with custom interfaces. The availability of local and global high bandwidth and low latency improves the performance of the many codes that leverage only a small fraction of the peak performance of commodity systems because of bottlenecks in access to local and remote memories. The availability of local and global high bandwidth can also simplify programming, because less programmer time needs to be spent in tuning memory access and communication patterns, and simpler programming models can be used. Furthermore, since memory access time is not scaling at the same rate as processor speed, more commodity cluster users will become handicapped by low effective memory bandwidth. Although increased performance must be weighed against increased cost, there are some applications that cannot achieve the needed turnaround time without custom technology.

> **Conclusion: Commodity clusters satisfy the needs of many supercomputer users. However, some important applications need the better main memory bandwidth and latency hiding that are available only in custom supercomputers; many need the better global bandwidth and latency interconnects that are available only in custom or hybrid supercomputers; and most would benefit from the simpler programming model that can be supported well on custom systems. The increasing gap between processor speed and communication latencies is likely to increase the fraction of supercomputing applications that achieve acceptable performance only on custom and hybrid supercomputers.**

Supercomputing systems consist not only of hardware but also of software. There are unmet needs in supercomputing software at all levels, from the operating system to the algorithms to the application-specific software. These unmet needs stem from both technical difficulties and difficulties in maintaining an adequate supply of people in the face of competing demands on software developers. Particularly severe needs are evident in software to promote productivity—that is, to speed the solution process by reducing programmer effort or by optimizing execution time. While many good algorithms exist for problems solved on supercomputers, needs remain for a number of reasons: (1) because the problems being attempted on supercomputers have difficulties that do not arise in those being attempted on smaller platforms, (2) because new modeling and analysis needs arise only after earlier supercomputer analyses point them out, and (3) because algorithms must be modified to exploit changing supercomputer hardware characteristics.

Conclusion: Advances in algorithms and in software technology at all levels are essential to further progress in solving applications problems using supercomputing.

Supercomputing software, algorithms, and hardware are closely bound. As architectures change, new software solutions are needed. If architectural choices are made without considering software and algorithms, the resulting system may be unsatisfactory. Because a supercomputing system is a kind of ecosystem, significant changes are both disruptive and expensive. Attention must therefore be paid to all aspects of the ecosystem and to their interactions when developing future generations of supercomputers.

Educated and skilled people are an important part of the supercomputing ecosystem. Supercomputing experts need a mix of specialized knowledge in the applications with which they work and in the various supercomputing technologies.

Conclusion: All aspects of a particular supercomputing ecosystem, be they hardware, software, algorithms, or people, must be strong if the ecosystem is to function effectively.

Computer suppliers are by nature economically opportunistic and move into areas of greatest demand and largest potential profit. Because of the high cost of creating a supercomputing ecosystem and the relatively small customer base, the supercomputing market is less profitable and riskier. Custom systems form a small and decreasing fraction of the supercomputer market and are used primarily for certain government applications. The commercial demand for such systems is not sufficient to support vendors of custom supercomputers or a broad range of commercial providers of software for high-performance science and engineering applications. As the commodity market has grown, and as the costs of developing commodity components have risen, government missions are less able to influence the design of commodity products (they might not succeed, for example, in having certain features included in instruction sets). Although spillovers from solutions to the technical problems facing supercomputing will eventually benefit the broader market, there is not sufficient short-term benefit to motivate commercial R&D.

The government has always been the primary consumer and funder of supercomputing. It has sponsored advances in supercomputing in order to ensure that its own needs are met. It is a customer both directly, through purchases for government organizations, and indirectly, through grants and contracts to organizations that in turn acquire supercomputers. Although supercomputing applications could be very important to industry in areas such as transportation, energy sources, and product design, industry is not funding the development of new supercomputer applications or the major scaling of current applications.

Conclusion: The supercomputing needs of the government will not be satisfied by systems developed to meet the demands of the broader commercial market. The government has the primary responsibility for creating and maintaining the supercomputing technology and suppliers that will meet its specialized needs.

The DoD has to assure the development and production of cutting-edge weapons systems such as aircraft and submarines, which are not developed or produced for the civilian market. To do this, it continuously undertakes to analyze which capabilities are needed in the defense industrial base, and it maintains these capabilities and has an ongoing long-term investment strategy to guarantee that there will always be suppliers to develop and produce these systems. Similarly, to ensure its access to specialized custom supercomputers that would not be produced without government involvement, DoD needs the same kind of analysis of capabilities and investment strategy. The strategy should aim at leveraging trends in the commercial computing marketplace as much as possible, but in the end, responsibility for an effective R&D and procurement strategy rests with the government agencies that need the custom supercomputers.

However, the analogy with aircraft and submarines breaks down in one essential aspect: Not only are custom supercomputers essential to our security, they can also accelerate many other research and engineering endeavors. The scientific and engineering discovery enabled by such supercomputers has broad societal and economic benefits, and government support of the R&D for these supercomputers may broaden their use by others outside the government. Broader use by industry is desirable and should be encouraged, because of the positive impact on U.S. competitiveness and the positive impact on supercomputing vendors.

Conclusion: Government must bear primary responsibility for maintaining the flow of resources that guarantees access to the custom systems it needs. While an appropriate strategy will leverage developments in the commercial computing marketplace, the government must routinely plan for developing what the commercial marketplace will not, and it must budget the necessary funds.

For a variety of reasons, the government has not always done a good job in its stewardship role. Predictability and continuity are important prerequisites for enhancing supercomputing performance for use in applications. Unstable government funding and a near-term planning focus can result in (and have resulted in) high transition costs, limiting the exploitation of supercomputing advances for many applications. Uneven and unpredictable acquisition patterns have meant fewer industrial suppliers of hardware and software, as companies have closed or moved into other areas of computing. Insufficient investment in long-term basic R&D and in research access to supercomputers has eroded opportunities to make major progress in the technical challenges facing supercomputing.

Conclusion: The government has lost opportunities for important advances in applications using supercomputing, in supercomputing technology, and in ensuring an adequate supply of supercomputing ecosystems in the future. Instability of long-term funding and uncertainty in policies have been the main contributors to this loss.

RECOMMENDATIONS

Taken together, the conclusions reached from this study lead to an overall recommendation:

Overall Recommendation: To meet the current and future needs of the United States, the government agencies that depend on supercomputing, together with the U.S. Congress, need to take primary responsibility for accelerating advances in supercomputing and ensuring that there are multiple strong domestic suppliers of both hardware and software.

The government is the primary user of supercomputing. Government-funded research is pushing the frontiers of knowledge and bringing important societal benefits. Advances in supercomputing must be accelerated to maintain U.S. military superiority, to achieve the goals of stockpile stewardship, and to maintain national security. Continued advances in supercomputing are also vital for a host of scientific advancements in biology, climate, economics, energy, material science, medicine, physics, and seismology. Because all of these are, directly or indirectly, the responsibility of the government, it must ensure that the supercomputing infrastructure adequately supports the nation's needs in coming years. These needs are distinct from those of the broader information technology industry because they involve platforms and technologies that are unlikely on their own to have a broad enough market any time soon to satisfy the needs of the government.

To facilitate the government's assumption of that responsibility, the committee makes eight recommendations.

Recommendation 1. To get the maximum leverage from the national effort, the government agencies that are the major users of supercomputing should be jointly responsible for the strength and continued evolution of the supercomputing infrastructure in the United States, from basic research to suppliers and deployed platforms. The Congress should provide adequate and sustained funding.

A small number of government agencies are the primary users of supercomputing, either directly, by themselves acquiring supercomputer hardware or software, or indirectly, by awarding contracts and grants to other organizations that purchase supercomputers. These agencies are also the major funders of supercomputing research. At present, those agencies include the Department of Energy (DOE), including its National Nuclear Security Administration and its Office of Science; the Department of Defense (DoD), including its National Security Agency (NSA); the National Aeronautics and Space Administration (NASA); the National Oceanic and Atmospheric Administration (NOAA); and the National Science Foundation (NSF). (The increasing use of supercomputing in biomedical applications suggests that NIH should be added to the list.) Although the agencies have different missions and different needs, they benefit from the synergies of coordinated planning and acquisition strategies and coordinated support for R&D. In short, they need to be part of the supercomputing ecosystem. For instance, many of the technologies, in particular the software, need to be broadly available across all platforms. If the agencies are not jointly responsible and jointly accountable, the resources spent on supercomputing technologies are likely to be wasted as efforts are duplicated in some areas and underfunded in others.

Achieving collaborative and coordinated government support for supercomputing is a challenge that many previous studies have addressed without effecting much improvement in day-to-day practice. What is needed is an integrated plan rather than the coordination of distinct supercomputing plans through a diffuse interagency coordination structure. Such integration across agencies has not been achieved in the past, and interagency coordination mechanisms have served mostly to communicate independently planned activities. A possible explanation is that although each agency needs to obtain supercomputing for its own purposes, no agency has the responsibility to ensure that the necessary technology will be available to be acquired.

Today, much of the coordination happens relatively late in the planning process and reflects decisions rather than goals. In order for the agencies to meet their own mission responsibilities and also take full advantage of the investments made by other agencies, collaboration and coordination must become much more long range. To make that happen, the appropriate incentives must be in place—collaboration and coordination must be based on an alignment of interests, not just on a threat of vetoes from higher-level management.

One way to facilitate that process is for the agencies with a need for supercomputing to create and maintain a joint 5- or 10-year written plan for high-end computing (HEC) based on both the roadmap that is the subject of Recommendation 5 and the needs of the participating agencies. That HEC plan, which would be revised annually, would be increasingly specific with respect to development and procurement as the time remaining to achieve particular goals decreased. Included in the plan would be a clear delineation of which agency or agencies would be responsible for contracting and overseeing a large procurement, such as a custom supercomputer system or a major hardware or software component of such a system. The plan would also include cost estimates for elements of the plan, but it would not be an overall budget. For example, planning for the development and acquisition of what the HECRTF report calls "leadership systems" would be part of this overall HEC plan, but the decisions about what to fund would not be made by the planners. Each new version of the plan would be critically reviewed by a panel of outside experts and updated in response to that review.

Appropriate congressional committees in the House and Senate would have the funding and oversight responsibility to ensure that the HEC plan meets the long-term needs of the nation. Both the House and Senate authorization and appropriation subcommittees and the Office of Management and Budget would require (1) that every budget request concerning supercomputing describe how the request is aligned with the HEC plan and (2) that an agency budget request does not omit a supercomputing investment (for which it has responsibility according to the HEC plan) on which other agencies depend. Similarly, House and Senate appropriation committees would ensure (1) that budgets passed into law are consistent with the HEC plan and (2) that any negotiated budget reductions do not adversely affect other investments dependent on them. Consistency does not imply that every part of every request would be in the plan. Mission agencies sometimes face short-term needs to meet short-term deliverables that cannot be anticipated. New disruptive technologies sometimes provide unanticipated opportunities. However, revisions to the plan would be responsive to those needs and opportunities.

The use of an HEC plan would not preclude agencies from individual activities, nor would it prevent them from setting their own priorities. Rather, the intent is to identify common needs at an early stage and to leverage shared efforts to meet those needs, while minimizing duplicative efforts. For example,

- Research and development in supercomputing will continue to be the responsibility of the agencies that fund research and also use supercomputing, notably NSF, DOE (the National Nuclear Security Administration and the Office of Science), DoD, NSA, NASA, NOAA, and NIH. A subset of these agencies, working in loose coordination, will focus on long-term basic research in supercomputing technologies. Another subset of these agencies, working in tighter coordination, will be heavily involved in industrial supercomputing R&D.
- Each agency will continue to be responsible for the development of the domain-specific technologies, in particular domain-specific applications software, that satisfy its needs.
- The acquisition of supercomputing platforms will be budgeted for by each agency according to its needs. Joint planning and coordination of acquisitions will increase the efficiency of the procurement processes from the government viewpoint and will decrease variability and uncertainty from the vendor viewpoint. In particular, procurement overheads and delays can be reduced with multiagency acquisition plans whereby once a company wins a procurement bid issued by one agency, other agencies can buy versions of the winning system.
- Tighter integration in the funding of applied research and development in supercomputing will ease the burden on application developers and will enhance the viability of domestic suppliers.

Until such a structure is in place, the agencies whose missions rely on supercomputing must take responsibility for the future availability of leading supercomputing capabilities. That responsibility extends to the basic research on which future supercomputing depends. These agencies should cooperate as much as they can—leveraging one another's efforts is always advantageous—but they must move ahead whether or not a formal long-term planning and coordination framework exists. More specifically, it continues to be the responsibility of the NSF, DoD, and DOE, as the primary sponsors of basic research in science and engineering, to support both the research needed to drive progress in supercomputing and the infrastructure needs of those using supercomputing for their research. Similarly, it is the responsibility of those agencies whose mission is the safety and security of the nation or the health and well-being of its citizens to plan for future supercomputing needs essential to their missions, as well as to provide for present-day supercomputing needs.

Recommendation 2. The government agencies that are the primary users of supercomputing should ensure domestic leadership in those technologies that are essential to meet national needs.

Some critical government needs justify a premium for faster and more powerful computation that most or all civilian markets cannot justify commercially. Many of these critical needs involve national security. Because the United States may want to be able to restrict foreign access to some supercomputing technology, it will want to create these technologies here at home. Even if there is no need for such restrictions, the United States will still need to produce these technologies domestically, simply because it is unlikely that other countries will do so given the lack of commercial markets for many of these technologies. U.S. leadership in unique supercomputing technologies, such as custom architectures, is endangered by inadequate funding, inadequate long-term plans, and the lack of coordination among the agencies that are the major funders of supercomputing R&D. Those agencies should ensure that our country has the supercomputers it needs to satisfy critical requirements in areas such as cryptography and nuclear weapon stewardship as well as for systems that will provide the breakthrough capabilities that bring broad scientific and technological progress for a strong and robust U.S. economy.

The main concern of the committee is not that the United States is being overtaken by other countries, such as Japan, in supercomputing. Rather, it is that current investments and current plans are not sufficient to provide the future supercomputing capabilities that our country will need. That the first-place computer in the June 2004 TOP500 list was located in Japan is not viewed by this committee as a compelling indication of loss of leadership in technological capability. U.S. security is not necessarily endangered if a computer in a foreign country is capable of doing some computations faster than U.S.-based computers. The committee believes that had our country made an investment similar to Japan's at the same time, it could have created a powerful and equally capable system. The committee's concern is that the United States has not been making the investments that will guarantee its ability to create such a system in the future.

Leadership is measured by a broad technological capability to acquire and exploit effectively machines that can best reduce the time to solution of important computational problems. From this perspective, it is not the

Earth Simulator system that is worrisome but rather the fact that its construction was such a singular event. It seems that without significant government support, custom high-bandwidth processors are not viable products. Two of the three Japanese companies that were manufacturing such processors do not do so anymore, and the third (NEC) may also bow to market realities in a not too distant future—since the Japanese government seems less willing now to subsidize the development of leading supercomputing technologies. The software technology of the Earth Simulator is at least a decade old. The same market realities prevail here at home. No fundamentally new high-bandwidth architecture has emerged as a product in the last few years in either Japan or the United States. No significant progress has occurred in commercially available supercomputing software for more than a decade. No investment that would match the time scale and magnitude of the Japanese investment in the Earth Simulator has been made in the United States.

The agencies responsible for supercomputing can ensure that key supercomputing technologies, such as custom high-bandwidth processors, will be available to satisfy their needs only by maintaining our nation's world leadership in these technologies. Recommendations 3 through 8 outline some of the actions that need to be taken by these agencies to maintain this leadership.

Recommendation 3. To satisfy its need for unique supercomputing technologies such as high-bandwidth systems, the government needs to ensure the viability of multiple domestic suppliers.

The U.S. industrial base must include suppliers on whom the government can rely to build custom systems to solve problems that are unique to the government role. Since only a few units of such systems are ever needed, there is no broad market for them and hence no commercial, off-the-shelf suppliers. Domestic supercomputing vendors are a source of both the components and the engineering talent necessary to construct low-volume systems for the government.

To ensure their continuing existence, the domestic suppliers must be able to sustain a viable business model. For a public company, that means having predictable and steady revenue recognizable by the financial market. A company cannot continue to provide cutting-edge products without R&D. At least two models of support have been used successfully: (1) an implicit guarantee of a steady purchase of supercomputing systems, giving the companies a steady income stream with which to fund ongoing R&D and (2) explicit funding for a company's R&D. Stability is a key issue. Suppliers of such systems or components often are small companies that can easily lose viability; uncertainty can mean the loss of skilled personnel to other sectors of the larger computing industry or the loss of investors. Historically, government priorities and technical directions have changed more frequently than would be justified by technology lifetimes, creating market instabilities. The chosen funding model must ensure stability. The agencies responsible for supercomputing might consider the model proposed by the British UKHEC initiative, whereby government solicits and funds proposals for the procurement of three successive generations of a supercomputer family over 4 to 6 years.

It is important to have multiple suppliers for any key technology, in order to maintain competition, to prevent technical stagnation, to provide diverse supercomputing ecosystems to address diverse needs, and to reduce risk. (The recent near-death experience of Cray in the 1990s is a good example of such risk.) On the other hand, it is unrealistic to expect that such narrow markets will attract a large number of vendors. As happens for many military technologies, one may typically end up with only a few suppliers. The risk of stagnation is mitigated by the continued pressure coming from commodity supercomputer suppliers.

The most important unique supercomputing technology identified in this report is high-bandwidth, custom supercomputing systems. The vector systems developed by Cray have been the leading example of this technology. Cray is now the only domestic manufacturer of such systems. The R&D cost to Cray for a new product has been estimated by IDC to be close to $200 million; assuming a 3-year development cycle, this results in an annual R&D cost of about $70 million, or about $140 million per year for two vendors. Note that Cray has traditionally been a vertically integrated company that develops and markets a product stack that goes from chips and packaging to system software, compilers, and libraries. However, Cray seems to be becoming less integrated, and other suppliers of high-bandwidth systems may choose to be less integrated, resulting in a different distribution of R&D costs among suppliers. Other suppliers may also choose high-bandwidth architectures that are not vector.

Another unique supercomputing technology identified in this report is that of custom switches and custom, memory-connected switch interfaces. Companies such as Cray, IBM, and SGI have developed such technologies and have used them exclusively for their own products—the Cray Red Storm interconnect is a recent example. Myricom (a U.S. company) and Quadrics (a European company) develop scalable, high-bandwidth, low-latency interconnects for clusters, but use a standard I/O bus (PCI-X) interface and support themselves from the broader cluster market. The R&D costs for such products are likely to be significantly lower than for a full custom supercomputer.

These examples are not meant to form an exhaustive list of leadership supercomputing technologies. The agencies that are the primary users of supercomputing should, however, establish such a list, aided by the roadmap described in Recommendation 5, and should ensure that there are viable domestic suppliers.

Similar observations can be made about software for high-performance computing. Our ability to efficiently exploit leading supercomputing platforms is hampered by inadequate software support. The problem is not only the lack of investment in research but also, and perhaps more seriously, the lack of sustained investments needed to promote the broad adoption of new software technologies that can significantly reduce time to solution at the high end but that have no viable commercial market.

Recommendation 4. The creation and long-term maintenance of the software that is key to supercomputing requires the support of those agencies that are responsible for supercomputing R&D. That software includes operating systems, libraries, compilers, software development and data analysis tools, application codes, and databases.

The committee believes that the current low-level, uncoordinated investment in supercomputing software significantly constrains the effectiveness of supercomputing. It recommends larger and better targeted investments by those agencies that are responsible for supercomputing R&D.

The situation for software is somewhat more complicated than that for hardware: Some software—in particular, application codes—is developed and maintained by national laboratories and universities, and some software, such as the operating system, compiler, and libraries, is provided with the hardware platform by a vertically integrated vendor. The same type of software, such as a compiler or library, that is packaged and sold by one (vertical) vendor with the hardware platform is developed and maintained by a (horizontal) vendor as a stand-alone product that is available on multiple platforms. Additionally, an increasing amount of the software used in supercomputing is developed in an open source model. The same type of software, such as a communication library, may be freely available in open source and also available from vendors under a commercial license.

Different funding models are needed to accommodate these different situations. A key goal is to ensure the stability and longevity of organizations that maintain and evolve software. The successful evolution and maintenance of complex software systems are critically dependent on institutional memory—that is, on the continuous involvement of the few key developers that understand the software design. Stability and continuity are essential to preserve institutional memory. Whatever model of support is used, it should be implemented so that a stable organization with a lifetime of decades can maintain and evolve the software. Many of the supercomputing software vendors are very small (tens of employees) and can easily fail or be bought out, even if they are financially viable. For example, several vendors of compilers and performance tools for supercomputing were acquired by Intel in the last few years. As a result, developers who were working on high-performance computing products shifted to work on technologies with a broader market. The open source model is not, per se, a guarantee of stability, because it does not ensure continuing stable support for the software.

It is also important to provide funding for software integration, as it is often a major source of function and performance bugs. Such integration was traditionally done by vertically integrated vendors, but new models are needed in the current, less integrated world of supercomputing.

As it invests in supercomputing software, the government must carefully balance its need to ensure the availability of software against the possibility of driving its commercial suppliers out of business by subsidizing their competitors, be they in government laboratories or in other companies. The government should not duplicate successful commercial software packages but should instead invest in technology that does not yet exist. When new commercial providers emerge, the government should purchase their products and redirect its own efforts toward technology that it cannot acquire off the shelf. HPSS and Totalview are examples of successful partnerships between government and the supercomputing software industry. NASTRAN and Dyna are examples of government-funded applications that were successfully transitioned to commercial suppliers.

Barriers to the replacement of application programming interfaces are very high owing to the large sunk investments in application software. Any change that significantly enhances our ability to program very large systems will entail a radical, coordinated change of many technologies, creating a new ecosystem. To make this change, the government needs long-term coordinated investments in a large number of interlocking technologies.

Recommendation 5. The government agencies responsible for supercomputing should underwrite a community effort to develop and maintain a roadmap that identifies key obstacles and synergies in all of supercomputing.

A roadmap is necessary to ensure that investments in supercomputing R&D are prioritized appropriately. The challenges in supercomputing are very significant, and the amount of ongoing research is quite limited. To make progress, it is important to identify and address the key roadblocks. Furthermore, technologies in different domains are interdependent:

Progress on a new architecture may require, in addition to computer architecture work, specific advances in packaging, interconnects, operating system structures, programming languages and compilers, and so forth. Thus, investments need to be coordinated. To drive decisions, one needs a roadmap of the technologies that affect supercomputing. The roadmap needs to have quantitative and measurable milestones.

Some examples of roadmap-like planning activities are the semiconductor industry's roadmap, the ASC curves and barriers workshops, and the petaflops workshops. However, none of these is a perfect model. It is important that a supercomputing roadmap be driven both top-down by application needs and bottom-up by technology barriers and that mission needs as well as science needs be incorporated. Its creation and maintenance should be an open process that involves a broad community. That community should include producers—commodity as well as custom, components as well as full systems, hardware as well as software—and consumers from all user communities. The roadmap should focus on the evolution of each specific technology and on the interplay between technologies. It should be updated annually and undergo major revisions at suitable intervals.

The roadmap should be used by agencies and by Congress to guide their long-term research and development investments. Those roadblocks that will not be addressed by industry without government intervention need to be identified, and the needed research and development must be initiated. Metrics must be developed to support the quantitative aspects of the roadmap. It is important also to invest in some high-risk, high-return research ideas that are not indicated by the roadmap, to avoid being blindsided.

Recommendation 6. Government agencies responsible for supercomputing should increase their levels of stable, robust, sustained multiagency investment in basic research. More research is needed in all the key technologies required for the design and use of supercomputers (architecture, software, algorithms, and applications).

The top performance of supercomputers has increased rapidly in the last decades, but their sustained performance has lagged, and the productivity of supercomputing users has lagged as well.[1] During the last decade the advance in supercomputing performance has been largely due

---

[1]See, for example, Figure 1 in the HECRTF report, at <http://www.hpcc.gov/pubs/2004_hecrtf/20040702_hecrtf.pdf>.

to the advance in microprocessor performance driven by increased miniaturization, with limited contributions from increasing levels of parallelism.[2]

It will be increasingly difficult for supercomputing to benefit from improvements in processor performance in the coming decades. For reasons explained in Chapter 5, the rate of improvement in single-processor performance is decreasing; chip performance is improved mainly by increasing the number of concurrent threads executing on a chip (an increase in parallelism). Additional parallelism is also needed to hide the increasing relative memory latency. Thus, continued improvement in supercomputer performance at current rates will require a massive increase in parallelism, requiring significant research progress in algorithms and software. As the relative latencies of memory accesses and global communications increase, the performance of many scientific codes will shrink, relative to the performance of more cache friendly and more loosely coupled commercial codes. The cost/performance advantage of commodity systems for these scientific codes will erode. As discussed in Chapter 5, an extrapolation of current trends clearly indicates the need for fundamental changes in the structure of supercomputing systems in a not too distant future. To effect these changes, new research in supercomputing architecture is also needed.

Perhaps as a result of the success of commodity-based systems, the last decade saw few novel technologies introduced into supercomputer systems and a reduction in supercomputing research investments. The number and size of supercomputing-related grants in computer architecture or computer software have decreased. As the pressure for fundamental changes grows, it is imperative to increase investments in supercomputing research.

The research investments should be balanced across architecture, software, algorithms, and applications. They should be informed by the supercomputing roadmap but not constrained by it. It is important to focus on technologies that have been identified as roadblocks and that are beyond the scope of industry investments in computing. It is equally important to support long-term speculative research in potentially disruptive technical advances. The research investment should also be informed by the "ecosystem" view of supercomputing—namely, that progress must come on a broad front of interrelated technologies rather than in the form of individual breakthroughs.

One of the needs of an ecosystem is for skilled and well-educated

---

[2]Surprisingly, the number of processors of top supercomputers did not scale up much in the last decade: The top system in the June 1994 TOP500 list had 3,680 processors; the top system in the June 2004 list had 5,120 processors.

people. Opportunities to educate and train supercomputing professionals should be part of every research program. Steady funding for basic research at universities, together with opportunities for subsequent employment at research institutions and private companies, might attract more students to prepare for a career in supercomputing.

Research should include a mix of small, medium, and large projects. Many small individual projects are necessary for the development of new ideas. A smaller number of large projects that develop technology demonstrations are needed to bring these ideas to maturity and to study the interaction between various technologies in a realistic environment. Such demonstrations projects (which are different from product prototyping activities) should not be expected to be stable platforms for exploitation by users, because the need to maintain a stable platform conflicts with the ability to use the platform for experiments. It is important that the development of such demonstration systems have the substantial involvement of academic researchers, particularly students, to support the education of the new generation of researchers, and that the fruits of such projects not be proprietary. In Chapter 9, the necessary investments in such projects were estimated at about $140 million per year. This does not include investments in the development and use of application specific software.

Large-scale research in supercomputing can occur in a vertical model, whereby researchers from multiple disciplines collaborate to design and implement one technology demonstration system. Or, it can occur in a horizontal model, in a center that emphasizes one discipline or focuses on the technology related to one roadblock in the supercomputing roadmap. A large effort focused on a demonstration system brings together people from many disciplines and is a good way of generating unexpected breakthroughs. However, such an effort must be constructed carefully so that each of the participants is motivated by the expectation that the collaboration will advance his or her research goals.

In its early days, supercomputing research generated many ideas that eventually became broadly used in the computing industry. Pipelining, multithreading, and multiprocessing are familiar examples. The committee expects that such influences will continue in the future. Many of the roadblocks faced today by supercomputing are roadblocks that affect all computing, but affect supercomputing earlier and to a more significant extent. One such roadblock is the memory wall,[3] which is due to the slower progress in memory speeds than in processor speeds. Supercomputers

---

[3]Wm. A. Wulf and S.A. McKee. 1995. "Hitting the Wall: Implications of the Obvious." *Computer Architecture News* 23(1):20-24.

are disproportionately affected by the memory wall owing to the more demanding characteristics of supercomputing applications. There can be little doubt that solutions developed to solve this problem for supercomputers will eventually influence the broad computing industry, so that investments in basic research in supercomputing are likely to be of broad benefit to information technology.

Recommendation 7. Supercomputing research is an international activity; barriers to international collaboration should be minimized.

Research has always benefited from the open exchange of ideas and the opportunity to build on the achievements of others. The national leadership advocated in these recommendations is enhanced, not compromised, by early-stage sharing of ideas and results. In light of the relatively small community of supercomputing researchers, international collaborations are particularly beneficial. The climate modeling community, for one, has long embraced that view.

Research collaboration must include access to supercomputing systems. Many research collaborations involve colocation. Many of the best U.S. graduate students are foreigners, many of whom ultimately become citizens or permanent residents. Access restrictions based on citizenship hinder collaboration and are contrary to the openness that is essential to good research. Such restrictions will reduce the ability of research and industry to benefit from advances in supercomputing and will restrict the transfer of the most talented people and the most promising ideas to classified uses of supercomputing.

Restrictions on the import of supercomputers to the United States have not benefited the U.S. supercomputing industry and are unlikely to do so in the future. Restrictions on the export of supercomputers have hurt supercomputer manufacturers by restricting their market. Some kinds of export controls—on commodity systems, especially—lack any clear rationale, given that such systems are in fact built from widely available COTS components, most of which are manufactured overseas. It makes little sense to restrict sales of commodity systems built from components that are not export controlled.

Although the supercomputing industry is similar in ways to some military industries (small markets, small ecosystems, and critical importance to government missions), there are significant differences that increase the benefits and decrease the risks of a more open environment.

A faster computer in another country does not necessarily endanger U.S. security; U.S. security requires a broad technological capability to acquire and exploit effectively machines that can best reduce the time to solution of important computational problems. Such technological capability is embodied not in one platform or one code but in a broad community of researchers and developers in industry, academia, and government who collaborate and exchange ideas with as few impediments as possible.

The computer and semiconductor technologies are (still) moving at a fast pace and, as a result, supercomputing technology is evolving rapidly. The development cycles of supercomputers are only a few years long compared with decades-long cycles for many weapons. To maintain its vitality, supercomputing R&D must have strong ties to the broad, open research community.

The supercomputing market shares some key hardware and software components with the much larger mainstream computing markets. If the supercomputing industry is insulated from this larger market, there will be costly reinvention and/or costly delays. Indeed, the levels of investment needed to maintain a healthy supercomputing ecosystem pale when they are compared with the cost of a major weapon system. A more segregated R&D environment will inevitably lead to a higher price tag if fast progress is to be maintained.

Supercomputers are multipurpose (nuclear simulations, climate modeling, and so on). In particular, they can be used to support scientific research, to advance engineering, and to help solve important societal problems. If access to supercomputers is restricted, then important public benefits would be lost. Moreover, the use of supercomputers for broader applications in no way precludes their use for defense applications.

Finally, advances in supercomputing technology can benefit the broader IT industry; application codes developed in national laboratories can benefit industrial users. Any restriction of this technology flow reduces the competitiveness of the U.S. industry.

Restrictions on the export of supercomputing technology may hamper international collaboration, reduce the involvement of the open research community in supercomputing, and reduce the use of supercomputers in research and in industry. The benefit of denying potential adversaries or proliferators access to key supercomputing technology has to be carefully weighed against the damage that export controls do to research within the United States, to the supercomputing industry, and to international collaborations.

Recommendation 8. The U.S. government should ensure that researchers with the most demanding computational requirements have access to the most powerful supercomputing systems.

Access to the most powerful supercomputers is important for the advancement of science in many disciplines. The committee believes that a model in which top supercomputing capabilities are provided by different agencies with different missions is a healthy model. Each agency is the primary supporter of certain research or mission-driven communities; each agency should have a long-term plan and budget for the acquisition of the supercomputing systems that are needed to support its users. The users should be involved in the planning process and should be consulted in setting budget priorities for supercomputing. Budget priorities should be reflected in the HEC plan proposed in Recommendation 1. In Chapter 9, the committee estimated at about $800 million per year the cost of a healthy procurement process that would satisfy the capability supercomputing needs (but not their capacity needs) of the major agencies using supercomputing and that would include the platforms primarily used for research. This estimate includes both platforms used for mission-specific tasks and platforms used to support science.

The NSF supercomputing centers have traditionally provided open access to a broad range of academic users. They have been responsive to their scientific users in installing and supporting software packages and providing help to both novice and experienced users. However, some of the centers in the PACI program have increased the scope of their activities, even in the face of a flat budget, to include research in networking and grid computing and to expand their education mission. The focus of their activity has shifted as their mission has broadened. The increases in scope have not been accompanied by sufficient increases in funding. The expanded mission and the flat budget have diluted the centers' attention to the support of computational scientists with capability needs. Similar difficulties have arisen at DOE's NERSC.

It is important to repair the current situation at NSF, in which the computational science users of supercomputing centers appear to have too little involvement in programmatic and budgetary planning. All the research communities in need of supercomputing have a continuing responsibility to help to provide direction for the supercomputing infrastructure that is used by scientists of a particular discipline and to participate in sustaining the needed ecosystems. These communities should prioritize funding for the acquisition and operation of the research supercomputing infrastructure against their other infrastructure needs. Further, such funding should clearly be separated from funding for computer and computational science and engineering research. Users of DOE and DoD centers have a similar responsibility to provide direction. This does not mean that supercomputing centers must be disciplinary. Indeed, multidisciplinary centers provide incentives for collaborations that would not occur otherwise, and they enable the participation of small communities. A multidisciplinary center should be supported by the agencies (such as NSF or NIH) that support the disciplines involved, but with serious commitment from the user communities supported by these agencies.

The planning and funding process followed by each agency must ensure stability from the users' viewpoint. Many research groups end up using their own computer resources, or they spend time ensuring that their codes run on a wide variety of systems, not necessarily because it is the most efficient strategy but because they believe it minimizes the risk of depending on systems they do not control. This strategy traps users into a lowest-common-denominator programming model, which in turn constrains the performance they might otherwise achieve by using more specialized languages and tools. More stability in the funding and acquisition process can ultimately lead to a more efficient use of resources. Finally, the mechanism used for allocating supercomputing resources must ensure that almost all of the computer time on capability systems is allocated to jobs for which that capability is essential. The Earth Simulator usage policies are illustrative. Supercomputers are scarce and expensive resources that should be used not to accommodate the largest number of users but to solve the largest, most difficult, and most important scientific problems.

Appendixes

A

Committee Member and Staff Biographies

COMMITTEE MEMBERS

SUSAN L. GRAHAM (NAE), *Co-chair*, is the Pehong Chen Distinguished Professor of Electrical Engineering and Computer Science at the University of California, Berkeley, and the chief computer scientist of the National Partnership for Advanced Computational Infrastructure (NPACI). Her research spans many aspects of programming language implementation, software tools, software development environments, and high-performance computing. As a participant in the Berkeley UNIX project, she and her students built the Berkeley Pascal system and the widely used program profiling tool gprof. Their paper on that tool was selected for the list of best papers from 20 years of the Conference on Programming Language Design and Implementation (1979-1999). She has done seminal research in compiler code generation and optimization. She and her students have built several interactive programming environments, yielding a variety of incremental analysis algorithms. Her current projects include the Titanium system for language and compiler support of explicitly parallel programs and the Harmonia framework for high-level interactive software development. Dr. Graham received an A.B. in mathematics from Harvard University and M.S. and Ph.D. degrees in computer science from Stanford University. She is a member of the National Academy of Engineering and a fellow of the Association for Computing Machinery (ACM), the American Association for the Advancement of Science (AAAS), and the American Academy of Arts and Sciences. In 2000 she received the ACM SIGPLAN Career Programming Language Achievement Award. In

addition to teaching and research, she has been an active participant in
the development of the computer science community, both nationally and
internationally, over the past 25 years. She was the founding editor in
chief of *ACM Transactions on Programming Languages and Systems*, which
continued under her direction for 15 years. She has also served on the
executive committee of the ACM special interest group on programming
languages and as a member and chair of the ACM Turing Award committee. Dr. Graham has served on numerous national advisory committees,
boards, and panels, including the National Research Council's (NRC's)
Computer Science and Telecommunications Board, the NRC's Commission on Physical Sciences, Mathematics, and Applications, the advisory
committee for the NSF Science and Technology Centers, and the advisory
committee of the NSF Center for Molecular Biotechnology. Dr. Graham is
a former member of the President's Information Technology Advisory
Committee (PITAC).

MARC SNIR, *Co-chair*, is Michael Faiman and Saburo Muroga Professor
and head of the Department of Computer Science at the University of
Illinois at Urbana-Champaign. Dr. Snir's research interests include large-
scale parallel and distributed systems, parallel computer architecture, and
parallel programming. He received a Ph.D. in mathematics from the Hebrew University of Jerusalem in 1979 and worked at New York University
on the Ultracomputer project from 1980 to 1982; at the Hebrew University
of Jerusalem from 1982 to 1986; and at the IBM T.J. Watson Research Center from 1986 to 2001. At IBM he headed research that led to the IBM
scalable parallel (SP) system; contributed to Power 4 and Intel server architecture; and initiated the Blue Gene project. Dr. Snir has published
more than a hundred papers on computational complexity, parallel algorithms, parallel architectures, interconnection networks, compilers, and
parallel programming environments; he was a major contributor to the
design of MPI. Dr. Snir is an ACM fellow and a fellow of the Institute of
Electrical and Electronics Engineers (IEEE). He serves on the editorial
boards of *Parallel Processing Letters* and *ACM Computing Surveys*.

WILLIAM J. DALLY received a B.S. degree in electrical engineering from
Virginia Polytechnic Institute, an M.S. degree in electrical engineering
from Stanford University, and a Ph.D. degree in computer science from
the California Institute of Technology (Caltech). He is currently the
Willard and Inez Bell Professor of Engineering at Stanford University,
where his group developed the Imagine processor, which introduced the
concepts of stream processing and partitioned register organizations, and
chair of the Computer Science Department. Dr. Dally and his group have
developed the system architecture, network architecture, signaling, rout-

ing, and synchronization technology that can be found in most large parallel computers today. While at Bell Telephone Laboratories he contributed to the design of the BELLMAC32 microprocessor and designed the MARS hardware accelerator. At Caltech, he designed the MOSSIM Simulation Engine and the Torus Routing Chip, which pioneered wormhole routing and virtual-channel flow control. While a professor of electrical engineering and computer science at the Massachusetts Institute of Technology (MIT), his group built the J-Machine and the M-Machine, experimental parallel computer systems that pioneered the separation of mechanisms from programming models and demonstrated very low overhead synchronization and communication mechanisms. Dr. Dally has worked with Cray Research and Intel to incorporate many of these innovations in commercial parallel computers and with Avici Systems to incorporate this technology into Internet routers. He cofounded Velio Communications to commercialize high-speed signaling technology, and he co-founded Stream Processors, Inc., to commercialize stream processing. He is a fellow of the IEEE and a fellow of the ACM and has received numerous honors, including the ACM Maurice Wilkes award. He currently leads projects on high-speed signaling, computer architecture, and network architecture. He has published over 150 papers in these areas and is an author of the textbooks *Digital Systems Engineering* (Cambridge University Press, 1998) and *Principles and Practices of Interconnection Networks* (Morgan Kaufmann, 2003).

JAMES W. DEMMEL (NAE) joined the computer science division and mathematics department at the University of California, Berkeley, in 1990, where he holds a joint appointment as the Dr. Richard Carl Dehmel Distinguished Professor. He is also the chief scientist of the Center for Information Technology Research in the Interest of Society (CITRIS), an interdisciplinary research center dedicated to applying information technology to societal-scale problems such as energy efficiency, disaster response, environmental monitoring, transportation, health care, and education. Dr. Demmel is an expert on software and algorithms to facilitate computational science, having contributed to the software packages LAPACK, ScaLAPACK, BLAS, and SuperLU. He is an ACM fellow and an IEEE fellow and has been an invited speaker at the International Congress of Mathematicians. He received a B.S. in mathematics from Caltech in 1975 and a Ph.D. in computer science from the University of California, Berkeley, in 1983.

JACK J. DONGARRA (NAE) is a University Distinguished Professor of Computer Science in the Computer Science Department at the University of Tennessee, a Distinguished Research Staff member in the Computer

Science and Mathematics Division at Oak Ridge National Laboratory, and an adjunct professor in the Computer Science Department at Rice University. He specializes in numerical algorithms in linear algebra, parallel computing, use of advanced computer architectures, programming methodology, and tools for parallel computers. His research includes the development, testing, and documentation of high-quality mathematical software. He has contributed to the design and implementation of the following open source software packages and systems: EISPACK, Linpack, the BLAS, LAPACK, ScaLAPACK, Netlib, PVM, MPI, NetSolve, TOP500, ATLAS, and PAPI. He has published approximately 300 articles, papers, reports, and technical memoranda and is coauthor of several books. He is a fellow of the AAAS, the ACM, and the IEEE. He earned a B.S. in mathematics from Chicago State University in 1972. A year later he finished an M.S. in computer science from the Illinois Institute of Technology. He received his Ph.D. in applied mathematics from the University of New Mexico in 1980. He worked at the Argonne National Laboratory until 1989, becoming a senior scientist.

KENNETH S. FLAMM is a professor and Dean Rusk Chair in International Affairs at the University of Texas Lyndon B. Johnson (LBJ) School of International Affairs. He joined the LBJ School in 1998, is a 1973 honors graduate of Stanford University, and received a Ph.D. in economics from MIT in 1979. From 1993 to 1995, Dr. Flamm served as principal deputy assistant secretary of defense for economic security and as special assistant to the deputy secretary of defense for dual-use technology policy. Defense Secretary William J. Perry awarded him the DoD's distinguished public service medal in 1995. Prior to and after his service at DoD, he spent 11 years as a senior fellow in the Foreign Policy Studies Program at the Brookings Institution. Dr. Flamm has been a professor of economics at the Instituto Tecnológico A. de México in Mexico City, the University of Massachusetts, and George Washington University. He is also currently a member of the National Academy of Science's Science, Technology, and Economic Policy Board, its Steering Group on Measuring and Sustaining the New Economy, and its Committee on Capitalizing on Science, Technology, and Innovation. He has served as member and chair of the NATO Science Committee's Panel for Science and Technology Policy and Organization, as a member of the Federal Networking Council Advisory Committee, the OECD's Expert Working Party on High Performance Computers and Communications, various advisory committees and study groups of the National Science Foundation, the Council on Foreign Relations, the Defense Science Board, and the U.S. Congress Office of Technology Assessment and as a consultant to government agencies, international organizations, and private corporations. Dr. Flamm teaches classes in microeconomic theory, international trade, and defense economics, has published extensively on the economic impacts of technological innovation in a variety of high-technology industries, and has analyzed economic policy issues in the semiconductor, computer, communications, and defense industries.

MARY JANE IRWIN (NAE) has been on the faculty at the Pennsylvania State University since 1977 and currently holds the A. Robert Noll Chair in Engineering in the Department of Computer Science and Engineering. Her research and teaching interests include computer architecture, embedded and mobile computing systems design, power-aware design, and electronic design automation. Her research is supported by grants from the MARCO Gigascale Systems Research Center, the National Science Foundation, the Semiconductor Research Corporation, and the Pennsylvania Pittsburgh Digital Greenhouse. She received an honorary doctorate from Chalmers University, Sweden, in 1997 and the Penn State Engineering Society's Premier Research Award in 2001. She was named an IEEE fellow in 1995 and an ACM fellow in 1996 and was elected to the National Academy of Engineering in 2003. Dr. Irwin is currently serving as a member of the Technical Advisory Board of the Army Research Lab, as the co-editor in chief of ACM's *Journal of Emerging Technologies in Computing Systems*, as a member of ACM's Publication Board, and on the steering committee of the Computing Research Association's (CRA's) Committee on the Status of Women in Computer Science and Engineering. In the past she served as an elected member of the CRA's Board of Directors, of the IEEE Computer Society's Board of Governors, of ACM's Council, and as vice president of ACM. She also served as the editor in chief of ACM's *Transactions on Design Automation of Electronic Systems* from to 1999 to 2004 and as chair of the NSF/CISE Advisory Committee from 2001 to 2003. Dr. Irwin has served in leadership roles for several major conferences, including as general chair of the 1996 Federated Computing Conference, general co-chair of the 1998 CRA Conference at Snowbird, general chair of the 36th Design Automation Conference, general co-chair of the 2002 International Symposium on Low Power Electronics and Design, and general co-chair of the 2004 Conference on Compilers, Architecture, and Synthesis for Embedded Systems. Dr. Irwin received her M.S. (1975) and Ph.D. (1977) degrees in computer science from the University of Illinois, Urbana-Champaign.

CHARLES KOELBEL is a research scientist in the computer science department at Rice University. Dr. Koelbel's area of expertise is in languages, compilers, and programming paradigms for parallel and distributed systems—in layman's terms, developing computer languages and algorithms that let several computers talk to each other and work together efficiently. He has contributed to many research projects while at Rice, mostly through the Center for Research on Parallel Computation, an NSF-funded Science and Technology Center with the mission to make parallel computation usable by scientists and engineers. These projects include the National Computational Science Alliance Technology Deployment Partners program, the DoD's high-performance computing modernization program, and the Fortran D programming language project. He was executive director of the High Performance Fortran Forum, an effort to standardize a language for parallel computing. More recently, he served for 3 years as a program director at the National Science Foundation, where he was responsible for the Advanced Computational Research program and helped coordinate the Information Technology Research program. He is coauthor of *The High Performance Fortran Handbook* (MIT Press, 1993) and many papers and technical reports. He received his Ph.D. in computer science from Purdue University in 1990.

BUTLER W. LAMPSON (NAE) is a Distinguished Engineer at Microsoft Corporation and an adjunct professor of computer science and electrical engineering at the Massachusetts Institute of Technology. He was on the faculty at the University of California, Berkeley; at the computer science laboratory at Xerox PARC; and at Digital's Systems Research Center. Dr. Lampson has worked on computer architecture, local area networks, raster printers, page description languages, operating systems, remote procedure call, programming languages and their semantics, programming in large, fault-tolerant computing, transaction processing, computer security, and WYSIWYG editors. He was one of the designers of the SDS 940 time-sharing system, the Alto personal distributed computing system; the Xerox 9700 laser printer; two-phase commit protocols; the Autonet LAN; Microsoft Tablet PC software; and several programming languages. He received an A.B. from Harvard University, a Ph.D. in electrical engineering and computer science from the University of California at Berkeley, and honorary science doctorates from the Eidgenoessische Technische Hochschule, Zurich, and the University of Bologna. Dr. Lampson holds a number of patents on networks, security, raster printing, and transaction processing. He is a former member of the NRC's Computer Science and Telecommunications Board. He has served on numerous NRC committees, including the Committee on High Performance Computing and Communications: Status of a Major Initiative. He is a fellow of the ACM and the AAAS. He received ACM's Software Systems Award in 1984 for his work on the Alto, IEEE's Computer Pioneer award in 1996, the Turing Award in 1992, the von Neumann Medal in 2001, and the NAE's Draper Prize in 2004.

ROBERT F. LUCAS is the director of the computational sciences division of the University of Southern California's Information Sciences Institute (ISI). He manages research in computer architecture, VLSI, compilers, and other software tools. Prior to joining ISI, he was the head of the High Performance Computing Research department in the National Energy Research Scientific Computing Center (NERSC) at Lawrence Berkeley National Laboratory. He oversaw work in scientific data management, visualization, numerical algorithms, and scientific applications. Prior to joining NERSC, Dr. Lucas was the deputy director of DARPA's Information Technology Office. He also served as DARPA's program manager for scalable computing systems and data-intensive computing. From 1988 to 1998, he was a member of the research staff of the Institute for Defense Analyses' (IDA's) Center for Computing Sciences. From 1979 to 1984, he was a member of the technical staff of the Hughes Aircraft Company. Dr. Lucas received B.S., M.S., and Ph.D. degrees in electrical engineering from Stanford University in 1980, 1983, and 1988, respectively.

PAUL C. MESSINA retired in April 2002 from Caltech, where he was assistant vice president for scientific computing, director of Caltech's Center for Advanced Computing Research, and faculty associate in scientific computing. He also served as principal investigator for the Distributed Terascale facility and Extensible Terascale facility projects at Caltech and was co-principal investigator of the National Virtual Observatory Project. From 2002 to 2004, Dr. Messina was a distinguished senior computer scientist (part time) at Argonne National Laboratory and until June 2003 was a senior advisor on computing to the director general of CERN, in Geneva. During a leave from Caltech from January 1999 to December 2000, he was Director of the Office of Advanced Simulation and Computing for Defense Programs in the NNSA at DOE. In that capacity he had responsibility for managing ASCI, the world's largest scientific computing program, which is defining the state of the art in that field. He held the position of chief architect for the NPACI, a partnership established by the NSF and led by the University of California, San Diego. His recent interests focus on advanced computer architectures, especially their application to large-scale computations in science and engineering. He has also been active in high-speed networks, computer performance evaluation, and petaflops computing issues. Prior to his assignment at DOE, he led the computational and computer science component of Caltech's research project, funded by the Academic Strategic Alliances Program (ASAP) of the ASC. In the mid-1990s he established and led the Scalable I/O (SIO) initiative. In the early 1990s, he was the principal investigator and project manager of the CASA gigabit network testbed. During that period he also conceived, formed, and led the Consortium for Concurrent Supercomputing, whose 13 members included several federal agencies, the national laboratories, universities, and industry. That consortium created and operated the Intel Touchstone Delta System, which was the world's most powerful scientific computer for 2 years. He also held a joint appointment at the Jet Propulsion Laboratory as manager of high-performance computing and communications from 1988 to 1998. Dr. Messina received a Ph.D. in mathematics in 1972 and an M.S. in applied mathematics in 1967, both from the University of Cincinnati, and a B.A. in mathematics in 1965 from the College of Wooster. In 1997 he was granted an honorary Ph.D. in computer engineering by the University of Lecce, Italy. He is a member of the IEEE Computer Society, the AAAS, the ACM, the Society for Industrial and Applied Mathematics, and Sigma Xi. He is coauthor of four books on scientific computing and editor of more than a dozen others.

JEFFREY M. PERLOFF is the chair of and a professor in the Department of Agricultural and Resource Economics at the University of California at Berkeley. His economics research covers industrial organization and antitrust, labor, trade, and econometrics. His textbooks are *Modern Industrial Organization* (coauthored with Dennis Carlton) and *Microeconomics*. He has been an editor of *Industrial Relations* and associate editor of the *American Journal of Agricultural Economics* and is an associate editor of the *Journal of Productivity Analysis*. He has consulted with nonprofit organizations and government agencies (including the Federal Trade Commission and the Departments of Commerce, Justice, and Agriculture) on topics ranging from a case of alleged Japanese television dumping to the evaluation of social programs. He has also conducted research in psychology. Dr. Perloff is a fellow of the American Agricultural Economics Association and a member of the board of directors of the National Bureau of Economic Research. He received his B.A. in economics from the University of Chicago in 1972 and his Ph.D. in economics from MIT in 1976. He was previously an assistant professor in the Department of Economics at the University of Pennsylvania.

WILLIAM H. PRESS (NAS) is a senior fellow at Los Alamos National Laboratory (LANL). From 1998 to 2004 he served as deputy laboratory director for science and technology. Before joining LANL in 1998, he was professor of astronomy and physics at Harvard University and a member of the theoretical astrophysics group of the Harvard-Smithsonian Center for Astrophysics. He is also the coauthor and co-maintainer of the Numerical Recipes series of books on scientific computer programming. Dr. Press was assistant professor of physics at Princeton University and Richard Chace Tolman research fellow in theoretical physics at Caltech, where he received a Ph.D. in physics in 1972. He is a member of the National

Academy of Sciences and was a founding member of its Computer and Information Sciences Section. He has published more than 140 papers in the areas of theoretical astrophysics, cosmology, and computational algorithms. He is also a fellow in the AAAS, a member of the Council on Foreign Relations, and a past recipient of an Alfred P. Sloan Foundation fellowship and the Helen B. Warner Prize of the American Astronomical Society. Dr. Press is a past co-chair of the Commission on Physical Sciences, Mathematics, and Applications of the NRC and a past member of the Chief of Naval Operations' Executive Panel, the U.S. Defense Science Board, NRC's Computer Science and Telecommunications Board, the Astronomy and Astrophysics Survey Committee, and a variety of other boards and committees. He has led national studies in subjects including high-bandwidth telecommunications (the Global Grid), national science and technology centers (especially for computational science), and a wide variety of national security issues. Dr. Press serves as a scientific advisor to the David and Lucille Packard Foundation and other foundations. He is a member of the board of trustees of the IDA and serves on its executive committee and on the external advisory committees of its CCS and CCR Divisions. He serves on the Defense Threat Reduction Agency's Science and Technology Panel.

ALBERT J. SEMTNER is a professor of oceanography at the Naval Postgraduate School in Monterey, California. He received a B.S. in mathematics from Caltech and a Ph.D. in geophysical fluid dynamics from Princeton. His prior professional positions were in UCLA's Meteorology Department and in the Climate Change Research Section of the NCAR. His interests are in global ocean and climate modeling and in supercomputing. Dr. Semtner has written extensive oceanographic codes in assembly language for shipboard use. He produced the first vectorized (Fortran) version of a standard ocean model in 1974 and the first parallel-vector version (in collaboration with Robert Chervin of NCAR) in 1987. He interacted with LANL scientists on transitioning the parallel-vector code to massively parallel architectures in the early 1990s. Under the leadership of Warren Washington of NCAR, he participated in the development of the DOE Parallel Climate Model using the Los Alamos Parallel Ocean Program and a parallel sea-ice model from the Naval Postgraduate School. That climate model has been ported to numerous parallel architectures and used as a workhorse climate model in numerous scientific applications. Dr. Semtner has been an affiliate scientist with NCAR for the last 12 years and simultaneously a member (and usually chair) of the Advisory Panel to the NCAR Scientific Computing Division. He is a winner (with R. Chervin) of a 1990 Gigaflop Performance Award (for the vector-parallel code) and the 1993 Computerworld-Smithsonian Leadership Award in Breakthrough Computational Science (for global ocean modeling studies that included ocean eddies for the first time). Dr. Semtner is an associate editor of *Ocean Modeling* and of the *Journal of Climate*. He is also a fellow of the American Meteorological Society.

SCOTT STERN graduated with a B.A. degree in economics from New York University. After working for a consulting company in New York, he attended Stanford University and received his Ph.D. in economics in 1996. From 1995 to 2001, Dr. Stern was assistant professor of management at the Sloan School at MIT. Also, from 2001 to 2003, Dr. Stern was a nonresident senior fellow of the Brookings Institution. Since September 2001, Dr. Stern has been an associate professor in the Kellogg School of Management at Northwestern University and a faculty research fellow of the National Bureau of Economic Research. He is also a co-organizer of the Innovation Policy and the Economy Program at the National Bureau of Economic Research. Dr. Stern explores how innovation—the production and distribution of ideas—differs from the production and distribution of more traditional economic goods and the implications of these differences for both business and public policy. Often focusing on the pharmaceutical and biotechnology industries, this research is at the intersection of industrial organization and economics of technological innovation. Specifically, recent studies examine the determinants of R&D productivity, the impact of incentives on R&D organization, the mechanisms by which firms earn economic returns from innovation, and the consequences of technological innovation for product market competition. A key conclusion from this research is that translating ideas into competitive advantage requires a distinct and nuanced set of resources and strategies. Effective management of innovation therefore requires careful attention to the firm's internal ability to develop truly distinct technologies and to subtle elements of the firm's external development and commercialization environment.

SHANKAR SUBRAMANIAM is a professor of bioengineering, chemistry, and biochemistry and biology and director of the Bioinformatics Graduate Program at the University of California at San Diego. He also holds adjunct professorships at the Salk Institute for biological studies and the San Diego Supercomputer Center. Prior to moving to the University of California, San Diego, Dr. Subramaniam was a professor of biophysics, biochemistry, molecular and integrative physiology, chemical engineering, and electrical and computer engineering at the University of Illinois at Urbana-Champaign (UIUC). He was also the director of the Bioinformatics and Computational Biology Program at the National Center for Supercomputing Applications and co-director of the W.M. Keck

Center for Comparative and Functional Genomics at UIUC. He is a fellow of the American Institute for Medical and Biological Engineering and is a recipient of Smithsonian Foundation and Association of Laboratory Automation awards. Dr. Subramaniam has played a key role in raising national awareness of training and research in bioinformatics. He served as a member of the National Institutes of Health (NIH) Director's Advisory Committee on Bioinformatics, which produced the report *Biomedical Information Science and Technology Initiative* (BISTI). The report recognized the dire need for trained professionals in bioinformatics and recommended the launching of a strong NIH funding initiative. Dr. Subramaniam serves as the chair of an NIH BISTI study section. He also served on bioinformatics and biotechnology advisory councils for Virginia Tech, the University of Illinois at Chicago, and on the scientific advisory board of several biotech and bioinformatics companies. Dr. Subramaniam served as review panel member of the Center for Information Technology (CIT) at NIH, and his focus was on how CIT should respond to the BISTI initiative. Dr. Subramaniam has served as a member of Illinois's governor's initiative in biotechnology and as advisor and reviewer of North Carolina's initiative in biotechnology. Dr. Subramaniam has published more than a hundred papers in the interdisciplinary areas of chemistry/biophysics/biochemistry/bioinformatics and computer science.

LAWRENCE C. TARBELL, JR., is the deputy director of the Technology Futures Office for Eagle Alliance, a company formed in 2001 by the Computer Sciences Corporation and Northrop Grumman to outsource part of the IT infrastructure (workstations, local area networks, servers, and telephony) for the NSA. His primary area of responsibility is IT enterprise management, with secondary responsibility in collaboration, distributed computing, and storage. Mr. Tarbell spent the previous 35 years at NSA with responsibilities for research and development of high-performance workstations, networks, computer security, mass storage systems, massively parallel processing systems, and systems software. For over 13 years, he managed and led supercomputing architecture research and development for NSA, sponsoring high-performance computing and mass storage research (both independently and jointly with DARPA and NASA) at many U.S. companies and universities. In 1990, he co-chaired Frontiers of Supercomputing II, sponsored jointly by NSA and LANL. For 3 years, he managed the development and procurement of the supercomputing and mass storage architecture at NSA. Mr. Tarbell received his M.S. in electrical engineering from the University of Maryland and his B.S. in electrical engineering (magna cum laude) from Louisiana State University.

STEVEN J. WALLACH (NAE) is vice president of technology for Chiaro Networks, an advisor to CenterPoint Venture Partners, and a consultant to the U.S. Department of Energy ASC program. Chiaro Networks provides major disruptive technologies in a high-end routing platform for reliability, scalability, and flexibility. Before that, he was cofounder, chief technology officer, and senior vice president of development of Convex Computers. After Hewlett-Packard bought Convex, Mr. Wallach became the chief technology officer of HP's Large Systems Group. He was a visiting professor at Rice University from 1998 to 1999 and manager of advanced development at Data General from 1975 to 1981. He was the principal architect of the 32-bit Eclipse MV supercomputer and, as part of this effort, participated in the design of the MV/6000, MV/8000, and MV/10000 (chronicled in the Pulitzer Prize-winning book *The Soul of a New Machine,* by Tracy Kidder). Mr. Wallach was an engineer at Raytheon from 1971 to 1975, where he participated in various hardware design efforts, including the computer used to control the launching of the Patriot missile system and various signal processors. He had primary responsibility for the design of the all-applications digital computer (AADC), which was intended for military specification airborne applications and was made up of gate arrays (one of the first such systems) and a vector instruction set based on APL. Mr. Wallach holds 33 patents. He was a member of PITAC. He is also a fellow of the IEEE. Mr. Wallach holds a B.S. in engineering from the Polytechnic Institute of Brooklyn, an M.S.E.E. from the University of Pennsylvania, and an M.B.A. from Boston University.

STAFF

CYNTHIA A. PATTERSON is a study director and program officer with the Computer Science and Telecommunications Board of the National Academies. Before the current study on the future of supercomputing, she completed several projects, including a study on critical information infrastructure protection and the law, a study that outlined a research agenda at the intersection of geospatial information and computer science, and a joint study with the Board on Earth Sciences and Resources and the Board on Atmospheric Sciences and Climate on public-private partnerships in the provision of weather and climate services. She also has been involved with a study on telecommunications research and development and a congressionally mandated study on Internet searching and the domain name system. Prior to joining CSTB, Ms. Patterson completed a M.Sc. from the Sam Nunn School of International Affairs at the Georgia Institute of Technology. In a previous life, Ms. Patterson was employed by IBM as an IT consultant for both federal government and private industry clients. Her work included application development, database administration, network administration, and project management. She received a B.Sc. in computer science from the University of Missouri-Rolla.

PHIL HILLIARD (through May 2004) was a research associate with CSTB. He provided research support as part of the professional staff and worked on projects focusing on telecommunications research, supercomputing, and dependable systems. Before joining the National Academies, Mr. Hilliard worked at BellSouth in Atlanta, Georgia, as a competitive intelligence analyst and at NCR as a technical writer and trainer. He earned an M.B.A. from Georgia State University (2000) and a B.S. in computer and information technology from the Georgia Institute of Technology (1986). He is currently working on a master's degree in library and information science through Florida State University's online program.

MARGARET MARSH HUYNH, senior program assistant, has been with CSTB since January 1999 supporting several projects. She is currently supporting, in addition to the present project, Wireless Technology Prospects and Policy Options, Internet Navigation and the Domain Name System, and Whither Biometrics. She previously worked on the projects that produced the reports *Beyond Productivity: Information Technology, Innovation, and Creativity, IT Roadmap to a Geospatial Future, Building a Workforce for the Information Economy*, and *The Digital Dilemma: Intellectual Property in the Information Age*. Ms. Huynh also assisted with the project Exploring Information Technology Issues for the Behavioral and Social Sciences (*Digital Divide* and *Democracy*). She assists on other projects as needed. Prior to coming to the National Academies, Ms. Huynh worked as a meeting assistant at Management for Meetings, from April 1998 to August 1998, and as a meeting assistant at the American Society for Civil Engineers, from September 1996 to April 1998. Ms. Huynh has a B.A. (1990) in liberal studies with minors in sociology and psychology from Salisbury State University (Maryland).

HERBERT S. LIN (May 2004 through December 2004) is senior scientist and senior staff officer at CSTB, where he has been study director of major projects on public policy and information technology. These studies include a 1996 study on national cryptography policy (*Cryptography's Role in Securing the Information Society*), a 1991 study on the future of computer science (*Computing the Future*), a 1999 study of Defense Department systems for command, control, communications, computing, and intelligence (*Realizing the Potential of C4I: Fundamental Challenges*), a 2000 study on workforce issues in high-technology (*Building a Workforce for the Informa-*

tion Economy), and a 2002 study on protecting kids from Internet pornography and sexual exploitation (*Youth, Pornography, and the Internet*). Prior to his NRC service, he was a professional staff member and staff scientist for the House Armed Services Committee (1986-1990), where his portfolio included defense policy and arms control issues. He received his doctorate in physics from MIT.

B

Speakers and Participants at Meetings and Site Visits

MEETING 1
March 6-7, 2003
Washington, D.C.

George Cotter, National Security Agency (NSA)
John Crawford, Intel Fellow, Intel Corporation
Robert Graybill, Program Manager, Information Processing Technology
   Office, Defense Advanced Research Projects Agency (DARPA)
John Grosh, Senior Staff Specialist (Computing and Software),
   Information Systems Directorate, Office of the Deputy Under
   Secretary of Defense (Science and Technology)
Daniel Hitchcock, Office of Advanced Scientific Computing Research,
   Department of Energy (DOE)
Gary Hughes, NSA
David Kahaner, Asian Technology Information Program
Jacob V. Maizel, Jr., Chief of the Laboratory of Experimental and
   Computational Biology, National Cancer Institute
José Muñoz, Office of Advanced Simulation and Computing, DOE
Clay Sell, Clerk, Senate Subcommittee on Energy and Water
   Development
David Turek, Vice President, IBM

MEETING 2
May 21-23, 2003
Stanford, California

Greg Astfalk, Chief Technical Officer, Hewlett-Packard
Gordon Bell, Senior Researcher, Microsoft Research
Debra Goldfarb, Vice President, IDC
James Gray, Senior Researcher, Microsoft Research
John Levesque, Senior Technologist, Cray Inc.
John Lewis, Technical Fellow, Boeing
Scott McClellan, Hewlett-Packard
William Reed, Director (retired), Office of Advanced Simulation and
    Computing, DOE
Mark Seager, Principle Investigator, Lawrence Livermore National
    Laboratory (LLNL)
Burton Smith, Chief Scientist, Cray Inc.

APPLICATIONS WORKSHOP AND MEETING 3
September 24-26, 2003
Santa Fe, New Mexico

Keynote Speakers

Phillip Colella, Senior Mathematician, Lawrence Berkeley National
    Laboratory (LBNL)
Charles McMillan, Defense and Nuclear Technologies Directorate,
    LLNL
Jeffrey Saltzman, Senior Director, Merck Research Laboratory
Warren Washington, Senior Scientist, National Center for Atmospheric
    Research (NCAR)

Participants

Cleve Ashcraft, Research Mathematician, Livermore Software
    Technology Corporation
William Carlson, Research Staff, Institute for Defense Analyses (IDA)
    Center for Computing Sciences
Michael Colvin, Senior Biomedical Scientist, LLNL
Stephen Eubank, Los Alamos National Laboratory (LANL)
Robert Harrison, Principal Architect, Oak Ridge National Laboratory
    (ORNL)

Bruce Hendrickson, Technical Staff and Acting Manager, Sandia
    National Laboratories
Gary Hughes, NSA
Anthony Jameson, Professor, Stanford University
John Killough, Senior Research Fellow, Landmark Graphics Corporation
Richard Loft, Application Engineer, NCAR
Gene Myers, Professor, University of California, Berkeley
Vincent Scarafino, Manager, Ford Motor Company
Francis Sullivan, Director, IDA Center for Computing Sciences
William Tang, Associate Director, Princeton University
Priya Vashishta, Professor, University of Southern California
Robert Weaver, Physicist, LANL
Paul Woodward, Professor, University of Minnesota

TOWN HALL BIRDS OF A FEATHER SESSION
November 19, 2003
Supercomputing Conference 2003
Phoenix, Arizona

Numerous conference attendees participated in the session and provided
comments to the committee.

NATIONAL SECURITY AGENCY SITE VISIT
December 2, 2003
Fort Meade, Maryland

Suzanne Banghart
William Carlson
Candice Culhane
Dave Harris
Eric Haseltine
Gary Hughes
Bill Johnson
Boyd Livingston
Mike Merrill
Baron Mills
Dave Muzzy
Tom Page
Steve Roznowski

MEETING 4
December 3-4, 2003
Washington, D.C.

Donald J. Becker, Founder and Chief Technical Officer, Scyld Computing Corporation
Francine Berman, Director, San Diego Supercomputer Center
Matt Dunbar, Principal Development Engineer, ABAQUS, Inc.
Earl Joseph, Program Vice President, High-Performance Systems, IDC
Kenichi Miura, Fujitsu Fellow, Professor and Project Leader, Center for Grid Research and Development, National Institute of Informatics
Cleve Moler, Chairman and Chief Scientist, The MathWorks, Inc.
Daniel Reed, Director, National Center for Supercomputing Applications
Roy F. Schwitters, S.W. Richardson Foundation Regental Professor of Physics and Chair of the Department of Physics, University of Texas, Austin
Horst D. Simon, Director, National Energy Research Scientific Computing (NERSC), LBNL
Srinidhi Varadarajan, Director, Virginia Polytechnic Institute and State University
Michael Wolfe, ST Fellow, STMicroelectronics, Inc.

LAWRENCE LIVERMORE NATIONAL LABORATORY SITE VISIT
January 9, 2004
Livermore, California

Welcome, Security Briefing, and Overview

Thomas F. Adams, Associate B-Program Leader for Computational Physics, Defense and Nuclear Technologies Directorate (DNTD)
Lynn Kissel, Deputy Program Leader, ASC
Michel G. McCoy, Program Leader, ASC
James A. Rathkopf, Associate A-Program Leader for Computational Physics, DNTD

Code Development Round Table

Katie Lewis, DNTD
Marty Marinak, DNTD
Thomas L. McAbee, DNTD
Rob Neely, DNTD
Brian Pudliner, DNTD
Michael Zika (facilitator), DNTD

Materials and Physics Modeling Roundtable

Grant Bazan, DNTD
Laurence E. Fried (facilitator), Chemistry and Materials Science
    Directorate
Randolph Q. Hood, Physics and Advanced Technologies Directorate
    (PATD)
Stephen B. Libby, PATD
Christian Mailhiot, Chemistry and Materials Science Directorate
Andrew K. McMahan, PATD
Paul L. Miller, DNTD
Albert L. Osterheld, PATD
John E. Reaugh, PATD
Eric R. Schwegler, PATD
Christine J. Wu, PATD

Designers' Roundtable

Robert E. Canaan, DNTD
Todd J. Hoover, DNTD
Juliana J. Hsu (facilitator), DNTD
Omar A. Hurricane, DNTD
Cynthia K. Nitta, DNTD
Peter W. Rambo, DNTD

Multiprogrammatic Capability Cluster in Production (Tour and Demo)

Robin Goldstone, Linux System Project Lead, Integrated Computing and
    Communications Department (ICCD)

Cyber Infrastructure Roundtable

Rob Falgout, ASC Institute for Terascale Simulation Leader
Randy Frank, Visualization Project Leader, ICCD
Mark Gary, Data Storage Group Leader, ICCD
Robin Goldstone, Linux System Project Lead, ICCD
John Gyllenhaal, Code Development Computer Scientist, ICCD
Steve Louis, ASC Data and Visualization Science Leader, ICCD
John May, ASC Performance Optimization and Modeling Project Leader
Mark Seager, Assistant Department Head for Advanced Technology
    and Terascale Computing, ASC Platform Leader, ICCD
Jean Shuler, ICCD Services and Development Deputy Division Leader,
    ICCD

Dave Wiltzius, ICCD Networks and Services Division Leader, ASC
    DisCom Leader, ICCD
Mary Zosel, ASC Problem Solving Environment Leader (facilitator),
    ICCD

LAWRENCE BERKELEY NATIONAL LABORATORY SITE VISIT
January 14, 2004
Berkeley, California

Overview of Computing Sciences at LBNL

Horst D. Simon, Associate Laboratory Director for Computing Sciences;
    Director, Computational Research Division (CRD); Director, NERSC
    Center Division

NERSC Issues

Bill Kramer, NERSC Center General Manager and Department Head for
    High-Power Computing (HPC)

New Technology Introduction at NERSC

Jim Craw, Group Leader, Computational Systems, Advanced Systems,
    and PDSF Systems, NERSC
Bill Saphir, Chief Architect, High Performance Computing Department,
    NERSC
Francesca Verdier, Group Leader, User Services, NERSC

Computing on the Earth Simulator

Andrew Canning, Computer Scientist, Scientific Computing Group,
    CRD

NERSC User Panel

John Bell, Group Leader, Center for Computational Science and
    Engineering, CRD
Julian Borrill, Computer Scientist, Scientific Computing Group, CRD
William Lester, Professor, Department of Chemistry, University of
    California, Berkeley
Doug Rottman, LLNL, Vice Chair of NERSC User Group
Rob Ryne, LBNL, Chair of NERSC User Group
Michael Wehner, Computer Scientist, Scientific Computing Group, CRD

Programming/Language Issues

Kathy Yelick, Professor, Computer Science Division, University of California, Berkeley

Scientific Discovery Through Advanced Computing (SciDAC)

Juan Meza, Department Head, High Performance Computing Research, CRD

Esmond Ng, Group Leader, Scientific Computing, CRD

Arie Shoshani, Group Leader, Scientific Data Management, CRD

SANDIA NATIONAL LABORATORIES SITE VISIT
February 26, 2004
Albuquerque, New Mexico

Nuclear Weapons Program Overview

Tom Bickel, Director, Engineering Sciences

George Novotony, Technical Assistant to the Vice President, Weapon Systems Division

Joe Polito, Director, Stockpile Systems Program

Art Ratzel

Paula Schoeneman, Protocol Officer

Robert Thomas, Manager, Advanced Simulation and Computing Program

Michael Vahle, Director, Simulation Enabled Product Realization Program

Microsystems/Science Applications for the Stockpile

Don Cook, Director, Microsystems and Engineering Sciences Applications Program Office

Code Development Strategies

Ken Alvin, Code Developer

Steve Bova, Code Developer

Arne Gullerud, Code Developer

Mike McGlaun (speaker/facilitator), Level II Manager, Systems Technology

Garth Reese, Code Developer

Solution Verification for Hyperbolic Equations

James Stewart, Manager, Production Computing/Sierra Architecture

Model/Code Validation

Chris Garasi, Analyst
Joel Lash, Analyst
Len Lorence, Analyst
Marty Pilch (speaker/facilitator), Manager, Validation and Uncertainty
    Quantification Process

Sandia's Long-Term Computer Architecture Strategies

Bill Camp, Director, Computation, Computers, and Math

*Supercomputer Issues, Including Operating System Software, Algorithms,
Capability/Capacity Strategies*

Rob Leland, Level II Manager, Computer and Software Systems

Sierra Frameworks

Carter Edwards, Advanced Computational Mechanics

LOS ALAMOS NATIONAL LABORATORY SITE VISIT
February 27, 2004
Los Alamos, New Mexico

LANL Overview and Strategic Directions

James S. Peery, Deputy Associate Director, Weapon Physics

Summary of Requirements/Drivers for Predictive Capability

Paul J. Hommert, Division Leader, Applied Physics

Performance Modeling

Adolfy Hoisie, Group Leader, Modeling, Algorithms, and Informatics

Science Appliance

Ronald G. Minnich, Team Leader, Cluster Research

Q Lessons Learned

John F. Morrison, Division Leader, Computing, Communications, and Networks

Visualization

Bob Tomlinson

Architecture, Partnerships, Technology Risks

Kyran B. Kemper (Chris), Deputy Division Leader, Computing, Communications and Networks

Flop Drivers

Jim Morel

**ARGONNE NATIONAL LABORATORY SITE VISIT,
WITH PARTICIPATION BY OAK RIDGE NATIONAL
LABORATORY STAFF**
March 2, 2004
Argonne National Laboratory
Argonne, Illinois

Advanced Computing Research

Rick Stevens, Director, Mathematics Computer Science, Argonne National Laboratory (ANL); Professor of Computer Science, University of Chicago

Scalability Studies of Selected Applications

Andrew Seige, ANL

Programming Models and Development Environments for HPC

Ewing Lusk, ANL

Leadership Class Computing for Science
Thomas Zacharia, ORNL

Overview and Status of Cray X1 Evaluation at CCS
Pat Worley, ORNL

Applications in Astrophysics and Materials
Tony Mezzacappa, ORNL
Jeff Nichols, ORNL
Thomas Schulthess, ORNL

High-Performance Information Technology Infrastructure Requirements for the National Academic Research Community
Michael Levine, Pittsburgh Supercomputer Center
Ralph Roskies, Pittsburgh Supercomputer Center

MEETING 5
March 3-4, 2004
Argonne, Illinois

Peter Freeman, Assistant Director, NSF
Shane Greenstein, Elinor and Wendell Hobbs Professor, Kellogg School
   of Management, Northwestern University
David Mowery, Milton W. Terrill Professor of Business, Walter A. Haas
   School of Business, University of California, Berkeley

JAPAN SITE VISIT
National Academy of Engineering–Engineering Academy of Japan
Joint Forum on the Future of Supercomputing
March 23, 2004

U.S. Co-chairs

Susan L. Graham (NAE), Pehong Chen Distinguished Professor,
   Electrical Engineering and Computer Science, University of
   California, Berkeley
Marc Snir, Michael Faiman and Saburo Muroga Professor and Head of
   Department of Computer Science, University of Illinois, Urbana-
   Champaign

U.S. Speakers

Jack J. Dongarra (NAE), Distinguished Professor of Computer Science, Computer Science Department, University of Tennessee
Albert J. Semtner, Professor, Oceanography Department, Naval Postgraduate School in Monterey
Scott Stern, Associate Professor, Kellogg School of Management, Northwestern University
Steven J. Wallach (NAE), Vice President and Co-Founder, Chiaro Networks

U.S. Participants

Maki Haraga, Interpreter
Cynthia Patterson, Study Director and Program Officer, National Research Council

Japan Co-chairs

Kenichi Miura, Professor and Project Leader, Center for Grid Research and Development, National Institute of Informatics
Tsuneo Nakahara, Engineering Academy of Japan (EAJ); Vice President, Advisor, Sumitomo Electric Industries, Ltd.

Japan Speakers

Hironori Kasahara, Professor, Department of Computer Science, Waseda University
Chisachi Kato, Professor, Institute of Industrial Science, University of Tokyo
Keiichiro Uchida, Professor, Department of Information and Computer Science, Science Faculty, Kanagawa University

Japan Participants

Mutsumi Aoyagi, Professor, Network Computing Research Division, Computing and Communication Center, Kyushu University
Taisuke Boku, Associate Professor, Institute of Information Sciences and Electronics, Center for Computational Physics, University of Tsukuba
Kozo Fujii, Professor, Department of Space Transportation Engineering, Institute of Space and Astronautical Science, Japan Aerospace Exploration Agency

Yoshinari Fukui, Information Technology Based Laboratory, Project
Leader, Technology Development Unit, Advanced Center for
Computing and Communication, Institute of Physical and Chemical
Research; Vice President, Japan Society for Industrial and Applied
Mathematics

Ryutaro Himeno, Head, Computer and Information Division, Advanced
Computing Center, Institute of Physical and Chemical Research

Kohichiro Hotta, Director, Core Technologies Department, Software
Technology Development Division, Software Group, Fujitsu Ltd.

Kozo Iizuka, EAJ; President, Japan Association for Metrology Promotion

Masanori Kanazawa, Professor, Academic Center for Computing and
Media Studies, Kyoto University

Sumio Kikuchi, Deputy General Manager, Enterprise Business Planning,
Software Division, Hitachi, Ltd.

Toshio Kobayashi, EAJ; President, Japan Automobile Research Institute;
Professor Emeritus, University of Tokyo; Member, Science Council
of Japan

Koki Maruyama, Senior Research Scientist and Director, Principal
Research Program on Global Warming Prediction and Measure,
Abiko Research Laboratory, Central Research Institute of the
Electric Power Industry

Yuichi Matsuo, Computation and Network Infrastructure Laboratory,
Computational Fluid Dynamics Technology Center, National
Aerospace Laboratory of Japan

Satoshi Matsuoka, Professor, Global Scientific Information and
Computing Center and Department of Mathematical and
Computing Sciences, Tokyo Institute of Technology

Masao Sakauchi, EAJ; Deputy Director General, National Institute of
Informatics; Professor, Institute of Industrial Science, University of
Tokyo

Tetsuya Sato, Director General, Earth Simulator Center, Japan Marine
Science and Technology Center

Satoshi Sekiguchi, Director, Grid Technology Research Center, National
Institute of Advanced Industrial Science and Technology

Masaru Tsukada, Professor, Department of Physics, Graduate School of
Science, University of Tokyo

Tadashi Watanabe, Vice President, High Performance Computing, NEC
Corporation

Genki Yagawa, EAJ; Professor, School of Engineering, Department of
Quantum Engineering and Systems Science, University of Tokyo;

Director, Center for Promotion of Computational Science and
Engineering, Japan Atomic Energy Research Institute
Ikuo Yamada, EAJ, Executive Director

UNIVERSITY OF TOKYO, SUPERCOMPUTER
RESEARCH CENTER
March 24, 2004

Obinata Kazuo

JAPAN AEROSPACE EXPLORATION AGENCY
March 24, 2004

Toshiyuki Iwamiya, Director, Information Technology Center
Yuichi Matsuo, Engineer, Information Technology Center

AUTO MANUFACTURER
March 25, 2004

Names withheld on request.

EARTH SIMULATOR CENTER
March 25, 2004

Tetsuya Sato, Director General
Kunihiko Watanabe, Program Director, Simulation Science and
Technology Research

UNIVERSITY OF TOKYO, GRAPE GROUP
March 26, 2004

Lab tour.

MINISTRY OF EDUCATION, CULTURE, SPORTS,
SCIENCE AND TECHNOLOGY
March 26, 2004

Toshihiko Hoshino, Director, Office for Information Science and
Technology
Harumasa Miura, Director, Information Division
Hiroshi Sato, Director, Office of Earth and Environmental Science and
Technology
Masaya Toma, Director, Office for Science Information Infrastructure
Development

C

List of White Papers Prepared for the Applications Workshop

Ashcraft, Cleve, Roger Grimes, John Hallquist, and B. Maker. "Supercomputing and Mechanical Engineering." Livermore Software Technology Corporation.

Colella, Phillip. "Computational Fluid Dynamics for Multiphysics and Multiscale Problems." Computing Sciences Directorate, Lawrence Berkeley National Laboratory.

Colvin, Michael. "Quantum Mechanical Simulations of Biochemical Processes." Lawrence Livermore National Laboratory.

Eubank, Stephen. "The Future of Supercomputing for Sociotechnical Simulation." Computer and Computational Sciences Division, Los Alamos National Laboratory.

Hendrickson, Bruce, William E. Hart, and Cindy Phillips. "Supercomputing and Discrete Algorithms: A Symbiotic Relationship." Discrete Algorithms and Math Department, Sandia National Laboratories.

Hughes, Gary D., William W. Carlson, and Francis E. Sullivan. "Computational Challenges in Signals Intelligence." National Security Agency (Hughes) and IDA Center for Computing Sciences (Carlson and Sullivan).

Keyes, David E. "Supercomputing for PDE-based Simulations in Mechanics." Department of Applied Physics and Applied Mathematics, Columbia University.

Killough, John. "High Performance Computing and Petroleum Reservoir Simulation." Landmark Graphics Corporation.

Loft, Richard D. "Supercomputing Challenges for Geoscience Applications." Scientific Computing Division, National Center for Atmospheric Research.

McMillan, Charles F., Thomas F. Adams, Michel G. McCoy, Randy B. Christensen, Brian S. Pudliner, Michael R. Zika, Patrick S. Brantley, Jeffrey S. Vetter, and John M. May. "Computational Challenges in Nuclear Weapons Simulation." Lawrence Livermore National Laboratory.

Myers, Gene. "Supercomputing and Computational Molecular Biology." University of California, Berkeley.

Saltzman, Jeffrey. "Pharmaceutical High Performance Computing Challenges." Merck & Co., Inc.

Scarafino, Vincent. "High Performance Computing in the Auto Industry." Ford Motor Company.

Tang, William M. "Plasma Science." Princeton University.

Washington, Warren M. "Computer Architectures and Climate Modeling." National Center for Atmospheric Research.

Weaver, Robert. "Computational Challenges to Supercomputing from the Los Alamos Crestone Project: A Personal Perspective." Los Alamos National Laboratory.

Woodward, Paul. "Future Supercomputing Needs and Opportunities in Astrophysics." University of Minnesota.

D

Glossary and Acronym List

ASC. Advanced Simulation and Computing program, the current name for the program formerly known as ASCI.

ASCI. Accelerated Strategic Computing Initiative, which provides simulation and modeling capabilities and technologies as part of DOE/NNSA Stockpile Stewardship Program.

automatic parallelization. The automatic creation of parallel code from sequential code by a compiler.

bandwidth. The amount of data that can be passed along a communications channel in a unit of time. Thus, memory bandwidth is the amount of data that can be passed between processor and memory in a unit of time and global communication bandwidth is the amount of data that can be passed between two nodes through the interconnect in a unit of time. Both can be a performance bottleneck. Bandwidth is often measured in megabytes (million bytes) per second (Mbyte/sec) or gigabytes (billion bytes) per second (Gbyte/sec) or in megawords (million words) per second (Mword/sec). Since a word consists (in this context) of 8 bytes, then 1 Gbyte/sec = 125 Mword/sec = 1,000 Mbyte/sec.

benchmark. An experiment that enables the measurement of some meaningful property of a computer system; a program or a computational task or a set of such programs or tasks that is used to measure the performance of a computer.

BLAS. Basic Linear Algebra Subprograms, a set of subprograms commonly used to solve dense linear algebra problems. Level 1 BLAS includes vector-vector operations, level 2 BLAS includes vector-matrix operations, and level 3 BLAS includes matrix-matrix operations. BLAS subroutines are frequently optimized for each specific hardware platform.

BG/L. Blue Gene/Light (IBM).

cache. A small, fast storage area close to the central processing unit (CPU) of a computer that holds the most frequently used memory contents. Caches aim to provide the illusion of a memory as large as the main computer memory with fast performance. They succeed in doing so if memory accesses have good temporal locality and good spatial locality.

cache line. The unit of data that is moved between cache and memory. It typically consists of 64 or 128 consecutive bytes (8 or 16 consecutive double words).

cache memory system. Modern computers typically have multiple levels of caches (named level 1, level 2, and so on) that are progressively larger and slower; together they comprise the cache memory system.

CAE. Computer-aided engineering. The construction and analysis of objects using virtual computer models. This may include activities of design, planning, construction, analysis, and production planning and preparation.

capability computing. The use of the most powerful supercomputers to solve the largest and most demanding problems, in contrast to capacity computing. The main figure of merit in capability computing is time to solution. In capability computing, a system is often dedicated to running one problem.

capacity computing. The use of smaller and less expensive high-performance systems to run parallel problems with more modest computational requirements, in contrast to capability computing. The main figure of merit in capacity computing is the cost/performance ratio.

CCSM. Community Climate System Model.

CDC. Control Data Corporation.

circuit speed. Time required for a signal to propagate through a circuit, measured in picoseconds per gate. It is a key aspect of processor performance.

CISE. The NSF Directorate for Computing and Information Science and Engineering. This directorate is responsible for NSF-funded supercomputing centers.

clock rate or **clock speed.** The frequency of the clock that drives the operation of a CPU, measured in gigahertz (GHz). Clock rate and instructions per cycle (IPC) determine the rate at which a CPU executes instructions.

cluster. A group of computers connected by a high-speed network that work together as if they were one machine with multiple CPUs.

CMOS. Complementary metal oxide semiconductor. CMOS is the semiconductor technology that is currently used for manufacturing processors and memories. While other technologies (silicon-germanium and gallium-arsenide) can support higher clock rates, their higher cost and lower integration levels have precluded their successful use in supercomputers.

commodity processor. A processor that is designed for a broad market and manufactured in large numbers, in contrast to a custom processor.

commodity supercomputer. A supercomputer built from commodity parts.

communication. The movement of data from one part of a system to another. Local communication is the movement of data between the processor and memory; global communication is the movement of data from one node to another.

composite theoretical performance. CTP is a measure of the performance of a computer that is calculated using a formula that combines various system parameters. CTP is commonly measured in millions of theoretical operations per second (MTOPS). Systems with a CTP above a threshold (currently 190,000 MTOPS) are subject to stricter export controls. The threshold is periodically raised. While CTP is relatively easy to compute, it bears limited relationship to actual performance.

computational fluid dynamics (CFD). The simulation of flows, such as the flow of air around a moving car or plane.

computational grid. Originally used to denote a hardware and software infrastructure that enables applying the resources of many computers to a single problem. Now increasingly used to denote more broadly a hardware and software infrastructure that enables coordinated resource sharing within dynamic organizations consisting of individuals, institutions, and resources.

control parallelism. Parallelism that is achieved by the simultaneous execution of multiple threads.

cost/performance ratio. The ratio between the cost of a system and the effective performance of the system. This ratio is sometimes estimated by the ratio between the purchase cost of a computer and the performance of the computer as measured by a benchmark. A more accurate but hard to estimate measure is the ratio between the total cost of ownership of a platform and the value contributed by the platform.

COTS. Commercial, off-the-shelf.

CPU. Central processing unit, the core unit of a computer that fetches instructions and data and executes the instructions. Often used as a synonym for processor.

CSTB. The Computer Science and Telecommunications Board is part of the National Research Council.

custom processor. A processor that is designed for a narrow set of computations and is manufactured in small numbers; in particular, a processor designed to achieve high-performance in scientific computing.

custom supercomputer. A supercomputer built with custom processors.

cyberinfrastructure. An infrastructure based on grids and on application-specific software, tools, and data repositories that support research in a particular discipline.

DARPA. Defense Advanced Research Projects Agency, the central research and development organization of the Department of Defense (DoD).

data parallelism. Parallelism that is achieved by the application of the same operation to all the elements of a data aggregate, under the control of one instruction. Vector operations are the main example of data parallelism.

dense linear algebra. Linear algebra computations (such as the solution of a linear system of equations) that involve dense matrices, where most entries are nonzero.

discretization. The process of replacing a continous system of differential equations by a finite discrete approximation that can be solved on a computer.

distributed memory parallel system. A parallel system, such as a cluster, with hardware that does not support shared memory.

DOD. Department of Defense.

DOE. Department of Energy. DOE is a major funder and user of supercomputing, through the ASC program and the various science programs of the Office of Science.

DRAM. Dynamic random access memory. The technology used in the main memory of a computer; DRAM is denser, consumes less power, and is cheaper but slower than SRAM. Two important performance measures are memory capacity, measured in megabytes or gigabytes, and memory access time, or memory latency. The memory access time depends on the memory access pattern; row access time (or row access latency) is the worst-case access time, for irregular accesses.

effective performance. The rate at which a processor performs operations (for a particular computation), often measured in operations per second. Often used as a shorthand for effective floating-point performance. More generally, the rate at which a computer system computes solutions.

efficiency or **processor efficiency.** The ratio between the effective performance of a processor and its peak performance.

ES. Earth Simulator, a large custom supercomputer installed in Japan in early 2002 in support of earth sciences research. The ES topped the TOP500 list from its intallation to June 2004 and still provides significantly better performance than the largest U.S. supercomputers on many application.

FFT. Fast Fourier transform.

FFTW. Fastest Fourier transform in the West.

floating-point operations. Additions and multiplications involving floating-point numbers, i.e., numbers in scientific notation.

floating-point performance. The rate at which a computer executes floating-point performance, measured in floating-point operations per second. In particular, peak floating-point performance and effective floating-point performance.

flops. Floating point operations per second. Flops is used as a metric for a computer's performance.

front-side bus (FSB). The connection of a microprocessor to the memory subsystem.

gigahertz (GHz). 1,000,000,000 cycles per second, often the unit used to measure computer clock rates.

grid. A synonym for computational grid.

grid computing. The activity of using a computational grid.

HECRTF. High End Computing Revitalization Task Force, a task force established in March 2003 to develop a roadmap for high-end computing (HEC) R&D and discuss issues related to federal procurement of HEC platforms.

high-bandwidth processors. A custom processor designed to provide significantly higher effective memory bandwidth than commodity processors normally provide.

high-end computing (HEC). A synonym for HPC.

high-performance computing (HPC). Computing on a high-performance machine. There is no strict definition of high-performance machines, and the threshold for high performance will change over time. Systems listed in the TOP500 or technical computing systems selling for more than $1 million are generally considered to be high-performance.

HPCCI. High Performance Computing and Communications Initiative, which was established in the early 1990s as an umbrella for federal agencies that support research in computing and communication, including HPC.

HPCS. High Productivity Computing Systems, a DARPA program started in 2002 to support R&D on a new generation of HPC systems that reduce time to solution by addressing performance, programmability, portability, and robustness.

HPF. High-Performance Fortran, a language designed in the early 1990s as an extension of Fortran 90 to support data parallelism on distributed memory machines. The language was largely discarded in the United States but continue to be used in other countries and is used for some codes on the Earth Simulator.

hybrid supercomputer. A supercomputer built with commodity processors but with a custom interconnect and a custom interface to the interconnect.

IDC. International Data Corporation.

IHEC Report. Formally, the *Report on High Performance Computing for the National Security Community*, a report requested by the House of Representatives from the Secretary of Defense and nominally submitted in July 2002. It describes an integrated high-end computing program.

instruction-level parallelism. The concurrent execution of multiple instructions in a processor.

instructions per cycle (IPC). Average number of instructions executed per clock cycle in a processor. IPC depends on the processor design and on the code run. The product of IPC and clock speed yields the instruction execution rate of the processor.

interconnect or interconnection network. The hardware (cables and switches) that connect the nodes of a parallel system and support the communication between nodes. Also known as a switch.

irregular memory access. A pattern of access to memory where successively accessed words are not equally spaced.

ISV. Independent software vendor.

LANL. Los Alamos National Laboratory.

LAPACK. Linear Algebra PACKage, a package that has largely superseded Linpack. The Linpack library makes heavy use of the BLAS subroutines.

latency. A measure of delay. Memory latency is the time needed to access data in memory; global communication latency is the time needed to effect a communication between two nodes through the interconnect. Both can be a performance bottleneck.

LBNL. Lawrence Berkeley National Laboratory.

Linpack. A linear algebra software package; also a benchmark derived from it that consists of solving a dense system of linear equations. The Linpack benchmark has different versions, according to the size of the system solved. The TOP500 ranking uses a version where the chosen system size is large enough to get maximum performance.

Linux. A version of the UNIX operating system initially developed by Linus Torvalds and now widely used. The Linux code is freely available in open source.

LLNL. Lawrence Livermore National Laboratory.

memory wall.   Faster increase in processor speed relative to memory access time. It is expected to hamper future improvements in processor performance.

mesh partitioners.   A program that partitions a mesh into submeshes of roughly equal size, with few edges between submeshes. Such a program is needed to map a computation on a mesh to a parallel computer.

message passing.   A method of communication between processes that involves one process sending data and the other process receiving the data, via explicit send and receive calls.

microprocessor.   A processor on a single integrated circuit chip.

MIPS.   Millions of instructions per second. A measure of a processor's speed.

MPI.   Message Passing Interface, the current de facto standard library for message passing.

MTOPS.   Millions of theoretical operations per second; the unit used to measure the composite theoretical performance (CTP) of high-performance systems.

MTTF.   Mean time to failure, the time from when a system or an application starts running until it is expected to fail.

multigrid.   A technique for the numerical solution of the linear systems that often arise from differential equations. It alternates the use of grids of various resolutions, achieving faster convergence than computations on fine grids and better accuracy than computations on coarse grids.

multilevel.   Numerical simulations that use multiple levels of discretization for a given domain, mixing coarser and finer discretizations; multigrid is an example of multilevel.

multiphysics.   A simulation that combines various physical models. For example, a simulation of combustion that combines a fluid model with a model of chemical reactions.

multiprocessor.   A system comprising multiple processors. Each processor executes a separate thread. A single-chip multiprocessor is a system where multiple processors reside on one chip.

multithreaded processor.   A processor that executes concurrently or simultaneously multiple threads, where the threads share computational resources (as distinct from a multiprocessor, where threads do not share computational resources). A multithreaded processor can uses its resources better that a multiprocessor: When a thread is idling, waiting for data to arrive from memory, another thread can execute and use the resources.

multithreading.   A form of parallelism where multiple threads run concurrently and communicate via shared memory.

NAS. NASA's Advanced Supercomputing Division (previously known as the Numerical Aerospace Simulation systems division). The NAS benchmarks are a set of benchmarks that were developed by NAS to represent numerical aerospace simulation workloads.

NASA. National Aeronautics and Space Administration.

NASTRAN. A structural analysis package developed in the mid-1960s at NASA and widely used by industry. It is now available both in open source and as a supported product.

NCAR. National Center for Atmospheric Research.

NCSA. National Center for Supercomputing Applications at the University of Illinois at Urbana-Champaign, one of three extant NSF supercomputing centers.

NERSC. National Energy Research Scientific Computation Center, a supercomputing center maintained by DOE at the Lawrence Berkeley National Laboratory to support basic scientific research.

Netlib. An online repository of mathematical software maintained by the University of Tennesse at Knoxville and by the Oak Ridge National Laboratory.

NIH. National Institutes of Health, the focal point for federally funded health research.

NITRD. Networking and Information Technology R&D, a federal program. The program includes (among other areas) the High End Computing Program Component Area. This involves multiple federal agencies (NSF, NIH, NASA, DARPA, DOE, the Agency for Healthcare Research and Quality (AHRQ), NSA, NIST, NOAA, EPA, the Office of the Director of Defense Research and Engineering (ODDR&E), and the Defense Information Systems Agency (DISA)). The National Coordination Office for Information Technology Research and Development (NCO/IT R&D) coordinates the programs of the multiple agencies involved in NITRD.

NNSA. National Nuclear Security Administration, the organization within DOE that manages the Stockpile Stewardship Program that is responsible for manufacturing, maintaining, refurbishing, surveilling, and dismantling the nuclear weapons stockpile.

NOAA. National Oceanic and Atmospheric Administration.

node. The building block in a parallel machine that usually consists of a processor or a multiprocessor, memory, an interface to the interconnect and, optionally, a local disk.

nonexcludable goods. Goods that suppliers cannot prevent some people from using while allowing others to use them.

nonrival goods. Goods that each consumer can enjoy without diminishing anyone else's ability to enjoy them.

NRC. The National Research Council is the operating arm of the National Academies.

NSA. National Security Agency, America's cryptologic organization. NSA is a major user of supercomputing.

NSF. National Science Foundation, an independent federal agency with responsiblity for scientific and engineering research. NSF funds research in computer science and engineering and supports three national supercomputing centers that serve the science community.

NWChem. A computation chemistry package developed at the DOE Pacific Northwest National Laboratory (PNNL).

ODE. Ordinary differential equation.

open source. Software that is available to users in source form and can be used and modified freely. Open source software is often created and maintained through the shared efforts of voluntary communities.

PACI. Partnership for Advanced Computational Infrastructure at NSF.

parallel efficiency. The ratio between the speedup achieved with p processors and the number of processors p. Parallel efficiency is an indication of scalability; it normally decreases as the number of processors increases, indicating a diminishing marginal return as more processors are applied to the solution of one problem.

parallel speedup. The ratio between the time needed to solve a problem with one processor and the time needed to solve it with p processors, as a function of p. A larger parallel speedup indicates that parallelism is effective in reducing execution time.

parallel file system. A file system designed to support efficiently a large number of simultaneous accesses to one file initiated by distinct processes.

parallelism. The concurrent execution of operations to achieve higher performance.

PDE. Partial differential equation.

peak performance. Highest performance achievable by a system. Often used as a shorthand for peak floating-point performance, the highest possible rate of floating-point operations that a computer system can sustain. Often estimated by considering the rate at which the arithmetic units of the processors can perform floating-point operations but ignoring other bottlenecks in the system. Thus, it is often the case that no program, and certainly no program of interest, can possibly achieve the peak performance of a system. Also known as never-to-exceed performance.

PETSc. A package for the parallel solution of sparse linear algebra and PDE problems developed at DOE's Argonne National Laboratory (ANL).

PIM. Processor in memory, a technique that combines DRAM and processor on the same chip to avoid the memory wall problem.

PITAC. President's Information Technology Advisory Committee, chartered by Congress in 1991 and 1998 as a federal advisory committee to provide the President with independent, expert advice on federal information technology R&D programs.

prefetching. The moving of data from memory to cache in anticipation of future accesses by the processor to the data, so as to hide memory latency.

process. An executing program that runs in its own address space. A process may contain multiple threads.

processor. See *CPU.*

programming model. An abstract conceptual view of the structure and operation of a computing system.

public goods. Goods that are nonrival and nonexcludable. Publicly available software that is not protected by a copyright or patent is an example of a public good.

put/get. A model of communication between processes that allow one process to read from (get) or write to (put) the memory of another process with no involvement of the other process.

R&D. Research and development.

scalar processor. A processor that operates only on scalar (i.e., single-word) operands; see *vector processor.*

scatter/gather. A type of memory access where multiple words are loaded from distinct memory locations (gather) or stored at distinct locations (scatter). Vector processors typically support scatter/gather operations. Similarly, a global communication where data are received from multiple nodes (gather) or sent to multiple nodes (scatter).

SCI. Strategic Computing Initiative, a large program initiated by DARPA in the 1980s to foster computing technology in the United States.

shared memory multiprocessor (SMP). A multiprocessor where hardware supports access by multiple processors to a shared memory. The shared memory may be physically distributed across processors.

SHMEM. A message passing library developed for the Cray T3E and now available on many systems that support put/get communication operations.

SPARC. Scalable processor architecture.

sparse linear algebra. Linear algebra computations (such as the solution of a linear system of equations) that involve sparse matrices, where many entries are zero. Sparse linear algebra codes use data structures that store only the nonzero matrix entries, thus saving storage and computation time but resulting in irregular memory accesses and more complex logic.

spatial locality. The property that data stored near one another tend to be accessed closely in time. Good (high) spatial locality ensures that the use of multiple word cache lines is worthwhile, since when a word in a cache line is accessed there is a good chance that other words in the same line will be accessed soon after.

SPECfp. Set of benchmarks maintained by the Standard Performance Evaluation Corporation (SPEC); see <http://www.spec.org>. SPECfp is the floating-point component of the SPEC CPU benchmark that measures performance for compute-intensive applications (the other component is SPECint). The precise definition of the benchmark has evolved—the official name of the current version is SPEC CFP2000. The changes are small, however, and the mean flops rate achieved on the benchmarks is a good measure of processor performance evolution.

speedup. See *parallel speedup.*

SRAM. Static random access memory. SRAM is faster but consumes more power and is less dense and more expensive than DRAM. SRAM is usually used for caches, while DRAM is used for the main memory of a computer.

Stockpile Stewardship Program. A program established at DOE by the FY 1994 Defense Authorization Act to develop science-based tools and techniques for assessing the performance of nuclear weapon systems, predicting their safety and reliability, and certifying their functionality in the face of a halt in nuclear tests. The program includes computer simulation and modeling (ASC) as well as new experimental facilities.

supercomputer. Refers to those computing systems (hardware, systems software, and applications software) that provide close to the best currently achievable sustained performance on demanding computational problems.

supercomputing. Used to denote the various activities involved in the design, manufacture, or use of supercomputers.

switch. See *interconnect.*

synchronization. Communication between threads with the effect of constraining the relative order that the threads execute code.

temporal locality. The property that data accessed recently in the past are likely to be accessed soon again. Good (high) temporal locality ensures that caches can effectively capture most memory accesses, since most accesses will be to data that were accessed recently in the past and that reside in the cache.

thread.   The basic unit of program execution.

time to solution.   Total time needed to solve a problem, including getting a new application up and running (the programming time), waiting for it to run (the execution time), and, finally, interpreting the results (the interpretation time).

TOP500.   A list, generated twice a year, of the sites operating the 500 most powerful computer systems in the world, as measured by the Linpack benchmark. While the list is often used for ranking supercomputers (including in this study), it is widely understood that the TOP500 ranking provides only a limited indication of the ability of supercomputers to solve real problems.

total cost of ownership.   The total cost of owning a computer, including the cost of the building hosting it, operation and maintenance costs, and so on. Total cost of ownership can be significantly higher than the purchase cost, and systems with a lower purchase cost can have higher total cost of ownership.

UNIX.   An operating system (OS) developed at Bell Laboratories in the late 1960s. UNIX is the most widely used OS on high-end computers. Different flavors of UNIX exist, some proprietary and some open source, such as Linux.

UPC.   Universal Parallel C.

vector operation.   An operation that involves vector operands (consisting of multiple scalars), such as the addition of two vectors, or the loading from memory of a vector. Vector loads and stores can be used to hide memory latency.

vector processor.   A processor that supports vector operations.

VTK.   Visualization toolkit.